The Environment: Confronting the Issues

The Environment: Confronting the Issues

Susan Curran

London: The Stationery Office

First published 1998 as *The Environment Handbook*.
Second revised edition 2001.

ISBN 0 11 310180 5

Printed in the United Kingdom for The Stationery Office
TJ030 C5 04/00 9385 13871

Published by The Stationery Office and available from:

The Stationery Office
(mail, telephone and fax orders only)
PO Box 29, Norwich NR3 1GN
General enquiries/Telephone orders 0870 600 5522
Fax orders 0870 600 5533

www.thestationeryoffice.com

The Stationery Office Bookshops
123 Kingsway, London WC2B 6PQ
020 7242 6393 Fax 020 7242 6394
68-69 Bull Street, Birmingham B4 6AD
0121 236 9696 Fax 0121 236 9699
33 Wine Street, Bristol BS1 2BQ
0117 926 4306 Fax 0117 929 4515
9-21 Princess Street, Manchester M60 8AS
0161 834 7201 Fax 0161 833 0634
16 Arthur Street, Belfast BT1 4GD
028 9023 8451 Fax 028 9023 5401
The Stationery Office Oriel Bookshop
18-19 High Street, Cardiff CF1 2BZ
029 2039 5548 Fax 029 2038 4347
71 Lothian Road, Edinburgh EH3 9AZ
0870 606 5566 Fax 0870 606 5588

The Stationery Office's Accredited Agents
(see Yellow Pages)

and through good booksellers

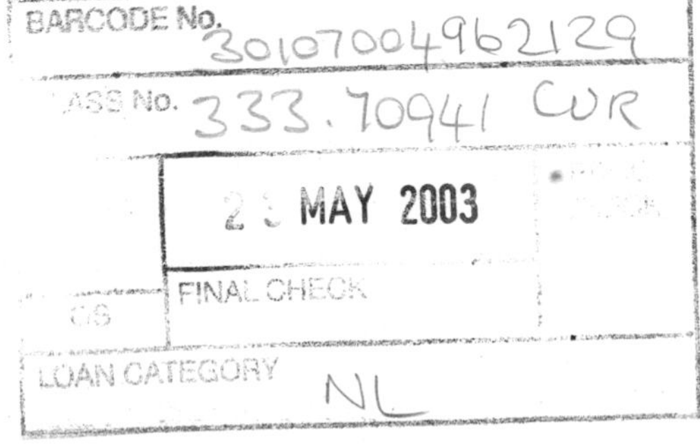

Contents

Acknowledgements

The following Crown copyright material has been adapted with the permission of the Controller of Her Majesty's Stationery Office. The Controller accepts no responsibility for the context in which the material has been presented.

Short extracts (some adapted) are taken from:

The Air Quality Strategy for England, Scotland, Wales and Northern Ireland
A Better Quality of Life: A Strategy for the Sustainable Development of the UK
Chemicals in the Environment
Digest of Energy Statistics 1999
Digest of Environmental Statistics 1998
Pesticides in Water
Recovery and Recycling Targets for Packaging Waste in 2001
Sustainable Business
Sustainable Development: Opportunities for Change
Transport 2010: The 10 Year Plan
UK Energy in Brief, 2000
UK Round Table on Sustainable Development *Fifth Annual Report*
Waste Strategy 2000 for England and Wales
Water: Nature's Precious Resource

Various tables have also been taken from information in Crown copyright sources. Full bibliographical details are listed at the end of the book.

Grateful thanks are due to Alan Cole, Rufus Curnow, Jackie Karas, Gwynne Lyons and Reg Walker, who provided assistance and advice during the research and writing of the first edition of this book; and to Alistair Marshall, who assisted with the research for this revised edition.

Susan Curran

December 2000

Acronyms and abbreviations

Organisations, agreements, acronyms etc.

ACE	Association for the Conservation of Energy
BAT	best available technology
BATNEEC	best available technology not entailing excessive cost
BRE	Building Research Establishment
CHP	combined heat and power
DETR	UK Department of the Environment, Transport and the Regions
DoE	UK Department of the Environment (now part of DETR)
DTI	UK Department of Trade and Industry
EA	UK Environment Agency
EEA	European Environment Agency
EC	European Community (used to refer here to both the European Community and the European Union)
EIA	environmental impact assessment
EIS	environmental information systems
EMAS	EC Eco-Management and Audit Scheme
ET	environmental technology
GDP	gross domestic product
GMO	genetically modified organism
IPCC	Intergovernmental Panel on Climate Change
IPPC	Integrated Pollution Prevention Control
ISO	International Organisation for Standardisation
JEMU	Joint Environmental Markets Unit
Ofwat	UK Office of Water Services
TEN	trans-European network
UNCED	United Nations Conference on Environment and Development
UNECE	United Nations Economic Commission for Europe
UNEP	United Nations Environment Programme
UNFCCC	United Nations Framework Convention on Climate Change
WHO	World Health Organisation

Measurements

GWh	Gigawatt hours
ha	hectare (1 ha = 10,000 sq m)
mSv	millisievert
MW	megawatt
ppb	parts per billion
ppm	parts per million
ppmv	parts per million by volume
TWh	Terawatt hours
μg	microgramme (0.001 gm)
μm	micrometre (0.001 mm)

Chemical compounds etc.

CFCs	chlorofluorocarbons (see page 209)
HBFCs	hydrobromofluorocarbons (see page 210)
HCFCs	hydrochlorofluorocarbons (see page 210)
HFCs	hydrofluorocarbons (see page 210)
PFCs	perfluorocarbons (see page 212)
PM_{10}	particulate matter with a diameter less than 10 μm
VOCs	volatile organic compounds (see page 214)

To Paul

Introduction

> *'Environmental issues are best handled with the participation of all concerned citizens at the relevant level.'*
>
> PRINCIPLE 10 OF THE RIO CONFERENCE

This book is designed primarily as an information resource. 'The environment' is a large and amorphous subject, and it would not be possible to cover every aspect of it exhaustively in any book, let alone one of this length. The intention is to provide an overview, concentrating on key facts, the legislative and regulatory framework and recent developments, and to point the reader to sources of further information.

The core target audience for this book consists of business people who are not environmental professionals, but who need a better general awareness of current environmental issues, environmental legislation, and environmental practices in a business context. The book should also be of interest to students and the general public, and professionals in environmental fields may find it useful as a general guide to topics beyond the scope of their specialism.

The coverage of the book broadly mirrors that of EC and UK government policies (and the legislation that arises from them) which affect the interaction between the enterprise and the natural world, and which attempt to implement the principle of sustainable development. The prime emphasis is on the quality of air, land and water. Very little space has been given to biodiversity and related issues.

The three main aims of each section are to:

- set the context
- outline current UK government policies, major international agreements to which the UK is a signatory, and the major pieces of UK and EC legislation
- offer practical suggestions which will enable organisations (and individuals, although the main focus is corporate) to improve their environmental performance.

The book does not claim to be an exhaustive source for information on current regulations. It concentrates on broad issues and there is much detailed legislation (for example, setting limits for the emission of specific pollutants) which is beyond its scope. It is in no way an adequate substitute for first-hand reference to the legislation.

The core emphasis is on English law. In large part the regulatory framework is similar in Scotland, Wales and Northern Ireland, but no attempt has been made to explain in detail the differences that apply.

The information in this second edition has been updated to September 2000. Inevitably environmental policies and laws are developing all the time, and it is hoped to continue to update the book on a regular basis.

Core environmental problems

A report for the EC prepared by the European Environment Agency in 1995 (*The Dobris Assessment*) identified various lists of environmental problems. *The Dobris Assessment* list of core environmental problems serves as one of the best summaries of the scale and scope of the environmental challenge facing the world today. The dozen core problems identified were:

- climate change
- stratospheric ozone depletion
- loss of biodiversity
- major accidents
- acidification
- tropospherical ozone and other photochemical oxidants
- management of freshwater resources
- forest degradation
- coastal zone threats and management
- waste reduction and management
- urban stress
- chemical risks.

As well as having individual impacts, these problems have cumulative impacts. Separately and in combination they affect the entire world and the quality of life of everyone. All of them require urgent action. Some of this action must be (and is) at a national or international level, but there are also actions that each organisation and each individual can take. Increasingly, regulations are being tightened and place new obligations on organisations; but to ensure continued compliance with regulations is only a part of the challenge. The environmentally concerned organisation will wish to go further, to participate in voluntary initiatives, and to undertake an environmental management plan that will not only improve its environmental performance, but will have a strong and positive impact on its overall management and performance.

Sustainable development

Of the many definitions of sustainable development that have been proposed over the years, the one which has achieved the widest currency is the definition given in the Brundtland Report of the World Committee on Environment and Development. That defined sustainable development as:

> *'Development which meets the needs of the present without compromising the ability of future generations to meet their own needs.'*

The UK government's recent definition, in its 1999 White Paper *A Better Quality of Life*, is:

'What is sustainable development? At its heart is the simple idea of ensuring a better quality of life for everyone, now and for generations to come.'

In that paper it defined the four core aims of its sustainable development strategy as:

- social progress which recognises the needs of everyone
- effective protection of the environment
- prudent use of natural resources
- maintenance of high and stable levels of economic growth and employment.

Among the government initiatives proposed or in hand to achieve these objectives are:

- the development of an integrated transport policy
- support for international action to combat climate change
- the work of the Social Exclusion Unit
- the Welfare to Work programme
- a programme for greening government
- devolved responsibilities which now lie with the Scottish Parliament, the Welsh Assembly and the Regional Development Agencies
- better management of water resources
- policies on sustainable international development.

This programme provides the framework within which organisations and individuals will need to work to develop their own approach to environmental issues.

Economic growth and sustainable development

The tenor of most environmental research and activism in the 1960s and 1970s, exemplified by the influential Club of Rome report *The Limits to Growth* (1972), was that there was an unbridgeable gulf between the economic philosophy and industrial system of the developed world, with its emphasis on continued economic growth, and the need for sustainability. This conviction persists among many radical environmentalists today.

The policy-makers of the West today tend to argue, however, that this is not necessarily the case. As will be apparent from the quotes above, 'sustainable development' in their vocabulary does not imply a revolutionary change in our industrial processes or in our overall way of life. Instead the argument is that the necessary changes can be achieved by a process of steady evolution. The UK government's stance is that sustainable development means a *reconciliation* of the two basic social aspirations: the achievement of higher living standards through economic development; and the protection and enhancement of the environment. Their policy is based on the assumption that this reconciliation is capable of being achieved.

In large part the environmental legislation that has been adopted to date has concentrated on measures that can be achieved through technological advance. Cars have become more fuel efficient, for example, and their harmful emissions have been reduced: this will clearly contribute to environmental improvement, but it will not have the radical impact of a major move to reduce reliance on the private motor car and persuade (or force) individuals to shift to public transport or to less polluting forms of transport such as the bicycle. Similarly, moves have been made to phase out materials and processes that have been shown to have harmful effects, but most progress has been made when adequate substitutes have been developed, and action has been limited or even non-existent where they have not.

Serious doubts remain as to whether the responses that have been made to today's pressing environmental problems are adequate in their scale or their scope. The conclusion of the UN General Assembly in reviewing progress on the Rio Conference Agreements at the Earth Summit II in June 1997, was that *'overall trends with respect to sustainable development are worse today than they were in 1992.'* Although it accepted that *'sustained economic growth is essential to the economic and social development of all countries, in particular developing countries,'* it also pointed out that *'unsustainable patterns of production and consumption, particularly in the industrialised countries, are ... the major cause of continued deterioration of the global environment.'*

It may be that, as projections turn into actualities, it will become still more apparent that the action which has been taken to date is insufficient and that more radical action is necessary. It is not the aim of this book to take a stance on these issues. It outlines the current evidence on the state of the environment, and the trends that it reveals. It describes the response of the government, and explains to what extent individuals and organisations will be forced by regulation to adapt. There is much more that can be done, by both individuals and organisations. Some of it requires no more than the attainment of current best practice within the constraints of the organisation's existing aims and objectives. Some of it undoubtedly requires more. Some individuals and organisations will argue that a more radical response at this stage is not only worthwhile because of its environmental effect, but is also desirable because it will enable them to adapt early to what will in time be required of the rest. Others may choose to adapt more slowly.

Whichever approach is taken, it will be clear from the information provided in this book that the environmental problems we face are real, and that if they are to be tackled, and negative trends reversed, immediate and positive action is necessary. I hope this book will help to increase awareness both of the issues, and of the responses that can be made to them.

1 The world environment

> *'The environment cannot be separated from the human condition but is one essential complement of sustainable human development.'*
>
> UNITED NATIONS ENVIRONMENT PROGRAMME, *GLOBAL ENVIRONMENTAL OUTLOOK 2000.*

This chapter provides a brief overview of the state of the environment, and of major environmental issues, on a global scale.

The information in this chapter is derived primarily from UK government and other official sources. For reasons of clarity and space, sources are not noted individually.

World population and health

World population is continuing to grow rapidly, particularly in major urban areas, giving rise to a range of environmental, social and political problems. Among the population-related issues that should be noted are:

- Continuing wide disparities in health standards and mortality rates world-wide.
- The prevalence of water-related diseases in developing countries.
- Acute and chronic human exposure to pesticides.
- The threat of AIDS, particularly in the undeveloped world. (AIDS killed about 14.3 million people in 1998.)
- The threat of vector-borne diseases such as malaria, which affects more than 500 million people, and causes between 1.5 and 2.7 million deaths a year.
- The spread of antibiotic-resistant infections.

Population (billions)

1800	1
1900	2
1950	2.5
1972	3.8
2000	6.08
2050	estimated: 8.9

Megacities (over 8 million people)

1950	2
1972	9
1997	25

It is thought that in the year 2000 there will be 23 cities with a population greater than 10 million.

Inequalities

In 1998 the richest 25% of the world population accounted for:

- 80% of global energy use
- 85% of global chemical use
- 90% of global automobile use.

Biodiversity

Many rare species of flora and fauna continue to be threatened (and to become extinct) because of:

- the destruction of large areas of wildlife habitat (for forestry, agriculture and other purposes)
- the continuing illegal trade in endangered and rare species
- climate change affecting habitats and the species they support
- pollution affecting habitats and the species they support.

Friends of the Earth estimate that between one and three species *per hour* have been lost in recent years because of tropical deforestation.

China tiger population

1950	**1999**
4,000	25

This sub-species of tiger is so endangered that the WWF do not even have a photograph of one. The total population of all tigers has decreased by over 95% since the last century and the numbers are still being depleted.

Food and fisheries

Although international food production is growing steadily, people in many parts of the world continue to be undernourished. The heavy use of fertiliser world-wide raises serious pollution issues.

World grain production per capita (kg per person):

1950	**1972**	**1999**
250	290	307

World grain production, in millions of tonnes:

1950	1972	1998/9
641	1,152	1,879

World fertiliser use in thousands of tonnes:

1991/2	1998/9
26,681.1	37,205.6

(an increase of 26% in 7–8 years)

The world availability of cropland continues to fall with increasing population: there are now about 0.24 ha per capita, compared with 0.32 ha per capita in 1975.

In 1997 an estimated 12 million ha world-wide were planted with genetically modified (GM) crops. This figure is increasing rapidly: for example, China is now thought to be growing over 1.6 million ha of GM tobacco and tomatoes. Nearly 15% of the 1997 US soya harvest was grown from GM seed.

Many fish stocks (including those in the North Sea) continue to be exploited at a greater than sustainable rate, and they suffer too from pollution caused by ocean dumping, oil spills, land run-off and atmospheric deposition. A WWF Marine Health Check in 2000 found that two-thirds of UK fish stocks were in decline and being fished unsustainably, while the common skate is now believed to be extinct in the Irish Sea and rare in the central and southern North Sea. UK river catches of the Atlantic salmon have declined by 82% in the last 25 years.

Annual global fish catch in millions of tonnes:

1950	1972	1997
19.3	58.9	95.5

The commercial exploitation of sharks has increased over the last 40 years from 272,000 tonnes in 1950 to 760,000 tonnes in 1996. Out of the 100 exploited shark species the FAO has stated that approximately 20 of these species are endangered. These include the Silky shark and the Basking shark.

Water supplies and water usage

With seas covering 71% of the earth's surface, freshwater represents only about 3% of global water resources, and easily accessible surface freshwater 0.3% of total water resources. Issues of concern regarding water supply and usage include:

- the very uneven distribution of water availability between countries, and in some cases a serious mismatch between supply and demand
- the salinisation of water supplies in some arid countries
- pollution of drinking water supplies
- inefficient farming methods and poor irrigation systems.

Annual global water use in cu km:

1950	1972	1997
1,300	2,600	4,200

Irrigation accounts for two-thirds of global water usage and produces 40% of the world's food. World farmers use approximately 160 billion cu m of water every year, and irrigated land produces 10% of the world's grain. The number of people in water-stressed countries is estimated to increase from 470 million in 1999 to 3 billion by 2025. This increase is shown by the increase in the number of countries importing grain; for example, Jordan imports as much as 91% of its grain and Israel 87%.

Forests and wood consumption

Many forests, and particularly tropical moist forests which supply hardwood, continue to be exploited at a more than sustainable rate. Since 1992 about 68 million ha of forest (an area more than five times the size of England) have been lost in developing countries. Deforestation in the Amazon Basin was running at about 15,000 sq km (annually) in 1994.

Particular issues of concern regarding forests and wood supplies are:

- the clearance of tropical moist forests
- monocultural reforestation in temperate zones, often using non-native softwood species
- soil erosion following the logging of closed forests
- tree damage (seriously affecting, for example, an estimated one-third of all trees in parts of central and Eastern Europe) caused by pollution, drought or disease.

Global rainforest cover (on an indexed basis: 1950 = 100)

1950	1972	1997
100	85	70

During the 1980s approximately 137,000 sq km of tropical forest were destroyed each year, 54,000 sq km in the Amazon Basin alone. By 1988, 6% of the total Brazilian rainforest had been lost to deforestation. The UK continues to import more than 1,400 tonnes of Amazonian plywood from Brazil each month, most of which is taken illegally.

Energy usage and supply

World energy usage continues to rise, with increasing usage in the developing world far outstripping the impact of fuel economies in the developed world. Particular issues are:

- limited world resources of fossil fuels
- the uneven availability and cost of fuels

- pollution from power generation (contributing to global warming, etc.)
- nuclear waste and the risk of radioactive pollution.

Global fossil fuel use in millions of tonnes of oil equivalent:

1950	1972	1998
1,742	5,494	7,996

Nuclear power installed generating capacity: in GW:

1960	1972	1998
1	32	343

World-wide in 1998 2,291 billion KW of electricity was generated by nuclear power, making 16% of the total power generated that year.

Renewable power sources are of increasing – although as yet limited – importance. The world-wide use of wind power increased by a factor of 26 in 1998, and geothermal energy use grew by 5.5% in 1996, mostly in the US and the Philippines.

Global wind power generating capacity in MW:

1980	1996	1999
10	6,070	13,400

Temperature and sea levels

Global average surface temperatures have increased by 0.3 to 0.6°C since the late nineteenth century, and in the same period there has been a rise of between 10–25 cm in the observed global sea level. Nine of the ten hottest years on record have occurred since 1983.

Experts now agree that there is clear evidence of global warming caused by the greenhouse effect.

Global average temperatures (actual and projected, in °C):

1950	1972	1998	2030	2099
14.86	15.00	15.32	est. 16.32	18.32

Between 1990 and 2000 the global temperature has increased by 2°C and the sea level has risen by, on average, 50 cm.

State of the ozone layer and ozone-destroying chemicals

The ozone layer has been seriously depleted, to the extent that there are now permanent holes in it in some parts of the world. This is caused by the build-up of ozone-destroying chemicals, for example chlorofluorocarbons (CFCs).

Average atmospheric concentration of CFCs in parts/billion:

1950	1972	1997
0	1.4	3.0

Other harmful emissions into the atmosphere

(The impact of these gases is outlined in Chapters 4 and 5.)

	1950	1972	1997
carbon dioxide emissions (billion tonnes p.a.)	1.6	4.9	7.0
sulphur emissions (million tonnes p.a.)	30.1	58.2	70.7
nitrogen emissions (million tonnes p.a.)	6.8	19.5	28.2

The concentration of carbon dioxide in the environment has increased from 265 ppm to 359 ppm in 150 years. This is the equivalent of an increase of 170 billion tonnes in the amount being discharged into the atmosphere. Deforestation accounts for around 20% of the total carbon dioxide in the air. and the US, which contains only 7% of the world's population, produces 22% of the total amount of carbon dioxide.

Methane has also increased drastically in the atmosphere since the industrial revolution: in 1850 the concentration of methane was thought to be approximately 650 ppm and today it is as high as 1,700 ppm.

Transport

In 1998 world car production was an estimated 38 million vehicles, and the figure is continuing to rise. If current trends continue, there will be more than 1,000 million vehicles on the road by 2025. Both the production and the use of motorised transport lead to pollution problems.

World car fleet in millions of vehicles:

1950	1972	1997
53	220	508

World annual bicycle production in millions:

1950	1972	1997
11	46	94

2 The regulatory framework

'The economies of the European Union are characterised by "underuse" of labour resources and "overuse" of natural resources. This situation has given rise to high unemployment and a heavy environmental impact.'

EUROPEAN COMMISSION, *BUILDING A SUSTAINABLE EUROPE* (18 NOVEMBER 1997)

'We continue to damage our environment. In some areas there have been improvements, but there is much to be done to reverse trends such as destruction of landscapes and wildlife, increases in the output of gases which cause climate change, orpoor air quality. We have to tackle pressures on the environment such as those from development, agriculture and transport. At the same time there will be limits to what we should do...'

SUSTAINABLE DEVELOPMENT: OPPORTUNITIES FOR CHANGE, DETR 1998

British law

British law has long had two roots. The first is statute law, which derives from Acts of Parliament, and lays down regulations, often with penalties for infringement. Increasingly over the past 20 years Statutory Instruments, subordinate legislation under powers conveyed by Acts of Parliament, have been used to implement and clarify detailed provisions. Although 'legislation' was once the term given to Acts of Parliament, it is now sometimes taken to include this 'delegated legislation' in the form of orders and regulations. Statute law also includes by-laws laid down by a local authority or other body in accordance with powers granted to them by an Act of Parliament.

The second root is common or case law, which does not derive from statutes, but from past court judgments. These are used as guidance as to how the law is interpreted in practice. The core principle of common law is the tort, a wrong that has remedies at civil law.

Although in much of this book the emphasis is on statute law, it should be borne in mind that common law can also be important in an environmental context. The torts of negligence and nuisance not infrequently form the bases of lawsuits against organisations causing environmental damage or annoyance. Nuisance would apply, for example, in cases of chemical pollution of adjoining land, or of excessive noise, and the damages awarded can be considerable, especially when negligence is also proven.

There is a now a third root for British law in the form of EC legislation, the framework of which is outlined below.

EC law: a brief general introduction

The Treaty of Rome 1957 set up the European Economic Community, which has been developed via the **Single European Act 1987** and the **Treaty on European Union 1992** (the Maastricht Treaty) into the European Community (EC). (The

Maastricht Treaty also provided for the establishment of the European Union, but most legal arrangements come under the auspices of the Community, not the Union, and for simplicity, if not absolute correctness, all references in this book are to the EC.) There have been various other amendments to the treaty framework over the years.

The UK joined the EC in 1973, and since then UK law has been shaped in part by the provisions of the treaties to which the UK is a signatory.

EC law – for which the effective law-making body is the European Council – takes two main forms:

- EC Regulations, which have general application and are binding and directly applicable in all Member States: that is, they take immediate effect throughout the EC, without any requirement for them to be translated into the national law of each Member State.
- EC Directives, which are also binding on all member countries, but do not take effect in individual Member States until they have been implemented: that is, their provisions have been put into effect by the government of each Member State. The method of implementation is at the discretion of the Member States, and depends not least on the framework of their legal system.

Directives typically set out:

- the results which are to achieved in each country
- dates by which either the results are to be achieved, or the directive is to be implemented formally.

In the past, EC legislation was frequently implemented in the UK administratively rather than legislatively. In other words, rather than a new piece of legislation being introduced, existing provisions would be adapted (using Statutory Instruments) to fulfil the requirements. Today it is acknowledged by the UK government that EC directives must be implemented in primary legislation.

Subsidiarity

A key feature of the Maastricht Treaty is the notion of subsidiarity, which states that in areas of activity which are not reserved for it exclusively, the EC *'shall take action, in accordance with the principle of subsidiarity, only if and so far as the objectives of the proposed action cannot be sufficiently achieved by the Member States and can therefore, by reason of the scale or the effects of the proposed action, be better achieved by the Community.'*

The environment is a field in which the EC does not have exclusive rights: that is, the Member States are free to make their own legislation in this area. However many environmental issues do have transnational impacts, and as a result there is a broad spectrum of environmental regulation which has been generally agreed to fall within the remit of EC law.

Harmonisation

There remains considerable freedom, for example for Member States to make provisions that are more stringent than those required by EC Directives. However, a degree of harmonisation is necessary, and it is perceived that national legislation can cause difficulties if its result is to create an obstacle to trade or to prevent or restrict free competition between Member States.

The **EC Standstill Directive** of 1983 required that Member States introducing new legislation that might have this effect should notify the Commission, which was then to be allowed time to decide whether Community action would be more appropriate. This followed on from a similar but more restricted agreement of 1973, which required Member States to notify the Commission if they were planning environmental legislation that could affect other Member States and the working of the EC. It was prompted by a number of individual pieces of legislation which prompted a need for harmonisation, including French measures on drinking water, German legislation on waste recycling and UK measures on control of pollution.

International agreements

Also significant in the environmental context are many international conventions and agreements which set out a framework for international co-operation in areas such as:

- sustainable development world-wide
- biodiversity and the protection of endangered species
- protection of tropical rainforests
- protection of the ozone layer
- action to combat global warming
- control over international shipping.

Both the UK and the EC can become signatories to such agreements, and once either party is a signatory, then the UK will be bound by the conditions of the agreement. Normally the requirements of the agreement will be met through appropriate statute law and other measures such as those outlined below.

The scope of environmental regulation

On an international, EC and national basis, sustainable development is about:

- conserving and enhancing the natural resource base
- ensuring a sustainable level of population
- meeting essential needs for jobs, food, energy, water and sanitation
- working towards an enhanced standard of living.

On an EC and UK level, environmental regulations cover, for example:

- the quality of air, land and water, and pollution which can affect it

- waste management, including waste production, recycling and disposal
- building and land use, with particular reference to its impact on the natural environment
- water abstraction
- transport, with particular reference to its impact on the natural environment
- energy usage, with particular reference to its impact on the natural environment and conservation of non-renewable energy sources
- usage of other non-renewable resources
- noise
- environmental management and reporting (primarily by businesses, also by other organisations, for example, public bodies)
- labelling for environmentally friendly products
- the encouragement of biodiversity and the protection of rare species
- genetically modified crops.

Legislation and other policy tools

Enforcement of regulations becomes an increasing problem – and an increasing expense – as the volume of regulations increases. This has proved a spur to the development of more imaginative ways of implementing environmental policy, especially ways that prove to be self-enforcing.

Ecotaxes

Although the term 'ecotaxes' applies specifically to taxes on polluting or otherwise damaging activities (such as the UK landfill tax), there is in fact a range of financial incentives and disincentives ('market-based instruments') which can be used to change behaviour in an environmentally sustainable direction. These include tax credits for environmental organisations. One of the aims is to ensure that, over time, the true environmental cost of a product or process will be reflected in the cost to the consumer.

Ecolabels and information schemes

The assumption is that better-informed consumers will prefer goods which are more environmentally friendly, so that better information (either on labels on goods, or provided separately) will bring about voluntary changes in behaviour.

Voluntary agreements with trade bodies

These are used to encourage rather than enforce improvements in the environmental performance of equipment and consumer goods: for example, tighter exhaust emission standards for cars or greater fuel efficiency from washing machines.

Changes in patterns of grant and subsidy

Not all existing patterns of subsidy and grant are well oriented to environmental objectives, but over time changes are being made which should bring them in line with the overriding policy of sustainable development. For example, agricultural grant measures that linked financial assistance to the volume of production tended to encourage intensive farming methods with a heavy use of fertilisers and pesticides; changes to separate the two aspects help to encourage more environmentally sustainable use of the land.

Trading in consents and limits

Where a body such as national government or a trade organisation has agreed to overall limits – for example, in their volume of emission of harmful gases, or of water abstracted – it can be possible for individual organisations within the body to 'trade' their contributions to this overall achievement. Organisations with a better performance can sell the proportion of their allowance that they do not require, while organisations unable to reach the overall limit can buy excess permission in this internal market. The 1997 Kyoto Protocol (an international agreement to reduce emissions of material which contribute to global warming) used international emissions trading as a policy tool, and subsequently there have developed trading proposals in a number of countries including Denmark, France, Australia and Canada. The UK government set up an Emissions Trading Group in 1999, with the remit to design an UK trading scheme, and the 2000 UK Budget set aside £30 million as an incentive to companies to commit to limits within the scheme.

Root sources of legislation

EC legislation is frequently prompted by international developments and agreements, including legislation in the US and in other non-member countries. The main source, however, is the draft legislation of Member States, which is referred to the EC under the Standstill Directive.

In some cases, measures intended for other purposes have been adapted to reflect increasing environmental concerns. For example, the EC legislation that sets down classifications for dangerous chemicals and specifies their labelling and packaging was intended initially to achieve an unified system for handling dangerous chemicals. Only on the sixth amendment of the original directive was there a specific category added for chemicals considered dangerous to the environment.

Another major spur to legislation on environmental issues is the practical emergence of environmental problems, and in particular, pollution-related and other disasters.

Not least because the EC has been so active in the environmental law field over the last ten to fifteen years, most if not all UK environmental law is now prompted by EC directives.

Rio and its outcomes

As noted above, the EC as a whole and the UK independently are signatories to a sizeable number of international agreements. These commitments play a major part in shaping environmental policy. Agreements specifically on particular subjects are referred to later in the book. The Rio Conference and its outcomes are noted here because they have an impact across a wide spread of environmental issues.

The Rio Conference 1992

The United Nations Conference on Environment and Development (UNCED) was attended by representatives of 172 governments, including 108 heads of state or government. The major outcomes included the adoption of three important agreements:

- Agenda 21, a comprehensive plan for global action in all areas of sustainable development.
- The Rio Declaration on Environment and Development, a series of principles defining the rights and responsibilities of states.
- Forest Principles, guidelines for the sustainable management of forests. These led to the setting up of the Intergovernmental Panel on Forests 1995.

The Rio Conference also led to the establishment of the UN Commission for Sustainable Development (UNCSD), and it opened for signature two international conventions:

- The UN Convention on Biodiversity, to protect biological diversity and ensure fair access and exploitation of genetic resources.
- The UN Framework Convention on Climate Change (UNFCCC), designed to spur international action to combat climate change. It committed developed countries to stabilise their emissions of carbon dioxide (a major cause of global warming: see Chapter 4) at 1990 levels by the year 2000. Coming into force in 1993, it has now been signed by 153 countries.

Agenda 21

Agenda 21 is a 700-page document which provides a non-binding framework for the signatories, who are expected to show their political commitment to implement the Rio programme into the twenty-first century. Each is intended to apply the programme at their own level and within their own means.

Agenda 21 is organised around a series of thirteen core themes:

- the atmosphere (covering climatic change and air quality)
- land management
- desertification
- mountains

- agricultural development
- biological diversity
- biotechnology
- oceans and coastal zones
- water resources
- toxic chemicals
- hazardous wastes
- solid wastes and sewage
- radioactive wastes.

Section III concentrates particularly on strengthening the role of groups seen as playing a major part in the sustainability process: women, children and young people, indigenous people, non-government organisations, local authorities, workers and unions, business and industry, the science and technology community, and farmers.

At the Rio Conference, the EU pledged US$4 billion to enable the early implementation of Agenda 21 in developing countries.

A core feature of the Rio agreements was the adoption of the precautionary principle, which is now echoed in the EC and UK sustainable development strategies: This specifies that the *'lack of full scientific certainty shall not be used as a reason for postponing cost-effective measures to prevent environmental degradation.'*

The term 'Local Agenda 21' refers to the application of Agenda 21 at a local level: for example (but not exclusively) by local authorities.

Earth Summit II, June 1997

The Earth Summit in June 1997 was a gathering of more than 100 heads of state or government to review progress on the Rio agreements five years later. It set a programme of work for the Commission on Sustainable Development for the period 1998 to 2002, based on the overriding theme of poverty/consumption and production patterns.

Other international agreements

Other key international conventions concerned with environmental issues, administered under the aegis of the UN, include:

- The UN Convention to Combat Desertification (UNECCD).
- The Convention on Wetlands of International Importance Especially as Waterfowl Habitat (Ramsar Convention).
- The Basel Convention on the Transboundary Movements of Hazardous Wastes and their Disposal.
- The Bonn Convention on Migratory Species.
- The Convention on International Trade in Endangered Species (CITES).

- The Vienna Convention for the Protection of the Ozone Layer.
- The Montreal Protocol on Substances that Deplete the Ozone Layer.
- The UNECE (UN Economic Commission for Europe) Protocols on volatile organic compounds (VOCs).

Kyoto Conference December 1997

This was the third Conference of Parties to the UNFCCC. It led to new agreement on the limitation of greenhouse gas emissions, setting an overall EC target which has since been translated into targets for the individual Member States. (See Chapter 4.)

EC and British environmental policy and regulations

It is generally accepted that many environmental issues have transnational implications and are an appropriate subject for regulation on an EC-wide, if not world-wide, basis. Article 3 of the Treaty of Rome specifies as one of the activities of the community, *'a policy in the sphere of the environment'*. This is the root of European law on environmental matters, and was reinforced by an affirmation of European heads of state or government in October 1972 that there was a need for a common environmental policy.

In the early 1980s a number of specific regulations were made, covering, for example, the disposal of batteries, a ban on CFCs in aerosols, the introduction of lead-free petrol, the transfrontier shipment of waste, and the halting of the proposed dumping of the Brent Spar oil platform in the North Sea.

The Treaty on European Union allowed the use of majority voting on environmental legislation and introduced as a principle of Treaty law the concept of sustainable growth. It states that Union policy should contribute to the pursuit of:

- preserving, protecting and improving the quality of the environment
- protecting human health
- ensuring a prudent and rational utilisation of natural resources
- promoting measures at the international level to deal with regional or world-wide environmental problems.

The Treaty requires Union policy to aim *'at a high level of protection'*, at rectifying environmental damage at source, and to be based on taking preventive action and making the polluter pay.

This commitment to environmental policy led to the development of five successive Community Action Programmes on the Environment, which have provided a framework for legislation. Within this framework more than 300 directives and regulations have been passed, representing a sizeable proportion of EC law. On the whole the EC environmental initiatives have been welcomed, and seen as one of the most successful areas of European integration.

Sustainability and economic development

The concept of sustainable development is now at the core of world-wide, EC and British environmental policies. It is outlined in the Introduction to this book.

It is undoubtedly the case that much current economic activity is not on a sustainable scale, in as far as:

- it consumes a large quantity of irreplaceable raw materials
- it consumes many renewable resources at a rate faster than that at which they can be replaced
- its use of energy pollutes the atmosphere to a degree which cannot be sustained without serious deterioration in atmospheric conditions
- it generates waste material, the disposal of which pollutes the planet.

A society with a high consumption and throwaway rate for material goods, with a fondness for imported foodstuffs, with a heavy reliance on private motorised transport, is not self-evidently a society that is pursuing a sustainable pattern of living. A naive observer might argue, therefore, that a move towards sustainable development requires a radical shift, away from our consumer-oriented society and towards one in which even our current level of economic development is seen as unaffordable in environmental terms.

In general, both within the EC and throughout the rest of the world, neither governments nor most individuals have shown any willingness to move away from a society based on high levels of consumption. Most people in developed societies wish to maintain their standard of living and their material conveniences, and people in developing societies wish to reach the same level.

In order to reconcile the two demands, for a sustainable approach that will conserve and improve the environment, and for economic development, most governments and international bodies have taken the view that there is no inherent conflict between them. They argue that technological developments will succeed in achieving most, if not all, of the changes that are required in order for a sustainable pattern to be achieved. It is questionable whether this is the case (and some of the arguments for and against it are presented in this book) but unquestionable that it is the basis on which most policy and regulations have been made.

This is true on a global scale, but it is also true that national governments are wary of introducing higher levels of regulation than are common elsewhere in the world, for fear that the burden of regulation will affect their national economy: threatening economic growth, foreign investment, export markets and employment creation. (This is discussed further in Chapter 3.) Conversely, there is international concern that some environmental regulations play a second role as trade barriers, protecting internal industries from competition particularly in the Third World, where the new standards are not easily achieved. The EC's policy is to ensure that there is a clear differentiation between environmental policies and trade measures which are intended to protect domestic industry.

There is also much concern on the part of Member States and the EC as a whole that their industrial sectors (in particular) should take full advantage of the opportunities created by the move towards sustainable development. Encouragement of the 'environment industry' (which again is outlined in Chapter 3) is another important strand of environmental policies. This achievement of 'strategic' or 'win-win' solutions is essential if environmental regulation is to be seen in a positive economic light.

In spite of the efforts that have been made to ensure harmonisation, it is evident that some recent environmental policies have led to distortions in the international market. As a result, intense political and legal battles have been waged over issues such as Danish bottle recycling programmes, German car emissions standards, packaging return schemes and ecolabelling schemes.

Differing industrial patterns have also caused political difficulties within the EC, since they can lead to differing attitudes to regulations which would have an effect on particular sectors. For example, HCFC compounds were introduced in the 1980s as a substitute for the highly damaging CFCs that were widely used in aerosols. HCFCs too had some harmful effects, and there were moves in the late 1980s and early 1990s to phase out their use in favour of the next generation of still less damaging CFC-substitutes. Regulations to achieve this were supported by the UK and Germany, who had tended not to invest in HCFC production but to invest in the next-generation technology; but they were opposed by France, which had chosen to invest in HCFCs.

The polluter pays

The concept of 'the polluter pays' is a core principle of EC environmental policy, and indeed an explicit provision of the 1987 Single European Act, although it was originated by the OECD in the early 1970s. The intention is that the cost of necessary environmental measures should be borne by the producer and not by society at large. It is not always easy to achieve this – or even, on occasion, to identify the polluter – but the principle is apparent in a wide range of recent legislative measures. Among its advantages are:

- it is perceived to be fairer
- it makes for greater efficiency in achieving objectives
- it can be more cost-effective in operation.

The 2000 European White Paper on *Environmental Liability* extended the principle of 'the polluter pays' – which until then had focused primarily on damage to persons, goods and contaminated sites – so that it also applies to damage to the wider environment, and set out proposals for EU legislation to put this into practice.

Other core principles of environmental policy

In general, the best environmental policy is based on prevention, and not on countering the effects of harmful activities. For example, a technology that prevents a process from emitting harmful gases is preferred to a technology which traps the gases after production.

The precautionary principle was outlined on page 17. In the UK White Paper *This Common Inheritance* (1990) it was defined as:

> *'Where there are significant risks of damage to the environment, the Government will be prepared to take precautionary action to limit the use of potentially dangerous materials or the spread of potentially dangerous pollutants, even where scientific knowledge is not conclusive, if the balance of likely costs and benefits justifies it.'*

Another set of principles is concerned with ensuring that the best available technology is used, and the least damaging environmental option is chosen, in any given set of circumstances. This has been refined into the concept of BATNEEC: Best Available Technology not Entailing Excessive Cost.

BATNEEC has been defined in detail in EC Directives. By 'available' it is meant that the technology, though not necessarily in general use, should be generally accessible. (It would still be regarded as generally accessible if it had to be imported, or if there was a monopoly supplier.) The concept of 'technology' includes not only plant and processes but staff numbers and quality, working methods, training, supervision, and the design, construction and layout of buildings.

Horizontal directives

In the 1970s and 1980s EC environmental legislation took shape mostly in the form of very specific directives, for example, setting limits on emissions of specific pollutants. A change of strategy occurred in the mid-1980s, and recent legislation has tended to concentrate on broader strategies. By the 1990s this change had led to the introduction of 'horizontal' directives: measures which regulated a range of different environmentally sensitive activities, providing the flexibility for Member States to implement them as they found appropriate.

EC Community Action Programmes on the Environment

To date there have been five Community Action Plans for the environment, which set out areas of activity and basic policy objectives.

The Fifth Action Plan (5th CAP) is embodied in the document *Towards Sustainability,* which was adopted in 1993. Many commentators perceived the significance of this plan in its move away from the suggestion that environmental problems can be solved by technological development alone, and towards an acceptance that technological progress alone will not solve all the problems, and that patterns of human consumption and behaviour must also be addressed. The EC's Progress Report of 1997 accepted that *'the road to sustainable development will be a long one.'*

The plan is based on the principle of shared responsibilities, and was designed to initiate action not only at the Community level and in Member States, but in the business world and from individual citizens.

The plan is also notable for its attempt to integrate environmental issues with the broad agenda of other policy areas. It advocated the use of a basket of measures to tackle environmental issues, including not only legislation, but also market-based instruments (that is, taxation and charges) aimed at altering environmentally damaging behaviour. It targeted five key sectors:

- industry
- tourism
- transport
- energy
- agriculture.

These were seen both as crucial sectors from an environmental viewpoint, and as sectors in which action at an EU level was particularly appropriate.

Its action plans were also oriented around a number of identified risks of particular importance:

- industrial risks including chemicals, biotechnology and animal use
- nuclear safety and radiation, including the problem of nuclear waste
- civil protection and environmental emergencies.

Specific targets of the Action Plan are noted in many places in this book.

The most recent progress report was issued in 1998. This decided on a set of priority areas in which efforts should be stepped up in order to give the plan new impetus:

- integrating the environment into other policy areas
- concentrating on agriculture, industry, transport, energy and tourism and laying down an action programme for these areas
- new initiatives to develop practical measures to put the plans into action
- better implementation and enforcement of environmental legislation
- encouraging better public awareness of environmental problems
- improving international co-operation
- developing the use of sustainable methods of production and consumption
- promoting regional and local initiatives.

However, as the EC's final communication on the review indicated, *'progress has been somewhat modest because the Member States and the various sectors covered by the programme have not really managed to take account of environmental concerns or to integrate them into their policies. The Union is still far from having achieved the broader objective of sustainable development laid down in the Treaty of Amsterdam.'* The intention is to remedy these defects in the sixth Environmental Action Plan, which is scheduled to be prepared in 2000. The keys aims of this, as well as more effective implementation, are to address key environmental priorities alongside main economic priorities, to develop more quantifiable objectives, indicators and control mechanisms, and to take fuller account of the EC enlargement process.

The European Environment Agency (EEA)

The EC agreed to create the EEA in 1990, and it became operational, based in Copenhagen, in 1994. Its broad aims are to:

- provide the EC, Member States and other countries with objective information to aid them in drawing up and implementing environmental protection policies
- supply technical, scientific and economic information as a basis for the drawing up and implementation of environmental regulation measures
- develop forecasting techniques so that environmental problems can be anticipated and appropriate and timely preventive measures taken
- ensure European environmental data are incorporated into international environmental programmes.

The EEA works through the European Information and Observation Network (Eionet) which consists of reference centres in every member state, co-ordinated by National Focus Points and various European topic centres which concentrate on research into specific areas such as:

- air quality and atmospheric emissions
- inland waters
- soils
- land cover and natural resources
- nature conservation
- the marine and coastal environment
- waste management.

Among its achievements have been the publication of the *Dobris Assessment*, an overview of the state of the environment which provided a baseline for future monitoring, a report, *The Environment in the EU*, which provided the basis for a review of the 5th CAP, and a 1997 report on *Air Pollution in Europe*.

Specific EC legislation

Among the great volume of EC environmental legislation, a few landmark pieces of legislation can be noted. In many cases these have been amended since their original introduction.

Directive of Conservation of Wild Birds, 1979

An estimated 28% of the bird species in the EC are under threat and this is designed to ensure their survival.

Directive on the Assessment of the Effects of Certain Public and Private Projects on the Environment, 1985

This lays down an ‘environmental impact assessment’ procedure, to be used as part of the planning and control process for new developments.

Directive on the Conservation of Natural Habitats and Wild Flora and Fauna, 1992/1997

Of the estimated 3,300 plant species in the core twelve EC nations, 10% are thought to be under threat of survival. This directive, implemented in stages over several years, is designed to protect them. The 1997 amendment set up an EU-wide ecological network known as 'Natura 2000' comprising 'special areas of conservation' and special protection areas for endangered species of wild birds.

Directive on Integrated Pollution Prevention and Control, 1996

Among a number of important directives designed to limit pollution, this is significant in its provision for an integrated pollution control procedure for major industrial processes, to prevent displacement of pollution from one medium to another (for example, from air to water).

The UK policy framework

The UK government's sustainable development strategy was originally developed in 1994 as a response to the Rio Conference. It has been developed and updated in a series of White Papers, including the core strategy document ***A Better Quality of Life: A Strategy for the Sustainable Development of the UK*** (1999). This sets out four core aims (outlined in the Introduction to this book), social progress, environmental protection, conservation of natural resources, and maintenance of high and stable levels of economic growth and employment. UK priorities include:

- reducing social exclusion
- developing a transport system which provides choice, minimises environmental harm, and reduces congestion
- improving larger towns and cities
- enhancing the countryside and wildlife
- improving energy efficiency and tacking waste.

It is also a priority to increase awareness of sustainability issues, a strategy being pursued by the Sustainable Development Education Panel.

As part of the strategy, a Sustainable Development Commission was set up in 2000 to monitor progress on sustainable development and to help build up a consensus on action to accelerate its achievement.

The key measure of progress is a system of sustainability indicators which identify the key issues and show what has been achieved. These have been developed from earlier sets of indicators, and now comprise about 150 items, including a subset of key headline indicators:

- GDP (total output of the country)
- investment in public, business and private assets
- proportion of people of working age who are in work

- qualifications at age 19
- expected years of healthy life
- homes judged unfit to live in
- level of crime
- emissions of greenhouse gases
- days when air pollution is moderate or high
- road traffic
- rivers of good or fair quality
- populations of wild birds
- new homes build on previously developed land
- waste arisings and management.

A final core indicator which is yet to be developed in detail is 'satisfaction with quality of life'.

Putting the policies into practice

Funds for sustainable development-related work

The government's main tool for providing funds to promote sustainable regeneration, economic development and competitiveness in England is the Single Regeneration Budget (SRB). The SRB Challenge Fund supports comprehensive regeneration strategies which are proposed by local partnerships between the public, private and voluntary sectors.

In deprived rural areas support is mainly channelled through the Rural Development Programme and Rural Challenge.

Taxation policies

The DETR's paper on **Sustainable Business**, published in 1998, affirmed the Government's strategy of reforming the tax system *'to shift the burden of tax from "goods" to "bads", to encourage innovation in meeting higher environmental standards, and deliver a more dynamic economy and a cleaner environment to the benefit of everyone.'*

A number of taxes have been introduced over the last few years with a view to encouraging greener actions. Among them are the Landfill Tax, introduced in 1996, the Fossil Fuel Levy, the Climate Change Levy, and changes to vehicle excise duty to encourage low emission and clean vehicles.

The Environmental Technology Best Practice Programme

This is a joint DETR/DTI initiative which has the overall target of stimulating cost savings of £320 million through the use of the best available technology by 2015.

Major UK legislation

A large number of pieces of UK legislation have some bearing on environmental issues, but the 1990s were dominated from an environmental viewpoint by two major Acts of Parliament which set the framework for environmental regulation.

Environmental Protection Act 1990

Part I covers integrated pollution control (see Chapter 5) and air pollution control by local authorities. It acts as the primary legislation for a range of Statutory Instruments which set out detailed provisions for specific substances and processes.

Part II concerns waste on land, with provisions covering:

- harmful deposits
- waste management licensing
- the collection and disposal or treatment of controlled waste
- waste recycling plans and waste disposal plans.

Part III covers statutory nuisances and clean air provisions.

Part IV concerns litter.

Part V amends the Radioactive Substances Act 1960.

Part VI concerns genetically modified organisms, with the *'purpose of preventing or minimising any damage to the environment which may arise from the escape or release from human control of genetically modified organisms'.*

Part VII set up the Nature Conservancy Councils for England and Scotland and the Countryside Council for Wales.

Part VIII has miscellaneous provisions including provisions covering:

- restrictions on the importation, use, supply or storage of injurious substances or articles
- restrictions on the importation or exportation of waste
- information on potentially hazardous substances
- public registers of contaminated land
- pollution of controlled waters
- deposits and incineration at sea
- stray dogs
- banning of straw and stubble burning
- financial assistance for environmental purposes, including assistance to the Groundwork Foundation.

Environment Act 1995

Part I of this Act concerns the setting up of the Environment Agency and the Scottish Environment Protection Agency.

Part II deals with contaminated land and abandoned mines.

Part III concerns changes in the regulations governing National Parks.

Part IV is concerned with air quality, including the establishment of a National Air Quality Strategy and the allocation of powers to the Environment Agencies (English/Welsh and Scottish) and local authorities.

Part V has miscellaneous provisions, including clauses covering:

- a National Waste Strategy
- producer responsibility provisions regarding packaging waste
- mineral planning permissions
- the protection of important hedgerows
- grants for certain drainage works
- and various fisheries regulations.

Many of the provisions of both of these major Acts are discussed later in the book.

3 The business framework

> *'Establishment and implementation of an organisation's EMS (environmental management system) is of central importance in determining the organisation's environmental policy, objectives, and targets.'*
>
> INTERNATIONAL ORGANISATION FOR STANDARDISATION
>
> *'Sustainable development has come a long way in the last ten years. If not yet part of everyday language (and is it reasonable to think that it ever will be?), it is now incontrovertibly entering the mainstream of politics and business.'*
>
> SIR JOHN HARMAN, UK ROUND TABLE ON SUSTAINABLE DEVELOPMENT *FIFTH ANNUAL REPORT*

This chapter looks at the patterns of regulation and commercial pressure which are encouraging, and in some cases forcing, organisations to take an environmental perspective into account in planning and controlling their activities. It looks initially at the framework under which all organisations now operate, and subsequently at the environmental business sector, and at the opportunities presented within it.

Although the emphasis is on commercial organisations, much of the information in this chapter is also relevant to public sector and voluntary organisations.

The green company

Virtually every aspect of a company's operations affects, and is affected by, the environment in which it operates. Accordingly, a company which wishes to operate in an environmentally friendly way must take into account every aspect of its operations. These should be considered in an integrated way, through the development and application of an environmental policy, which will take into account, for example:

- the selection of operating site(s)
- the design of new, and the redesign of existing, buildings and other structures
- the choice of products
- the design of individual products (discussed further in Chapter 15)
- the choice of suppliers – of raw materials, components and services
- the use and handling of raw materials and components
- the design of production processes, including the handling of any emissions
- supply and distribution systems
- waste management (reuse, recycling, disposal)
- supply and distribution systems
- all aspects of transport and communications
- management and accounting procedures
- plant and building maintenance.

Environmental aspects are of course only one aspect of an organisation's policies and procedures, and the environmentally conscious organisation will look to balance its effect on the environment with its economic performance and its effects on society as a whole.

It is undeniable that some environmental protection measures add to an organisation's costs. Recent studies suggest that in many industrial sectors (for example, oil, steel, chemicals, power generation and paper manufacturing) environmental protection consumes from 5% to 20% of overall production costs, and accounts for an even higher proportion of current investment. It has been estimated that up to 15% of a merchant vessel's total annual costs are taken up by measures to meet international and national standards; and that this figure is 1% or 2% lower for ships registered in countries with less demanding environmental regulations.

Clearly this gives a competitive advantage to the organisations and vessels which do not have to comply, and in theory at least it can lead to 'ecological dumping', or the movement of dirty industries to countries with lower environmental standards (sometimes referred to as 'pollution havens'). It also contributes to the rapid decline of some dirty industries and processes, and the equally rapid rise of replacement industries using cleaner technologies.

Greater standardisation of regulations (for example, throughout the EC) can help to reduce the risk, but there are instances of industries shifting location. One example is the European phosphate fertiliser industry, which collapsed in the late 1980s, largely under the weight of EC regulation, with its products being replaced by cheaper fertilisers manufactured largely in North Africa. There are also many examples of firms with a heavy investment in older and dirtier technologies failing to make the technological transition required to cope with tighter new regulations.

However, some studies, particularly those that have explored the Eastern European experience over recent years, suggest that low environmental standards act as a deterrent rather than an incentive to potential foreign investors. This may in part be because lower environmental standards tend to be allied to poor infrastructures, low standards of living, and social and political instability. Certainly it is true that high environmental standards tend to be the norm across the developed world, although there is evidence too of governments taking into account local industrial patterns when agreeing to international regulations. For example, in the last years of the twentieth century the UK and some other EC countries had strong industrial sectors involved in manufacturing or using CFCs and this undoubtedly slowed EC attempts to agree to international proposals to phase out CFCs very rapidly.

More significantly, there has been a shift in recent years away from the perception that environmentally friendly businesses are expensive to run, and towards the perception (borne out by research) that there are many business benefits to pursuing a positive and proactive environmental policy.

Both the EC and the UK government (and other international and national regulatory bodies) take this more positive approach. They argue that a company which plans carefully in order to improve its environmental performance is also likely to improve its overall performance. For example:

- the organisation will find it easier to meet international (and foreign national) regulations, assisting its exports

- the organisation will find it easier to obtain planning permission and other types of operating consent
- increasingly significant green investment funds will become available as a possible source of finance
- environmental management techniques will contribute to an altogether tighter and more efficient management system
- redesign of products and processes may result in lower raw material and component costs, providing an opportunity to improve profit margins
- redesign of products and processes, and general energy efficiency measures, will reduce fuel bills
- better control of production and cleaner work processes will reduce the risk of pollution and other incidents, minimising disruption to production, staff absences and insurance premiums
- green policies will contribute to employee morale and thus to employee productivity
- green policies and products will appeal to consumers, enhancing brand identity and possibly opening up new markets among environmentally-conscious organisations and individuals
- cleaner processes will result in a better relationship with the surrounding community and fewer complaints
- redesign of products and processes may result in less waste, reducing waste disposal costs
- opportunities may arise to reuse or recycle waste material, providing significant new income streams.

Environmental management and auditing

Three linked steps enable a company to shift to a green perspective:

- drawing up and adopting an environmental policy
- environmental management techniques designed to put the environmental policy into practice
- environmental auditing, to track achievements against policies.

This three-stage process was developed originally in the US in the late 1970s and early 1980s, and is now well established, with a solid core of theory and much practical experience to guide companies going down this route.

Environmental policies

The list of aspects of an organisation's activities that affect the environment on page 29 provides an outline of the scope of the organisation's environmental policy. The first aim of the policy should be to ensure that the organisation is fully in compliance with all relevant statutory requirements. It should include a general mission statement, reinforcing the organisation's general intention to take an environmentally (and socially) responsible approach both to existing activities and to possible new developments. It should also include clear and quantified targets. For example:

- to reduce energy or water requirements by a specific or percentage amount
- to reduce harmful emissions by a specific or percentage amount
- to reduce raw materials requirements by a specific or percentage amount
- to reuse or recycle a specific amount or percentage of waste material.

Aspects of an organisation's operations which could be covered in its environmental policy include:

- materials and components sourcing and handling (avoiding non-renewable sources, and taking full account of the environmental impact of transporting goods and materials)
- choice of suppliers and contractors, taking account of their social and environmental policies
- buildings and other structures (maintaining or improving their appearance and energy efficiency)
- information (providing full and appropriate information to employees, customers and other stakeholders including the general public)
- product design
- product use (providing information and facilitating procedures to ensure that products are used, stored and disposed of at the end of their life in the most environmentally favourable way)
- packaging materials (minimising use and maximising opportunities for reuse and recycling)
- process design or redesign
- new developments (ensuring that proper environmental impact assessments are carried out – see pages 165–8)
- transport (reviewing the need for journeys and the choice of transport type by all employees and contractors)
- waste generation, handling and disposal
- post-operation disposal and remediation or reuse of sites, equipment and residues
- accident and emergency plans.

The organisation's environmental policy should be formalised in writing. It should receive active support at board level, and it should be disseminated to all those affected by it, including not only staff, but suppliers, contractors, customers, investors and so on.

Environmental management

The purpose of environmental management is to ensure that the organisation's environmental policy is put into practice. Environmental management should be practised throughout the organisation, but it should also receive specific attention from designated individuals, with a board member taking ultimate responsibility. Its core tasks are:

- to disseminate the organisation's environmental policy and ensure that all members of staff comply with it
- to monitor existing activities and ensure that they are run efficiently and are in compliance with existing and new regulations, and with specific consents granted to the organisation
- to ensure that existing products are in compliance with existing and new regulations
- to review existing products, processes and other corporate aspects, and consider where there is room to achieve an environmental improvement
- to assess proposals for new sites, new processes and new products from an environmental standpoint
- to ensure that accident and emergency arrangements are kept fully operational and up to date, and to manage actual accidents and emergencies should they occur
- to report on progress to the organisation's management, regulators and stakeholders.

Environmental management should be an ongoing activity, with all products and processes being put under regular review so that full advantage can be taken of emerging opportunities to improve on current practice. It should be fully integrated with all other aspects of the organisation's management, and it should take account of the standards for environmental management that already exist and are being further developed.

The environmental manager will want to pay particular attention to sources of pollution, including both point and diffuse sources of emissions to air, land or water. Monitoring arrangements should be planned and implemented for each source.

The environmental manager will also want to take account of experience elsewhere in his/her sector, and to make use of benchmarks of environmental performance.

Environmental auditing

While environmental management is an ongoing activity, an environmental audit is a snapshot review of the organisation's performance from an environmental standpoint. The aim is to compare performance against policies and against regulatory requirements, to provide a benchmark for future comparisons, and to provide information to managers or stakeholders.

There are numerous types of environmental audit; some examples follow.

Compliance audits assess the organisation's compliance with regulations and with the conditions of specific consents (for example, emissions limits and water abstraction permissions).

Corporate audits consider the organisation as a whole and its environmental policy.

Issues audits consider the organisation's policy on one or more general environmental issues, for example, recycling or ethical sourcing.

Site audits review activity on a specific site, focusing on, for example, emissions from point locations, arrangements to recycle materials, accident and emergency preparations.

Activity audits focus on one or more corporate activities.

Product/service analyses focus on one or more products or services, analysing their cradle-to-grave environmental impact.

Raw materials audits specifically assess the organisation's sourcing, handling and use of raw materials.

Energy audits specifically assess the organisation's use of energy.

Health and safety audits are concerned with these aspects of the environmental policy.

Associate audits assess the environmental policies and performance of suppliers, contractors or agents.

Aquisitional and transactional audits assess the environmental policies and performance of organisations with which the parent organisation may become involved, for example in takeovers or joint ventures.

Divestiture liability audits concern post-use issues such as disposal, demolition and site remediation.

Environmental accounting and reporting

The discipline of environmental accounting is concerned with clarifying the impact of environmental factors on:

- the costs of the organisation
- the revenues of the organisation
- the assets of the organisation
- the liabilities, including contingent liabilities, of the organisation.

Environmental management accounting is a part of the environmental manager's toolkit, concerned with providing a sound financial basis on which to make decisions that have an environmental dimension. Environmental financial accounting is an essential reactive activity, concerned with reporting on the company's performance from a financial/environmental standpoint.

There are limited legal requirements for companies to report on social and ethical issues, and at its lowest level an environmental report is a means of fulfilling these requirements. More widely, an environmental report can become the organisation's vehicle for publishing its environmental policies and reports on its environmental performance, either as a section of the annual financial reports, or as a separate report which is made available to stakeholders on a similar basis to annual financial reports.

Most of the UK's top 100 companies currently report on environmental matters, but environmental reporting is less common for smaller organisations. About one in five of the top 100 (mostly companies whose activities have a heavy impact on the environment) produce separate environmental reports, while the remainder devote a section of their annual report to environmental issues. The content and detail of these reports varies widely. Many companies are happy to publish their environmental mission statements, but far fewer are prepared to publish information beyond that required by law, for example on clean-up liabilities or on failures to meet regulatory requirements, which could affect the financial performance of the company or lay it open to possible litigation. In many instances information on contingent liabilities is not readily obtainable or quantifiable.

Since there are no statutory benchmarks for environmental policies, the organisation typically assesses its performance against standards and targets which it has set itself, weakening the value of these reports for comparative purposes.

It seems clear that environmental reporting will become more widespread and more systematic in future. In a 1998 consultation paper on *Sustainable Business*, the DETR commented that:

> *'There is a need to widen the take up and extent of environmental reporting so that the public, investors and the City can judge how effective companies are at managing their impact on the environment.'*

The Association of Chartered and Certified Accountants (ACCA) makes an annual Environmental Reporting Award.

Standards for environmental management and reporting

The EC Eco-Management and Audit Scheme (EMAS)

This is a voluntary scheme with statutory backing, which was formally launched in the UK in May 1995. It is aimed primarily at manufacturing companies, although it is also possible for local authorities and other organisations to register using slightly different criteria. A site-specific scheme, it registers organisations on a site by site basis when they meet its criteria after independent verification.

EMAS consists of seven core steps:

- formalising an environmental policy
- carrying out an environmental review
- establishing an environmental programme to put the policy into practice
- managing the programme, including organising and documenting it, ensuring that responsible staff are trained, and integrating it into the company's existing management structure
- audits of performance at regular intervals
- issuing annual public environmental statements linked to the audit process
- validation of the environmental statement by an accredited verifier.

Take-up of EMAS in the UK has been relatively slow, with only about 3% as many sites becoming certified as have become certified in Germany.

British, European and international non-statutory standards

British Standard (BS) 7750, *Specification for Environmental Monitoring Schemes*, was the world's first environmental monitoring standard. Published in 1992, it took a quality systems approach, linking with other BSI and European standards for quality management. In 1997 BS 7750 was superseded by the introduction of a more comprehensive set of International Organization for Standardisation (ISO) standards covering aspects of environmental management and monitoring.

ISO 14001 is the standard on *Environmental Management Schemes–Specification with Guidance for Use,* the core standard which assists organisations in formulating an environmental management system, policy and objectives. It was introduced in 1996, and more than 650 UK organisations are now certified to the standard. Recent reviews are looking to bring ISO 14001 more closely in line with EMAS (discussed above).

Among the supporting standards are:

ISO 14004 which provides additional guidance on developing and maintaining an environmental management system.

ISO 14010, BSI EN ISO 14011 and **BSI EN ISO 14012** which are all concerned with environmental auditing.

ISO 14015 (under development) which concerns the environmental assessment of sites and entities.

ISO 14020, 14021 and 14024 which are concerned with environmental labels and declarations.

ISO 14040, 14041, 14042, 14032, 14048, 14049 and 14950 which are all concerned with environmental management lifecycle assessment.

Future standards will concentrate on environmental labelling and on procedures in small and medium-sized enterprises.

These are all standards concerned with environmental management practices, which must be audited and certified by a third party before the standard is met. They do not however set specific standards for the environmental achievements of the organisation. They are complementary to, and compatible with, the EMAS scheme outlined above.

Other standards and assessment tools

The **Index of Corporate Environmental Engagement** is an assessment carried out by the business-led environmental organisation Business in the Environment. It measures and compares the extent to which FTSE 100 companies manage their environmental affairs, using criteria such as:

- whether the company has adopted a corporate environmental policy and environmental management system
- whether senior management have been assigned responsibility for environmental performance
- whether corporate environmental objectives are published
- whether corporate targets for improvement have been adopted and are being audited

- the terms of engagement of suppliers, employees and other stakeholders
- the environmental stewardship of products, processes and services.

77 of the top FTSE 100 firms were assessed in the fourth Index, for which they were surveyed in 1999/2000.

CONTOUR is a CBI initiative, launched in September 1997. It provides a benchmarking tool for companies to assess how they fare on environment, health and safety issues, with the emphasis on practice rather than policy.

Ethical trading and ethical sourcing

The sourcing of raw materials from sustainable sources is only one of a complex of issues concerned with the performance of organisations throughout the supply chain. Other issues of great concern to many organisations (and their customers) include:

- the use of child labour
- payment of fair wages to labourers
- general environmental standards in associate companies.

Social Accountability 8000, the universal standard for ethical sourcing, is an initiative of the Council on Economic Priorities. It provides a common framework for ethical sourcing for companies of any size and any type, anywhere in the world. By setting out specific requirements on such issues as trade union rights, use of child labour, working hours and fair pay, companies can demonstrate their commitment to best practice.

Business opportunities and job creation

As noted above, environmental protection is not seen today as a negative factor, a burden placed on organisations that makes them less competitive. Rather, the emphasis both institutionally and corporately is on finding win-win solutions: taking advantage of improving technology and improving standards to find and exploit business opportunities. Some of these are in 'green' sectors, specifically concerned with improving environmental standards, while some are concerned with product development in all sectors of industry and commerce.

Business in the Environment estimate that the environmental technology market is worth US$200 billion and will grow up to US$600 billion. The Joint Environmental Markets Unit (JEMU) estimated it to be even larger: currently at US$280 billion, and likely to rise to US$640 billion by 2010. An estimated 3.5 million workers in the EC are already employed in the environmental sector. In the UK, the JEMU database lists about 4,000 firms (mostly small and medium sized) with a total of 140,000 employees and an annual turnover of £5 billion. This already represents 1% of GDP.

JEMU sees as the core 'green' industries:

- air pollution control
- environmental services including consultancy and training
- waste management

- environmental monitoring and instrumentation
- water and waste water treatment
- noise and vibration control
- contaminated land remediation
- energy management
- renewable energy
- marine pollution control.

Energy efficiency

There will be continuing regulatory pressure to improve energy efficiency, upgrading energy-using appliances and improving building insulation. The estimate of the European Foundation for the Improvement of Living and Working Conditions is that if all sectors were required to use energy conservation best available technologies, an extra 500,000 jobs would be created in the EC. The Association for the Conservation of Energy estimates that 1,200,000 new jobs could be created if energy conservation in the UK was taken seriously. Much of the poorest energy-efficient performance is in run-down areas with high unemployment, which makes the potential impact even more significant.

Power generation using new technologies and renewable fuel sources

Friends of the Earth estimate that if half the EC's renewable energy potential was realised by 2020 (enabling this sector to meet 14% of primary energy demand) there would be a net gain of around 515,000 jobs. Concentrating on developing and exploiting renewable sources of energy would, according to some studies, create five times more jobs than would be created by improving fossil fuel-based technology.

The renewable energy industry consists predominantly of small and medium-sized organisations which are recognised as being a major source of new job opportunities in the EC. Biomass fuel sources are largely available in rural areas with employment problems. Up to 160,000 new jobs could be created from the development of power generating facilities using biomass as a fuel.

The emerging UK wind generation industry has already created over 3,500 direct and indirect jobs. Employment in operation and maintenance activities per unit of electricity generated is sixteen times greater for wind farms than for typical fossil fuel generation technologies. Greenpeace's estimate is that if wind energy is exploited to meet 10% of the country's electricity demands, it could lead to the creation of 36,000 jobs.

Environmentally friendly transport

Among the employment opportunities in this sector are jobs concerned with:

- the construction and maintenance of rail (including light rail and trams), cycling and walking infrastructures

- the manufacture of trains, buses and bikes
- operation of buses and trains.

A study by the German Road League and the construction union IG Bau Steine Erden found that investing DM100 billion in road building would yield only 1,201 to 1,630 person-years of employment, while the same sum could generate 1,880 jobs in railway construction or 1,992 in local public transport initiatives such as light rail schemes. Another recent study by Friends of the Earth suggests there could be net job gains of 130,000 in the UK if there was a switch to public transport and cycling sufficient to reduce passenger road traffic by 10% from 1990 levels by 2010.

Biotechnology

Although biotechnology is viewed as a potentially major field with significant employment potential, it is also regarded with some caution from an environmental viewpoint. Many environmentalists feel that the safety of products such as genetically-modified crops is not yet proven beyond doubt. The EC's policy is that it is crucial to ensure the safety of biotechnology ('biosafety'), and it has been developing mechanisms for risk assessment, management and control with this in mind.

The DTI's Manufacturing for Biotechnology initiative is a two-year programme launched in 1998, to help small and medium-sized enterprises develop in the biotechnology market. It provides advice, information and training grants.

'Biowise' is a major DTI-funded programme to improve the competitiveness of UK industry through the use of biotechnology, and support the development of the UK biotechnology supplier industry. It provides information, consultancy and advice, and grant support to companies to demonstrate the benefits of biotechnology.

Government policies

Numerous EC and UK policies are concerned with the impact of organisations and businesses on the environment. Many are covered in more specific contexts elsewhere in this book, and the emphasis here is on general policies.

Overall, both EC and UK policies centre on the concept of sustainable development outlined in the Introduction. The UK *Sustainable Business* consultation paper, published in 1998, introduces the concept of 'market transformation'. This is seen as a way of transforming market sectors and the use of best available products by consumers, by a combination of:

- negotiated agreements with industry sectors, to encourage them to improve the environmental performance of products
- incentives for consumers to encourage them to replace old and inefficient appliances more rapidly (including public sector procurement initiatives)
- regulated minimum standards to remove the worst-performing products from the market

- information initiatives including labelling schemes, to encourage consumers to purchase the best-performing products.

The stated intention is to set a framework of long term (20–30 year) objectives, looking to negotiate both framework agreements and detailed commitments with business sectors. The five main themes of the document are:

- the development of goods and services which meet people's needs while consuming fewer natural resources
- involving business in developing sustainable communities for people to live and work in
- policies to manage and protect the environment and resources, encouraging businesses both to avoid harmful impacts by using the best available current technology, and to develop innovative new products and processes
- sending the right signals to the public, firstly by ensuring that environmental costs are reflected in the market price of goods and services, and secondly by enlarging and stimulating consumer choice
- supporting international action where it is necessary and appropriate.

Also included in the paper is a list of the environmental indicators that are perceived in the document as being most relevant to businesses. These give an indication of the scope of the government's concern with the business/environment interface.

National core indicators:

- measures of eco-efficiency and waste minimisation in production and distribution
- energy consumption/carbon/greenhouse gas emissions compared to GDP (by key sector)
- water consumption compared to GDP
- materials consumption compared to GDP
- freight traffic compared to GDP, by mode
- empty running of vehicles
- total industrial and commercial waste compared to output
- recycling ranges for industrial and commercial waste
- environmental engagement of companies, including target-setting, reporting, and the take-up of environmental management systems.

Measures of how we meet consumer needs and aspirations while using fewer natural resources:

- average energy efficiency of selected consumer goods, including cars
- energy and water use in the home
- household waste per person/household.

Measures of our management and protection of our environment and resources:

- emissions of pollutants to air and water
- reduction in the use of toxic materials
- pollution incidents.

Measures of the signals and information we provide to the consumer:

- extent of verifiable information provided to the consumer, for example, through labelling
- extent of consumer understanding of key issues and impacts.

Measures of competitiveness and economic growth:

- economic output
- value of exports
- employees in key sectors.

Measures of impacts overseas:

- trade in 'sensitive' resources, for example, tropical hardwoods
- green/ethical investment.

The Joint Environmental Markets Unit (JEMU)

JEMU is a DTI/DETR initiative to help support and develop the environmental industry, looking to compensate for its current rather fragmented structure and to encourage export opportunities. It maintains a database of companies in this sector, encourages effective communications, and supports the Technology Partnership Initiative (TPI) which aims to support the transfer of environmental technologies to the developing world.

The Environmental Technology Best Practice Programme

This is a transfer programme, run jointly by the DTI and the DETR, to promote better environmental performance and to increase the competitiveness of UK industry and commerce. It collects, analyses and publicises information on the most effective technology, especially in the areas of waste minimisation and cost-effective cleaner technology.

Particular areas of focus, perceived as being most likely to generate substantial environmental and commercial benefits, include chemicals, foundries, glass, paper and board making, printing, textiles and the use of VOCs.

The programme supports research and development, on three bases:

- exploiting current good practice
- the first commercial application of new technology or techniques

- more exploratory programmes provided there is a clear route to the exploitation of the results.

DETR ET Best Practice Programme: Making a Corporate Commitment Campaign

This campaign, launched in 1991, and now in its second phase (MACC2), is particularly focused on energy efficiency strategies. It is a membership campaign – now with over 2,000 members – which encourages organisations to assess and develop their use of resources and management of waste and ensure that their environmental strategy is given support and attention at board level.

4 Climate change and the ozone layer

> *'The international community has confirmed its recognition of the problem of climate change as one of the biggest challenges facing the world in the next century.'*
>
> UN GENERAL ASSEMBLY, *PROGRAMME FOR THE FURTHER IMPLEMENTATION OF AGENDA 21*, 1997

Global warming and other related climate changes, and damage to the ozone layer, are two of the most serious and intractable environmental problems facing the world today. They are in large part caused by atmospheric pollution, but climate change in particular also has other causes, so they are considered here separately. Further information on many of the chemicals mentioned in this chapter is to be found in Chapter 5.

Climate change

Global average surface temperatures have increased by between 0.3°C and 0.6°C since the late nineteenth century. Nine out of the ten hottest years on record have occurred since 1983. In the UK, the 1990s brought four of the five warmest years in a 340-year record, with 1999 being the joint warmest year ever recorded. These are statistically significant trends, supported by the fact that the global sea level has risen between 10 and 25 cm over the same period. Although the first Report of the **Intergovernmental Panel on Climate Change** (IPCC) in 1990 concluded that there was insufficient evidence that the variations were caused by human activity and not by natural variability, new findings led the IPCC to state in its 1995 Assessment that *'The balance of evidence suggests a discernible human effect on climate.'*

The earth's temperature is controlled by a complex set of natural processes. Solar radiation (in visible, ultraviolet and near-infrared wavelengths) is absorbed by the earth, mostly at the surface, and redistributed by the atmosphere and the oceans. At the same time, energy is radiated outwards in longer infra-red wavelengths. Some of this outwards radiation is absorbed by gases in the atmosphere – a natural process known as the greenhouse effect – and the rest is lost to space. The heat gain from the solar radiation is balanced by the heat loss from the outgoing infra-red radiation. If the amount of incoming or outgoing radiation changes, or if the distribution of energy alters within the Earth-atmosphere system, this can lead to changes in the earth's climate.

The earth's atmosphere is divided into layers according mostly to their temperature. The layer nearest the earth, the troposphere, stretches to between 8 km (at the poles) and 16 km (at the equator) above the surface. It contains 75% of the gaseous matter in the atmosphere, including virtually all the water vapour and aerosols (small particles of matter). Above this is the stratosphere, which stretches to approximately 50 km. (The outer layers, the mesosphere and the ionosphere, do not have a significant impact on the earth's climate.) The stratosphere contains much of the total of atmospheric ozone (O_3), and includes what is commonly referred to as the 'ozone layer'.

The naturally occurring 'greenhouse gases' which absorb outgoing radiation include:

- water vapour
- carbon dioxide (CO_2)
- ozone (O_3)
- methane (CH_4)
- nitrous oxide (N_2O).

Concentrations of greenhouse gases in the atmosphere are now rising rapidly due to human activities. This rise is expected to increase the greenhouse effect, forcing up global average temperature and bringing about a global climate change.

Human activities affect levels of naturally occurring greenhouse gases in two ways. One way is by emission of the gases (or substances which combine in the atmosphere to create them), from industrial processes involving the burning of fossil fuels and, to a lesser extent, cement production, and from vehicles powered by fossil fuels. This is the largest cause of recent changes in the composition of the atmosphere. (The process of atmospheric pollution is discussed in detail in Chapters 5 and 6.)

The second way is by changes in the pattern of plant life (and to a smaller extent, animal life) on earth. Vegetation (especially trees) and soils act as 'carbon sinks', absorbing and thus storing large quantities of carbon. Changes in land use can both release carbon dioxide into the atmosphere and reduce the size of the carbon store. The most significant change in global plant cover over recent years has been the large-scale destruction of tropical rainforests.

In addition, new gases have been created by industrial processes which also contribute to the greenhouse effect. Among the most significant of these are:

- halocarbons: including halons, chlorofluorocarbons (CFCs: compounds containing chlorine, fluorine and carbon) and methyl chloroform
- hydrochlorofluorocarbons (HCFCs: compounds containing hydrogen, chlorine, fluorine and carbon), which were introduced as a less-damaging alternative to CFCs, and stay in the atmosphere for up to twenty years
- hydrofluorocarbons (HFCs: compounds containing hydrogen, fluorine and carbon) which are also being used to replace ozone depleting substances and have atmospheric lifetimes ranging from one to over 250 years
- perfluorocarbons (PFCs) and sulphur hexafluoride (SF_6) which are produced in very small quantities but are very powerful greenhouse gases and remain accumulating in the atmosphere for thousands of years, so are likely to influence the climate long into the future.

The contribution of the main greenhouse gases to the enhanced greenhouse effect since pre-industrial times is as follows:

- carbon dioxide 64%
- methane 19%

- CFCs and HCFCs 10%
- nitrous oxide 5.7%
- others 1.3%

SOURCE: FRIENDS OF THE EARTH

The following table indicates how their current levels in the atmosphere compare with estimated pre-industrial levels, and how they are tending to change.

	pre-industrial annl atmos concentration (ppmv)	**1994 ave. atmospheric concentration**	**Current change % per annum**
Carbon dioxide	280	358	0.4
methane	0.7	1.72	0.6
nitrous oxide	0.275	0.312	0.25
HCFC-22	0	0.00011	5

SOURCE: *DIGEST OF ENVIRONMENTAL STATISTICS 1998*, TABLE 1.1

These continuing increases in concentration mask the fact that for carbon dioxide, methane and nitrous oxide, the level of UK emissions fell throughout the 1980s and early 1990s, though for carbon dioxide and nitrous oxide this trend was reversed in the mid-1990s, and in the absence of strong action, UK emissions are projected to continue on an upward course through the early years of this century. For carbon dioxide the fall was almost entirely owing to a shift from coal fired to gas fired power stations. Despite this drop-off, UK emissions of greenhouse gases per person are still higher than those, not only of developing countries but of many developed countries.

Increases in aerosols (such as sulphates and soot) and related changes in clouds slightly offset the effect of increases in greenhouse gases. As far as possible, such complexities are allowed in recent calculations of the possible effect of human activities on climate.

Ozone levels

Ozone is a form of oxygen and is found throughout the atmosphere, with 90% of its occurrence in the stratosphere, between 10 and 50 km above the ground (the so-called ozone layer). Ozone is toxic to living matter, and in the lower atmosphere (the troposphere) it can be regarded as a serious pollutant. However the ozone in the stratosphere has a positive role to play, as a filter for harmful ultraviolet radiation (UV-B). It also acts as a greenhouse gas.

Ozone levels are maintained through a complex series of chemical reactions as ozone is constantly being broken down and reformed in the atmosphere. This process is naturally in balance, but there is now evidence that human activities have upset this balance causing ozone concentrations to increase in the troposphere (see Chapter 6) and to decrease in the upper atmosphere.

Levels of ozone in the stratosphere vary from year to year owing to fluctuations in meteorological conditions, but it is indisputable now that a general reduction has occurred, to such an extent that there are now 'holes' in the ozone layer. The first clear signs of damage were detected in Antarctica in 1985, and now ozone loss is apparent everywhere except at the equator. Holes now form each winter and spring (when the ozone loss over Antarctica in the lower stratosphere is now almost total), although they are partly repaired in the summer when the polar stratospheric clouds disperse and comparatively ozone-rich warm air comes in from other parts of the globe. Nasa reported that in September 2000 the hole over Antarctica had reached a record size of about 18 million sq km.

Average total ozone values over Antarctica in October are now 50–70% lower than those of the 1960s. In the UK and across the northern mid-latitudes the overall trend for the past twenty years is for a reduction of about 5–6% in stratospheric ozone per decade. There has been no ozone loss in the tropics.

Reduced levels of stratospheric ozone affect crop yields and have negative effects on human (and animal) health, including sunburn, skin cancers, damage to the eye and to the immune system. The depletion of ozone recorded so far over the UK is unlikely to have any significant negative effect, but very much further depletion would undoubtedly have an impact.

It is now generally accepted that the reduction in stratospheric ozone is caused by the emission of man-made compounds containing chlorine and bromine–one molecule of chlorine can destroy many thousands of molecules of ozone. These ozone depleting chemicals include:

- CFCs, used as aerosol propellants and in refridgerators
- HCFCs and HFCs, used as substitutes for CFCs
- methyl chloroform (also called 1,1,1 trichloroethane), used in adhesives and as a solvent for cleaning metals
- carbon tetrachloride, used as a solvent and in the production of CFCs
- methyl bromide, used as a fumigant
- halons, used in fire extinguishers
- hydrobromofluorocarbons (HBFCs), which have various uses.

International agreements to phase out or limit the main ozone depleting substances have resulted in substantial drops in production and consumption. As a result the chlorine loading of the atmosphere probably reached its peak around the end of the 1990s. However, it could take until the latter part of this century for chlorine levels to return to pre-ozone-hole levels.

The problem of stratospheric ozone depletion is connected to that of climate change both by source and by impact. On the one hand, CFCs, halons and their replacements are greenhouse gases and as well as destroying ozone, they contribute to the risk of climate change. On the other hand, ozone itself is a greenhouse gas, and scientists believe that reductions in stratospheric ozone slightly offset the warming effect of rises in concentrations of other greenhouse gases. Despite this, there is widespread agreement that because of the serious threats to human and ecosystem well-being posed by the destruction of the ozone layer, it is essential to stop this destruction.

Likely effects of the climate changes

Because the changes in atmospheric concentrations outlined above have time lags, it is impossible to halt global warming entirely: the best that can be achieved is to keep it within tolerable bounds.

The current estimate by the IPCC and other bodies, based on projections of future emissions of greenhouse gases, is that if nothing is done to curb emissions, the global average temperature could increase by between 1 and 3.5°C (with a best-estimate of 2°C) by the end of this century. The IPCC note that *'In all cases the average rate of warming would probably be greater than any seen in the last 10,000 years*.' This general warming would affect climate world-wide, with prospects for more severe droughts and floods in some places and less severe conditions in others. The global mean sea level is also projected to rise by between 15 and 95 cm (with a best-estimate of 50 cm) by 2100, owing to thermal expansion of sea water and melting of glaciers and ice-sheets. Such changes will not be a smooth gradual process. As the IPCC observe, *'the more likely outcome will include surprises and unanticipated rapid changes.'*

Most human activities are sensitive to changes in climate. While the effects of climate change may be beneficial in some places, the overall impact is expected to be adverse. Anticipated impacts include:

- a poleward spread of malaria and other tropical diseases
- reductions in biodiversity, including large-scale losses of boreal forest – and the goods and services ecosystems provide
- more extreme desert conditions
- an increased risk of hunger particularly in subtropical and tropical areas
- major impacts on regional water resources.

In addition, coastal areas could experience major negative effects on tourism, freshwater supplies, fisheries and biodiversity, while a 50 cm rise in sea level would increase the number of people world-wide at risk from flooding from 46 million to 92 million.

Regional projections of climate change are hugely uncertain owing to the limitations of the computer models used to predict future changes. Nevertheless, most models suggest that the south-east of the UK may become drier and the north-west may become wetter. However, recent results indicate a possibility that the Gulf Stream could change, with conditions becoming more like Newfoundland than the Mediterranean. Such uncertainty is a major problem in trying to anticipate and adapt to climate change. Overall sea level in the UK is expected to rise by about the global average, but this masks strong regional variations owing to uplift and subsidence around the coast. The worst affected areas are likely to be along the low-lying east coast, where erosion and flood risks would increase markedly.

Given the uncertainties inherent in regional climate prediction, it is impossible to be precise over the possible implications for the UK. However, results from one study suggest impacts will be mixed, with benefits for forestry, for pastoral agriculture and for tourism, and a negative impact on soil moisture content, wildlife, water resources, arable agriculture, the insurance industry, and human health. There could be an increased spread of weeds, pests and diseases that have not been common in the UK.

With drier soils, the foundations of more buildings could be destabilised. Existing problems such as coastal erosion, the degradation of wetlands and groundwater contamination could be worsened.

Actions to alleviate the situation

Two kinds of action are necessary. The first, and in the UK by far the most important, is a concerted move to reduce man-made emissions of the gases which contribute to the greenhouse effect and which destroy the ozone layer. The second is a change in land-use patterns to halt or reverse the destruction of carbon sinks, by moving to the sustainable management of biomass resources.

Changes in patterns of energy generation have already made a significant impact, and further changes in fuels used for power and transportation could bring about further improvements. Among the most important elements are:

- The use of comparatively low-carbon-content fossil fuels. (Natural gas has only 60% the carbon content of coal. Coal production in the UK fell from 92.8 million tonnes of oil equivalent in 1970 to 25.2 million tonnes in 1999, while natural gas production rose from 10.5 million tonnes in 1970 to 99.6 million tonnes in 1999.)
- A move from fossil fuel usage to forms of renewable energy generation. (See Chapter 10.)
- The development and exploitation of alternative fuels for transport.

Perhaps more important however is a reduction in overall energy usage. This can be achieved through:

- Energy efficiency measures, by enterprises and by individual households.
- A reduction in transport usage. (See Chapter 11.)
- More efficient power plants. (Gas-fired plants have an efficiency rating of up to 55%, compared to 38% for the average coal-fired plant.)

The final method of reducing emissions is by technological and process changes. For example:

- Some greenhouse gases used in industrial and chemical processes have less-damaging or non-ozone depleting alternatives, which can be used to replace them. EC policy now is to prevent all but essential uses of CFCs and other ozone-depleting chemicals.
- Clean-up technology can in some circumstances help to reduce emission levels: for example, catalytic converters on cars reduce their methane emissions.
- Reduction in the use of landfill (which can generate methane) as a waste disposal method.
- The burning of methane (either as a fuel or simply by flaring methane from landfill), to convert it to carbon dioxide, which is up to 60 times less powerful as a greenhouse gas.

Carbon sink measures which can be taken in the UK include:

- more afforestation

- possible changes in the EC set-aside regulations, to ensure that set-aside land is not rotated on a frequent basis and is used to grow non-food crops (such as biofuels).

International agreements

Global warming and the depletion of the ozone layer are international problems, and to a large extent national policies are determined by the framework of international agreements. In large part these agreements accept that it is up to the industrialised nations to take the lead in reducing greenhouse and ozone-depleting gases. It is likely that developing countries, in contrast, will continue to see their emissions levels (which are substantially below those of the developed world) increase over the next 20 years or more. It is of real concern that this understandable development will negate the progress in the developed world, and that overall the actions agreed are insufficient to combat the threat of global climate change.

As the UN General Assembly commented in its 1997 review of the Rio Conference, '*the emission and concentration of greenhouse gases continue to rise, even as scientific evidence assembled by the Intergovernmental Panel on Climate Change and other relevant bodies continues to diminish the uncertainties and points ever more strongly to the severe risk of global climate change. So far, insufficient progress has been made by many developed countries...*'

The UK is a signatory to all the following agreements:

The Vienna Convention on Protection of the Ozone Layer, 1985

The first international agreement on ozone depletion. Under this Convention, governments committed themselves to protect the ozone layer and to co-operation in developing scientific understanding of atmospheric processes.

Montreal Protocol on Protection of the Ozone Layer, 1985

Definite actions aimed at tackling the problem of stratospheric ozone depletion were agreed under this protocol. Agreed in 1987 and coming into force in 1989, the Protocol aims to reduce and eventually eliminate the emissions of man-made ozone depleting substances through controls on the production and supply.

The range of chemicals covered and speed of reductions required were increased progressively through **Amendments to the Protocol**: in London in 1990, in Copenhagen in 1992, in Vienna in 1995, in Montreal in 1997 and in Beijing in 1999. Under the Protocol and its Amendments, parties agreed to phase out of production and consumption of bromochloromethane, CFCs, carbon tetrachloride, halons, methyl chloroform and HBFCs before the end of the twentieth century, and to a progressive phase out of production and consumption of HCFCs by 2030 and of methyl bromide by 2005.

Within the Protocol and its Amendments, special dispensations are given for essential uses and, in the case of methyl bromide, quarantine applications. A certain amount of production is also permitted to meet the needs of developing countries which have a ten-year grace period for compliance. There is no agreement on HFCs which are seen as long-term substitutes in some applications, which is significant as these are greenhouse gases.

UN Framework Convention on Climate Change 1992 (UNFCCC)

This was one of the outcomes of the Rio Conference, and came into force in March 1993. Under the Convention, developed countries committed to stabilising their emissions of carbon dioxide and other greenhouse gases at 1990 levels by 2000. Commitments for developing countries were less – relating mostly to reporting requirements and development of national programmes – on account of their lesser contribution to the problem to date and their lower level of development.

At the first Meeting of Parties in Berlin in 1994, it was agreed that existing commitments were inadequate and negotiations to come up with a new agreement were initiated, culminating in the **Kyoto Protocol** in December 1997. The Protocol sets out for the first time legally binding emissions targets for developed countries for six greenhouse gases: carbon dioxide, methane, nitrous oxide, hydrofluorocarbons, perfluorocarbons, and sulphur hexafluoride. These vary from country to country but, if achieved, are expected to achieve an overall reduction in greenhouse gas emissions from developed countries of about 7%, with the EU agreeing to a target of reducing greenhouse gas emissions by an overall 8% by 2010 compared with 1990 levels, and to making demonstrable progress towards this target by 2005.

The UK's current targets are to cut greenhouse gas emissions to 12.5% below 1990 levels by 2009–2012, and to move towards a 20% cut in carbon dioxide emissions below 1990 levels by 2010.

Current commitments should be viewed in terms of the ultimate objective of the Climate Convention which is: '*stabilisation of greenhouse gas concentrations in the atmosphere at a level that would prevent dangerous anthropogenic interference with the climate system.*' Achieving this objective could require deep cuts in global emissions of greenhouse gases. According to the IPCC, stabilisation of concentrations at current levels would require instantaneous cuts in global emissions of over 50% in the case of carbon dioxide and nitrous oxide and of 8% in methane, and the elimination of all emissions of long-lived gases such as the perfluorocarbons.

Various conferences have followed up the Kyoto Protocol and firmed up its agreements, including meetings in Kuala Lumpur in March 2000 and Bonn in June 2000. Schemes are being developed for Joint Implementation and Clean Development Mechanism projects, which will earn emissions trading credits from 2000 onwards.

EC regulations

EC regulations on ozone-depleting chemicals over more recent years have tended to give effect to the international agreements outlined above. As a result, production of CFCs, halons, carbon tetrachloride and methyl chloroform in the EC has now virtually ceased, except for limited essential uses. Regulations for phasing out HCFCs and reducing methyl bromide have also been agreed and are tighter than the terms of the Montreal Protocol.

The 'bubble' of total reductions agreed by the EU under the Kyoto Protocol has been broken down into targets for the individual Member States, which vary widely according to their capabilities and degree of industrialisation. The UK target is to reduce emissions by 12.5%. (Other Member State targets include Germany minus 21%, Luxembourg minus 28%, Greece plus 25% and Portugal plus 27%.) Overall, the aim is to reduce the emissions of greenhouse gases by 8% compared to 1990 levels, by the period 2008 to 2012.

The EU climate target is backed up by other relevant directives and research programmes on, for example, emission and efficiency standards, methane emissions from landfill, alternative energy sources and transport. Nevertheless achievement of national targets will hinge critically on further action by individual countries.

The UK government's policy

Climate Change: The UK Programme, outlining the first UK programme on climate change was published in 1994, and was intended as a report on the UK government's response to its Rio commitments. The most recent **Draft Programme on Climate Change was** published in 2000. The government's current targets include, in addition to the EC targets mentioned above:

- to reduce emissions of carbon dioxide by 20% from its 1990 level by 2010
- to reduce emissions of greenhouse gases other than carbon dioxide to 12.5% below 1990 levels by 2008–2012.

Also relevant is the National Air Quality Strategy.

Recent initiatives in the energy and transport sectors are discussed in Chapters 10 and 11.

The climate change levy

Among the measures introduced to help meet the Kyoto targets is the climate change levy, which was introduced in the Budget in March 2000, and is intended to come into effect from April 2001. This is effectively a carbon tax, charged on most energy used in the industrial, commercial and public sectors, with the estimated revenue of around £150 million being spent on energy efficiency measures. (See also Chapter 10.)

The Climate Change Challenge Fund

This fund was launched as a government/business partnership in February 1999, and aims to provide a flexible source of funding to help business and developing countries to take action to meet the challenges of climate change, and to develop and take advance of British expertise in clean technologies and renewable energies. Projects supported to date, for example, include feasibility studies for landfill gas use in Malaysia, and vehicle emissions testing in India.

The UK's performance to date

Carbon dioxide emissions in 2000 are expected to be from 4–8% below the 1990 level, and emissions of all greenhouse gases are expected to be 15% below 1990 levels. However, recent improvements that have been achieved – mostly by the reduction of coal usage – may not easily be sustainable at the same rate in the future. Moreover, emissions from traffic growth may rise rapidly if growth is not curbed. For the improvements to be sustained and the required cuts to be made, other methods of reduction must be found, and to some degree these are likely to require changes in current patterns of behaviour from both individuals and organisations.

For other greenhouse gases, the UK remains on target. The government expects emissions in 2000 of methane to be 18% below the 1990 level, and of nitrous oxide to be 70% below.

Significant progress too has been made in achieving targets to increase tree cover in the UK, which has so far doubled this century, and increased by one-third since the early 1970s, through incentive schemes such as the Woodland Grant Scheme and Farm Woodland Premium Scheme. The government target is for a further doubling over the next half-century.

5 Pollution

> *'The Government is... concerned that we do not have even a basic assessment of the possible risks of most chemicals released into the environment in large quantities.'*
>
> DETR, *CHEMICALS IN THE ENVIRONMENT*, 1999.

By pollution is meant here the presence of substances, whether they result from human activity or occur naturally, which have adverse effects on man and/or the environment. Pollution of the environment is a cause of many environmental and health problems, including damage to crops and the problems of climate change and ozone depletion discussed in Chapter 4.

Pollution can affect the air, the land or water supplies, and in some cases the same source of pollution can affect more than one medium: for example, pollutants in the air are the cause of acid rain which in turn pollutes water and land. After a general introduction, this chapter looks at a number of particular pollution problems of this kind. The chapter concludes with a review of regulations and policies to control pollution.

Subsequent chapters specifically consider air pollution, water pollution and the contamination of land. A glossary of common pollutants is on page 207.

Sources of pollutants

Not all pollution is man-made: natural sources too contribute to the volume of noxious substances in the environment. Among these are:

- radiological decomposition
- forest fires
- volcanic eruptions.

Bacteria and allergens too rate as pollutants, and are found in the air, in water, in contaminated materials and foodstuffs.

There are numerous sources of man-made pollution, but a short list of some of the major ones may help to outline the scale of the problem:

- Processes involving the combustion of fossil fuels, including power generation and motorised transport, which emit harmful gases to the atmosphere.
- Other combustion processes which can give off harmful gases, including the incineration of waste plastics and other materials.
- The evaporation of fumes from liquids being stored or used: for example, natural gas leakage in the national distribution network, motor spirit evaporation and solvent evaporation.
- Chemical processes which produce (as their main product or as by-products) toxic substances.

- Spills of dangerous substances contaminating the land and/or water supplies.
- Waste disposal to landfill tips, slag heaps and so on. As well as contaminating the landfill site itself, the refuse may generate harmful gases, and other harmful substances may leach out to contaminate water supplies.
- Sewage and its treatment.
- The use of pesticides and fertilisers in agriculture.

The effects of pollution

The effect on human (and animal) health

Pollutants can affect human beings and animals:

- by their direct effect on the skin
- when they are inhaled
- when they are ingested, typically in food or drink
- indirectly, by affecting the global climate and altering the spread of diseases (see Chapter 4)
- indirectly, by affecting the ozone layer and its protective capabilities (see Chapter 4).

Acute episodes of pollution account for relatively few human deaths and serious illnesses, but the effect of chronic long-term pollution is much more significant. The Department of Health judge air pollution to be responsible each year for 12–24,000 premature deaths; for 14–24,000 hospital admissions; and for many thousands of lesser impacts, including:

- minor illnesses
- reduced levels of activity
- general distress and discomfort.

Serious effects are most common among particularly sensitive groups (the very young and old, and those with existing health problems) and in areas such as congested urban centres where air quality can become particularly poor under certain climatic conditions.

In assessing many substances it is very difficult to establish a direct relationship between the concentration that is found in the air or in water, and the possible toxic effects. Other substances are known to be highly toxic or acute carcinogens to which no level of exposure can be considered safe.

Among the complaints which pollution is thought either to cause or to worsen are:
Allergies and chemical sensitivity. Allergies can be triggered, for example, by house dust mites, cockroach skin scales and particles, pet hair, saliva, urine, skin, pollen and moulds, all of which are found particularly in the indoor environment. Chemical sensitivity, sometimes specific and sometimes widespread, is caused by

exposure to toxic chemicals and has effects that range from mild discomfort to total disability.

Asthma and other respiratory diseases. The incidence of asthma has roughly doubled in the last twenty years, and although this may in part be due to greater willingness to classify cases, it certainly represents a real increase. It affects approximately 6% of the UK population and up to 20% of primary school children. Chronic asthma can be fatal. Among the triggering factors is cigarette smoking. Other respiratory diseases, from coughs to bronchitis, can be triggered or worsened by pollutants that affect the mucous membranes, including ozone, formaldehyde, VOCs, nitrous oxide, environmental tobacco smoke and airborne fibres, and by viral infections.

Cancers. Among the common carcinogens found in the environment are environmental tobacco smoke, radon, benzene and asbestos. The destruction of the ozone layer has led to an increase particularly in skin cancers.

Cardiovascular disease is affected by exposure to carbon monoxide and environmental tobacco smoke.

Cryptosporidiosis results from exposure to cryptosporidium, a microscopic parasite spread by contact and in food and water. Properly operated water treatment processes can partially (but not entirely) remove the risk. It causes diarrhoea, and in some cases more serious illness.

Hormone disruption and damage to the reproductive system. The endocrine system is critical to the functioning of both animals and plants, controlling their growth, maintenance and reproduction. Certain substances appear to interfere with the synthesis and action of hormones in the body. As a result they may have either feminising effects in males, or masculinising effects in females. There is good evidence that reproductive abnormalities have been caused by pollution, particularly in water-based species such as dog whelks. One known cause is the use of tributyl tin (TBT) as an antifouling agent on boats. Some argue that related effects are apparent in the human population, including an increase in testicular and breast cancer, birth defects and declining sperm counts.

Legionnaire's disease is caused by inhaling air in which legionellae bacteria are suspended in water droplets. Air conditioning systems and humidifiers are among the devices which help to spread the disease. It can be fatal.

The effect on plant life

Pollutants can stunt growth, limit the abilities of plants to photosynthesise, or kill them outright. The effects are caused primarily by:

- gases which cause damage to leaves and shoots of plants
- particles which settle on leaves
- particles which settle on soil and are ingested by the plant
- ultraviolet radiation damage owing to ozone layer depletion (see Chapter 4)
- damage to habitats and ecosystems through climate change (see Chapter 4).

The effect on overall quality of life

Among the negative effects of high levels of pollution:

- air pollution can screen out sunlight
- air, land and water pollution can give rise to noxious smells.

The effect on buildings and other inanimate objects

Damage to structures is caused particularly by:

- corrosion by acidic air (or water)
- abrasion of fine or coarse airborne or waterborne particles
- soiling, for example by black smoke
- cleaning-related damage.

Economic effects

Among the economic effects of pollution are the following.

- Pollution affects human health, and contributes to reduced efficiency at work and to sickness absences, causing costs both to individual organisations and to society at large.
- Damage to buildings has a direct economic effect.
- Damage to crops and trees has a direct economic effect.
- Measures to control pollution (for example, flue gas extraction techniques) are a direct charge on polluting industries.
- The clean-up of incidents which cause pollution (such as oil spills) is a charge both on polluting industries and on society at large.
- The remediation of contaminated land involves charges, which may fall on its owners or on society at large.
- Dealing with waste material containing pollutants is costly both to industry and to society at large.
- Pollution can be visually offensive and smell noxious, and this discourages tourism and economic investment in affected areas.

Regulating and reducing pollution

Pollution problems can take a variety of different forms. The pollution might, for example, be:

- acute – that is, a high-level but short-term problem – or chronic – a low-level, long-term problem
- localised or widespread
- caused by a single pollutant or by a combination of different substances

- affecting the air, the land, water, or any combination of these
- from a fixed point source, diffuse sources, or a mobile source
- derived from one or several industrial sectors.

The exact nature of the problem will in large part determine the kind of regulation that is appropriate.

Substance-oriented regulations are most appropriate to deal with individual substances which are used – and can cause pollution – in a variety of different contexts. Examples of these are lead, asbestos, and dioxins.

Source-oriented regulations are most appropriate as a method of controlling specific industries or industrial sectors, which give rise to a range of pollution problems.

Integrated pollution control is a necessary approach when the substance may pollute a combination of air, land or water; or when control of emissions to one of these media may lead to displacement pollution of another kind.

The restraint on the pollutant can also be expressed in various ways, for example as:

Emission limits: that is, the quantity or proportion of a pollutant that it is acceptable for a process to emit. These are applied, for example, to car exhausts and to emissions from incinerators.

Exposure standards and critical loads: that is, the maximum amount of exposure to a pollutant that it is acceptable for an individual or organism to receive. (These are used, for example, to define acceptable limits for radiation.)

Biological standards: that is, the dose of a pollutant that it is acceptable for an individual to receive over a certain time frame, or the maximum amount of a pollutant that may be found in an individual or organism. These are also particularly applicable when an individual or organism builds up its internal level of a substance, rather than excreting it over time.

Operational standards, which concentrate on methods of operation. The argument is that if operations are kept within defined limits, then their polluting capacity will also be controlled.

Reducing pollution

There are two aspects to the question of reducing pollution. One is technological: finding less-polluting alternatives to existing substances and processes. The other is behavioural: enforcing current standards, and persuading or forcing organisations and individuals to change patterns of production, consumption, usage and disposal.

Technological change encompasses:

- changes in material usage, to substitute safer materials for those which offer particular hazards (for example, asbestos or CFCs)
- changes in production processes, to make them 'cleaner' and reduce the quantity of emissions and of hazardous waste
- changes in emission control technology and procedures, using, for example, flue gas desulphurisation, scrubbing and filtration systems.

Behavioural change is achieved through a combination of:

- enforcing existing regulations more tightly, and increasing the penalties for infringement
- introducing new and tighter regulations
- using fiscal incentives, grants and other financial methods of encouraging the use of more environmentally friendly technologies and substances, and discouraging the use of those that are particularly damaging
- voluntary agreements with specific industry sectors to improve the standards of processes and of products
- better environmental management within organisations, including the management of polluting accidents and spills
- information campaigns, to inform both producers and users of polluting materials about the risks and encourage them to change their products and usage patterns.

Specific EC and UK policies and regulations are discussed on pages 68–70.

Acid rain

This is the name given to various processes which cause man-made emissions of acidic substances to be deposited on land and water, often hundreds of kilometres from the pollution source. Acid deposition occurs through wet processes (polluted rain) and through dry processes (direct deposition at surface).

The main effects of acid rain are:

- To acidify the soil in geologically sensitive areas, inhibiting its ability to nourish plant life, and leading to a restricted range of flora and fauna. Upland areas tend to be among the most vulnerable, including those in the north and west of Britain.
- To acidify fresh water, making it toxic to aquatic plant and animal life. Acidification in Scandinavia has led to the reduction or extinction of the fish population in many waters: in over 600 lakes in Norway, for example.
- To corrode building materials including stone, concrete and metals.

Acid rain is caused particularly by sulphur dioxide and oxides of nitrogen, although other contributors include ammonia, volatile organic compounds (VOCs) including dioxins, and heavy metals. The EC and the UK have targets to reduce all these pollutants.

Industrial chemicals

There are now about 70,000 chemicals in use, and 500 to 1,000 are added each year. These include both naturally occurring elements and compounds, and man-made compounds. Naturally-occurring as well as man-made chemicals can cause pollution problems, particularly when they are concentrated as the result of man's activities.

Chemicals not naturally occurring in the environment can enter it, and the proportions of naturally-occurring chemicals can be increased:

- by deliberate release as a product
- as liquid or solid waste matter, or gaseous emissions, from industrial processes, containing (for example) excess raw material, by-products, catalysts or solvents, particularly where filtering and disposal arrangements are not adequate
- through spillages or other accidents
- as waste after the end of product life.

There are several ways in which chemicals can be classified according to the risks they pose. EC regulations require manufacturers and suppliers to classify chemicals according to their intrinsic hazards (for example, whether they are flammable, toxic or carcinogenic). They must provide appropriate packaging and labelling, and industrial and professional users must be provided with written health and safety information.

The WHO classifies chemicals according to their likely carcinogenic effect:

- Group 1 chemicals: clear evidence exists that they are carcinogenic in humans.
- Group 2A chemicals: limited evidence exists that they are carcinogenic in humans, or evidence exists that they are carcinogenic in animals.
- Group 2B chemicals: limited evidence exists that they are carcinogenic in humans, or less than sufficient evidence exists that they are carcinogenic in animals
- Group 3 chemicals: cannot adequately be classified for the lack of sufficient evidence, but there may be some risk.
- Group 4 chemicals: are thought not to be carcinogenic.

The UK government's strategy paper, *Chemicals in the Environment: The Chemicals Strategy* was published in 1999, with the goals of:

- making full information publicly available about the environmental risks of chemicals
- continuing to reduce the risks chemicals pose to the environment and human health, while maintaining industrial competitiveness
- phasing out chemicals posing an unacceptable risk.

Among the actions proposed are speeding up the process of hazard assessments leading to risk management strategies for high-production volume chemicals by 2005, establishing a Stakeholder Forum of those concerned with chemical risks, and the phasing out of chemicals posing unacceptable risk within five years.

The Chemical Industries Association's Responsible Care programme, which was adopted by the UK chemicals industry in 1989, now operates in forty-two countries. Member companies are required to make a commitment to improve their performance constantly, in both health and safety and environmental areas. They may display a Responsible Care symbol.

The DETR's National Centre for Toxic and Persistent Substances (TAPS) provides expertise on toxic and persistence substances to both the government and outside organisations. Chapter 19 of Agenda 21 also deals with the environmentally sound management of toxic chemicals.

Chemical handling and chemical spillages

All chemicals should be kept in a properly designed store, and clearly labelled.

Equipment for dealing with spillages should be maintained in readiness. This should include shovels, drain bungs, and absorbent materials (for example, sand or sawdust) to soak up the spill. There should also be clear records of the site drainage system. It is useful to mark manhole covers and gullies, using blue for surface water and red for foul water. Where possible, shut-off valves should be fitted.

Spillages should never be washed away, and nearby drains, manholes and gullies should immediately be blocked and valves shut, to prevent their entering the water system.

Pollution problems caused by landfill of waste

The anaerobic decomposition of putrescible waste generates a significant volume of gas, principally methane (55%) and carbon dioxide (45%), two powerful greenhouse gases. A tonne of biodegradable waste generates about 6 cubic metres of landfill gas per year. Landfill gas emissions accounted for an estimated 46% of all UK methane gas emissions in 1996.

Leaching is also a significant landfill problem. Chemicals dumped in the landfill, or created by reactions within it, are dissolved in rainwater which then percolates out of the landfill and may join watercourses, or enter the water distribution system through groundwater supply sources.

Oil pollution

Oil pollution can cause considerable damage. Five litres of oil can form a film on the surface of a small lake, drastically reducing the level of oxygen in the water, and making it difficult for fish to breathe. Oil and grease also deoxygenate water as they are broken down. Oil can coat plants and animals, is difficult or impossible to remove without damage, and frequently causes injury or death. Oil-contamination renders drinking water sources unfit for use, and oil spills at sea have been among the greatest environmental disasters of recent years. Commercial oils contain polycyclic aromatics and phenols, and these too are pollutants.

In 1998 oil and fuel became the most frequent type of water pollutant since Environment Agency records began. In 1999 there were over 3,750 substantiated incidents, making up 26% of the total number of around 14,500 substantiated water polluting incidents.

Most oil spillage incidents are caused by:

- spillage during delivery or tank filling
- tank leaks, owing to poor maintenance or to vandalism
- poorly designed tanks
- oil separators either not used on rainwater drains, or poorly maintained and not functioning adequately
- waste oil being disposed of improperly, for example poured into drains or sewers.

Other sources of pollution include corroding pipelines, below and above the surface, and illegal oil discharges at sea.

Handling oil and oil spills

Careful handling significantly reduces the risk of oil pollution, and pre-planning can limit the impact if a spill does occur.

Oil pipelines should for preference be above ground, so they can be inspected regularly, and adequate measures should be taken to protect them against corrosion and physical damage.

Fuel delivery areas should be surrounded by a raised kerb, with the drainage passing through a suitable oil separator. Oil separators should also be used to filter the drainage from petrol filling station forecourts and large car parks.

Oil storage tanks should be sited on an impervious base and surrounded by an oil-tight bund wall with no drainage outlet. The bunded area should be large enough to contain 110% of the volume of the tank and all the pipes and gauges should be enclosed within it. The vent pipe should be directed downwards into the bund.

Oil should be disposed of correctly, and never by discharge into the foul sewer, water drainage system or watercourses. Even domestic quantities of waste oil (for example, from amateur mechanics changing the oil in their car) should be collected and sent for recycling. The Environment Agency can provide the location of oil banks: their Freephone number is 0800 663366.

Preparations to deal with oil spills should include the provision of dry sand or earth which can be used to absorb them.

When an oil spill occurs, every effort should be made to stop the oil from entering drains or watercourses. It should be diverted until earth or sandbags can be used to absorb it. Oil spills should never be hosed down, and any contaminated wash water used to clean up slight oil spillages (for example, on garage forecourts) must not be discharged to the water drainage system, but to the foul sewer, or collected for disposal off sight. The Environment Agency should be notified, and can give advice: their oil spill hotline number is 0800 807060.

Regulations to control oil pollution

In addition to general pollution control-regulations, these include:

- A ban on all deliberate discharges of oil in harbours and coastal waters, and discharges of ballast water in harbours.
- Oil spill regulations came into force in 1998 to implement obligations in the 1990 International Convention on Oil Spill Preparedness, Response and Co-operation (OPRC). They require ports, harbours, oil handling facilities and offshore installations to prepare and submit detailed oil spill contingency plans, and expand the existing regulations covering the reporting of oil spills (at sea or in harbours to the nearest Coastguard Station).

The Marine Pollution Control Unit is the regulatory body for oil pollution at sea.

New oil storage guidelines were issued by the DETR in April 2000.

Finally, the risk of pollution can be lowered considerably when polluting oils are replaced by environmentally considerate lubricants, or ECLs. They can cost around four times as much as conventional mineral-based lubricants, but they tend to last longer, which contributes to their environmentally friendly performance. They are now widely used in Germany, Austria and Scandinavia, and an increase in their use in the UK would be welcome.

Pesticides

There are about 800 different active ingredients approved for use in pesticides in the UK. In addition, there remain traces in the environment of pesticides whose active ingredients are no longer approved for use. The external costs associated with pesticide use have been estimated to be up to £300 million per year.

Particular concerns have been raised about organochloride pesticides, including aldrin, lindane, dieldrin and DDT, and organophosphorus pesticides such as diazonin. Most of these are now banned (aldrin, dieldrin and endrin were banned in 1989) and others are in declining (and severely restricted) use. Among the other substances banned in recent years are non-agricultural uses of atrazine and simazine (banned 1993), which had been widely used as weedkillers.

Applications and patterns of use

Insecticides, herbicides and fungicides are used, for example:

- to kill agricultural and horticultural pests
- as slug killers in gardens
- as rat poison
- to control weeds in parks and gardens, and on roads and railways
- to control pest infestations in buildings
- as masonry and timber preservatives
- in anti-fouling paints
- in mothproofing materials
- as mould killing agents
- as soil sterilants
- as food storage protectors
- as plant growth regulators
- as desiccants
- in tanning and wool processing
- as bird and animal repellents
- and as headlice killers.

Some veterinary products (sheep dip, for example) share common characteristics with them.

The term 'pesticide' is strictly applicable to agricultural products; 'biocides' is the term used for non-agricultural products. Most of the information here applies to both types of product.

Agriculture and horticulture together account for about 88% of the domestic market, and in terms of areas treated, the products used are:

- 45% fungicides
- 32% herbicides and desiccants
- 14% insecticides
- 7% growth regulators
- 2% others.

SOURCE: DEPT. OF THE ENVIRONMENT, *PESTICIDES IN WATER*, 1996.

In terms of weight of active ingredients, the most used is sulphuric acid, used as a desiccant on potatoes and bulbs.

After agriculture, the next largest users are local authorities, who use pesticides mostly for weed control.

The risks of pesticide use

Pesticides are generally accepted to have an useful function: the Pesticides Safety Directorate estimates that were they not used, 30% of world crops would be lost each year to insect activity, weed infestation or plant disease. They can very easily cause pollution, however, particularly when they are not properly used and disposed of.

A major risk is damage to the health of non-target organisms, either through direct ingestion of the pesticide, or via contaminated water, contaminated soil, or food grown in contaminated soil. Among the outcomes are acute poisoning and chronic problems such as cancer, genetic mutations and foetal damage. Some pesticides have hormone-disrupting properties.

There is also a concern that elimination of one part of the food chain may bring about imbalances elsewhere, and result in new infestations by non-target organisms; and there is a significant problem of resistance developing in target organisms, leading on occasion to higher pesticide usage (the 'pesticide treadmill'). One argument in favour of genetically modified crops (there are also arguments against them) is that they can be particularly herbicide-resistant and pest-resistant, reducing the requirement for pesticide usage.

Contamination can derive from:

- direct use of pesticides
- contaminated effluent from pesticide manufacturing facilities
- incorrect disposal which directly or indirectly contaminates water supplies or the sewage system (for example, by leaching from disposal sites)
- spray drift or accidental overspray
- surface runoff and sub-surface drain flow, following rainfall after application

- contaminated rainfall
- the inflow of contaminated groundwater.

Regulation of pesticide use

Government policy is to minimise pesticide usage, which has been falling since the mid-1980s (from around 35,000 tonnes in 1987 to around 27,000 tonnes in 1997) but which remains at a level that raises serious concerns. The 1999 report from the UK government's Working Party on Pesticide Residues indicated that 43% of fresh fruit and vegetable samples were found to contain traces of pesticides.

The EC **Dangerous Substances Directive 1976** underpins most recent legislation. It is discussed on page 68. The core UK legislation to control pesticide use is Part III of the **Food and Environmental Protection Act 1985**, which introduced controls on their advertisement, sale, supply, storage and use. There are also Statutory Instruments amending this legislation and setting out more detailed provisions, largely in order to conform with EC legislation, including the **Control of Pesticides Regulations 1986**. Also significant in this context are the **Control of Substances Hazardous to Health (COSHH) Regulations 1994.**

The use of agricultural pesticides is controlled by the Pesticides Safety Directorate, an agency of the Ministry of Agriculture Fisheries and Food, which also runs the Wildlife Incident Investigation Scheme to investigate cases of wildlife and pet poisoning where pesticides may be involved. Non-agricultural uses are controlled by the Pesticides Registration Section of the Health and Safety Executive. The approval of pesticide manufacture is regulated by five different government departments, acting on acting on the advice of the independent Advisory Committee on Pesticides (ACP) which was set up under the Food and Environmental Protection Act 1985.

Methods of usage

Pesticides should be used only when other methods cannot combat the problem. In agriculture, Integrated Crop Management (ICM) offers a range of practices intended to balance economic crop production and measures to preserve and enhance the environment, which can bring about a reduction in usage. Techniques such as cutting, harrowing, mulching and delayed sowing can help to protect crops from pests and disease.

Where pesticides are to be used, it is important to:

- Correctly identify the problem (the pest, weed or disease).
- Select the correct product, and assess the risks involved using the COSHH regulations as a framework.
- Use non-persistent pesticides wherever possible.
- Purchase no more pesticide than is required, and store it to the correct standard.
- Ensure that the materials are handled and applied by properly trained staff. (In some cases Certificates of Competence are required.)

- Apply pesticides only when conditions are suitable (that is, not when winds could cause spray drift, when the ground is waterlogged or heavily cracked, or when heavy rain is forecast).
- Ensure that all equipment is cleaned after use, following the manufacturer's instructions (particularly important for pesticides that react with water), and using techniques that minimise any water requirement.
- Ensure that any surplus pesticide is disposed of properly. Under no circumstances should it be flushed down the drain or added to landfill waste. In some cases the supplier may take back unused quantities; otherwise, a specialist waste disposal contractor should be employed.
- Ensure that empty containers are disposed of safely. Again, manufacturers may take them back; otherwise they should be punctured and crushed to prevent reuse, and either burned or buried in strict accordance with the appropriate Code of Good Agricultural Practice, or disposed of using a specialist contractor. They should not be sent to general landfill sites.

The BASIS Standard defines how professional users (for example, farmers and crop spraying contractors) should store pesticides. Stores should be carefully located, in a site where any spills or leakages will not immediately contaminate water supplies. Small quantities may be kept in a secure weather-proof vault or container, but for large quantities a purpose-built store should be provided. It should be fire resistant, have an impermeable chemical resistant floor, be bunded or kerbed, and kept locked. The stores should be clearly marked, and a record of their contents should be kept separately. Metal containers should be kept off the ground to reduce the risk of rusting.

Containers should be filled and washed in a prepared area well away from drains and watercourses, with proper provision for containing any spills. Closed chemical tanker systems minimise the risk of spillage and ensure the container is rinsed effectively.

Particular care should be taken to avoid contaminating surface waters. Pesticides (except those specifically intended for aquatic use) should not be sprayed over ditches, watercourses or open drains, or close enough to them that spray drift could contaminate them. Run-off can be prevented by:

- Leaving a no-spray zone near open water.
- Leaving a strip of natural vegetation. (This also provides a valuable wildlife habitat.)

The Environment Agency must generally be consulted, and approval obtained, before any pesticides are used on or near water (including aerial spraying within 250 m of any watercourse or lake).

Radioactivity

All active radioactive substances are capable of causing harm to humans and animals, and thus can be classed as pollutants. Radiation can be absorbed directly from the air, or it can be ingested in contaminated food or drink, or other substances (for instance, soil ingested by children playing, or seawater swallowed by bathers).

There is a natural background level of radioactivity, which causes the average UK citizen to receive a dose of 2.2 mSv (millisieverts) per year, although in areas with high quantities of natural radon the dose can be considerably higher. (In several West Country areas the average dose is up to 8 mSv per year, and in West Cornwall it can reach 100 mSv per year.) The government has an 'action level' roughly equivalent to 10 mSv/year, above which it advises householders to take remedial action to reduce the level of naturally occurring radiation in their homes.

Medical treatment also contributes, with the average dosage from this source at 0.37 mSv per year.

Other sources of radioactive exposure are man-made, and include:

- various industrial processes in which radioactive materials are used
- nuclear power generating stations
- nuclear waste processing facilities
- leaching from contaminated landfill sites
- the residual fallout from testing nuclear weapons.

Radiation can be carried considerable distances from the original polluting source: for example, there was fallout from the Chernobyl disaster in areas to the west of the British Isles.

The government sets dose limits for the public. The limits take account of advice from the National Radiological Protection Board (NRPB) which in turn is based on the recommendations of the International Commission on Radiological Protection (ICRP). The methods of calculating dose rates, and the recommended limits for the public, have both been progressively revised downwards. Currently the limit for exposure of the public from all man-made sources of radioactivity (other than medical exposure) is 1 mSv per year, a figure which is enshrined in EC legislation. This is considerably less than the background rate in some areas, but the low limit reflects the fact that this represents additional exposure. The government's current targets include a reduction in maximum exposure from authorised radioactive discharges to no more than 0.02 mSv a year from 2020 onwards.

The average member of the public receives a radiation dose of only about 0.0004 mSv per year from man-made sources. The dosage is higher to critical groups, including workers in facilities where radioactive material is handled, and those living close to nuclear installations, but still within the 1 mSv limit.

Discharges from nuclear facilities, including discharges to the air, liquid discharges, and solid radioactive wastes, are controlled by authorisations issued under the **Radioactive Substances Act 1993,** which specify discharge limits and require operators to use the best practicable means to limit the radioactive content. Together these controls ensure that doses to the public are as low as reasonably achievable (economic and social factors having been taken into account) and that doses to the critical group (that small group of the public representative of those receiving the highest doses from a source) are well within the 1 mSv annual dose level recommended by NRPB as a limit.

Discharges from nuclear facilities peaked at around 2 mSv per year in 1981, but had fallen by 1999 to less than 0.2 mSv a year.

Levels of exposure are monitored by a number of different bodies. The Environment Agency monitors most environmental sources of exposure, producing an annual report for its Radioactive Substances Monitoring Programme, while MAFF monitors concentrations of radionuclides in foods, publishing an annual report on Radioactivity in Food and the Environment.

The UK government published its proposed *UK Strategy for Radioactive Discharges 2001–2020* in 2000.

Information on nuclear waste is in Chapter 9.

What to do in the event of an incident that causes pollution

Although some requirements are specific, there are also general guidelines that apply to all single incidents which are liable to lead to air, water or ground pollution.

All organisations dealing with hazardous substances should have an emergency action plan which should be followed.

Measures should be taken swiftly to limit harm, for example, by soaking up the material using an absorbent solid, and by blocking drains and diverting flow to prevent it entering the water and sewage systems.

Many incidents must be reported promptly to the relevant authorities. It is also important to notify insurers without delay.

Finally, details of the incident should be retained on record.

Integrated pollution control

At the core of current thinking on pollution prevention and control is the concept of integrated pollution control, or IPC (sometimes defined as integrated pollution prevention and control, or IPPC). Integrated pollution control looks to take a comprehensive and unified approach to the processes through which pollution is created, and the ways in which various media – air, water and soil – are polluted as a result. It ties in to integrated initiatives in other fields of environmental control and management, such as integrated product policy (discussed in Chapter 15) and the various environmental management initiatives discussed in Chapter 3. IPC and IPPC have been the subject of a number of major and minor pieces of EC and UK legislation which are discussed below.

Regulations governing pollution

This is a general introduction only. Some more specific regulations concerning air and water pollution and contaminated land are referred to in Chapters 6, 7 and 8, and those concerned with global warming and damage to the ozone layer are in Chapter 4.

International agreements to limit persistent organic pollutants (POPs) and heavy metals

International progress is now being made on developing agreements to minimise and eventually eliminate emissions and releases of these pollutants, which do not affect either global warming or the ozone layer. A first round of talks on developing an international agreement was hosted by the UN in Montreal in July 1998, and international protocols to curb both types of substance were signed by the UK government in Aarhus in June 1998.

EC regulations

A very large number of EC regulations cover various aspects of dangerous substances and pollution risks, and they cannot all be mentioned here. Specific regulations and policies concerning the quality of air, land and water are covered in Chapters 6, 7 and 8.

The EC has had regulations covering the classification, packaging and labelling of dangerous substances since 1967, and classifies substances on the European Inventory of Existing Commercial Chemical Substances, or EINECS, which contains more than 100,000 chemical substances, about 2,500 of which are classified as dangerous.

The EC Directive on Pollution caused by the Discharge of Certain Dangerous Substances into the Aquatic Environment 1976

This core measure divided 129 dangerous substances into two lists, List 1 (the most hazardous in terms of their toxicity, persistence and tendency to bioaccumulate) and List II (still hazardous, but less so). The measure required Member States to eliminate pollution by List 1 substances and reduce pollution by List II substances. These lists have been revised in various successor legislation.

Most List I substances – which include DDT, the 'Drins' and hexochloro-cyclohexane (HCH), or lindane – are no longer in use, although lindane continues to have some limited applications.

The UK has implemented this directive by developing Environmental Quality Objectives (EQOs) which set acceptable concentrations for the List I substances. These are enforced in UK legislation as EQSs or Environmental Quality Standards. In addition, the UK has drawn up a 'Red List', more limited than the EC List I, of substances for priority action. This contains 23 substances or groups of substances, including seventeen pesticides. Among them are atrazine, lindane and DDT.

Directive on Integrated Pollution Prevention Control (IPPC) 1996

The requirements of this major directive had to be applied to new industrial plants in the UK by spring 2000, with existing plants progressively having IPC authorisations replaced by IPPC authorizations up to October 2007. Designed to meet some of the core targets of the Fifth Community Action Plan on the Environment, the directive sets out an integrated approach intended to reduce emissions to air, water and soil from stationary sources. The Directive does not set specific emission limit values but requires those responsible for issuing permits that authorise processing causing emissions to base them on Best Available Techniques in the context of the effect on the environment as a whole (see below), which might, for instance, include factors such as the noise generated. The option which minimises the impact on the environment as a whole is known as the Best Practicable Environmental Option (BPEO). It includes a requirement for measures to be taken to avoid any pollution risk when an installation closes down permanently.

The range of processes covered by IPPC is similar to, but slightly broader than, those covered by Integrated Pollution Control under the UK legislation described below.

UK legislation and policies

Among the measures which should be noted are:

The Control of Pollution Act 1974 which has given rise to subsidiary regulations including regulations on antifouling paints in 1987.

The Food and Environment Protection Act 1985 is the legislative source for a variety of directions controlling pesticides (for example, the Control of Pesticides Regulations (COPR) 1986).

The Environmental Protection Act 1990 (EPA)

Part I of the EPA introduces the concept of integrated pollution control (IPC), replacing previous measures which tended to concentrate on pollution of either air, land or water, and not to cover adequately changes of technique which might simply shift the pollution from one medium to another. As such, it is likely be superseded by the legislation that implements the IPPC regulations noted above.

A core concept is Best Available Technology not Entailing Excessive Cost. (BATNEEC): the technology that must be used by installations requiring a permit that allows emitting processes to take place. The aim is either to prevent releases of prescribed substances into the environment, or where they cannot completely be prevented, to keep them to a minimum and render the substances harmless.

'Available' in this context is taken to mean that the technology need not be in general use, but it must be generally accessible. Technology is not ruled out from consideration if it is available only from sources outside the UK, or if it has only one monopoly supplier. By 'technology' is meant all plant and processes, including staff numbers and quality, working methods, training, supervision, and the design, construction and layout of buildings. 'Excessive cost' is largely a matter of agreement between the regulator and the operator. It is up to the regulating authority to decide what constitutes the BATNEEC and to translate it into requirements of the conditions of authorisation.

BATNEEC is not identical to Best Available Techniques as defined in the IPPC Regulations, although the two are similar. The BATNEEC definition limits costs to those of the operator of the process, while the IPPC definition includes a wider range of social costs and benefits.

The DETR and the Department of Trade and Industry jointly operate an Environmental Technology Best Practice Programme (ETBPP), launched in 1994 and extended in 1999 for a further five years, which advises organisations on how to achieve BATNEEC.

Environmental Protection (Prescribed Processes and Substances) Regulations 1991

These regulations implemented the IPC provisions in the EPA, specifying which industrial processes are subject to IPC (naturally, those involving substances most dangerous to the environment or most difficult to control). Six broad categories of process are involved:

- fuel and power
- the waste disposal industry
- the mineral industry
- the chemical industry
- the metal industry
- others including paper and coating manufacture.

In total the regulations cover about 2,000 specific processes (known as Part A processes) in England and Wales. The Environment Agency is responsible for inspecting these and issuing licences, while processes not covered (Part B processes) remain under non-IPC regulation which includes local authority air pollution control (LAAPC).

These regulations also control the release of a wide variety of substances, including solvents, halogens, pesticides and various metals.

Radioactive Substances Act 1993

One of a sequence of acts dealing with the control of activities involving radioactive material, this Act covers the Environment Agencies' responsibility for regulating the use of radioactive substances and the disposal of radioactive waste.

Control of Substances Hazardous to Health Regulations (COSHH) 1994

These important health and safety regulations require employers to assess the risk to health (of employees and others) from exposure to hazardous substances, and to establish measures to prevent and control exposure.

Pollution Prevention and Control Act 1999

This is the primary UK legislation which brings into effect the EC's IPPC Directive.

6 Air pollution and air quality

> *'Air pollution hits hardest the most vulnerable in our society. The young and the old, in particular those suffering from asthma and heart and lung diseases... Along with the right to clean air, we all have a responsibility to do what we can to keep it clean.'*
>
> JOHN PRESCOTT, FOREWORD TO *THE AIR QUALITY STRATEGY FOR ENGLAND, SCOTLAND, WALES AND NORTHERN IRELAND,* 2000.

The terms 'air quality' and 'air pollution' are not synonymous. 'Air pollution' refers to the presence of pollutants in the air (of the type outlined in Chapter 5) which give rise to a range of problems, including problems of air quality but also including, for example, ozone depletion, climate change (both discussed in Chapter 4) and acid rain. 'Air quality' is the more specific term for local and regional air pollution problems (generally of the troposphere, the lower atmosphere) which have direct impacts particularly on human health, but also on the wider environment.

Local and regional air pollution problems include:

- acid rain
- 'photochemical smog' made up of ozone and other pollutants, which can cause respiratory and other health problems
- unacceptably high (in health or environmental terms) atmospheric levels of certain gases, particulates or chemicals in the atmosphere.

Their impacts include:

- Adverse effects of many kinds on human and animal health. The Department of Health estimated in 1998 that short-term air pollution caused between 12,000 and 24,000 premature deaths in Great Britain each year.
- Damage to plant life, from gases and from particulate matter which can clog plants and hinder their ability to photosynthesise.
- Damage to buildings, from chemical reactions, from soiling and from the abrasive action of airborne particles.

The degree of air pollution is determined partly by the type and quantity of pollutants that enter the air, and partly by weather conditions. Stagnant weather tends to increase the proportion of pollutants in the lower atmosphere, while winds help to disperse pollution. Some pollutants have short lives in the atmosphere, while some persist for a very long time.

Specific Pollutants

The pollutants of greatest concern are:

Benzene

A volatile organic compound (VOC), benzene enters the air mostly from vehicle emissions, and from evaporation losses during the handling, distribution and storage of petrol. It is a known human carcinogen particularly associated with leukaemia. UK standards for the amount of benzene in the air are regularly exceeded for short periods.

Butadiene

A hydrocarbon used in the production of synthetic rubber for tyres, and emitted in car exhausts, butadiene is a suspected human carcinogen. UK standards for the amount of butadiene in the air are regularly exceeded for short periods.

Carbon monoxide

A colourless, odourless gas produced by the incomplete combustion of carbon, and by some industrial and biological processes. Most emissions of carbon monoxide come from power stations and road transport, other sources are industrial processes, incinerators, domestic heaters and tobacco smoke. Inhaling it causes hypoxia (that is, it interferes with the absorption of oxygen) which at low levels slows reflexes, impairs thinking, causes drowsiness, affects fertility and general levels of health, and at higher levels leads to death. About 100 deaths per year are caused in the UK by carbon monoxide release from faulty gas appliances, and it is also a health problem in urban areas where 'cocktails' of pollutants result in photochemical smog and surface ozone. It is an ingredient of acid rain.

Emission levels have been reduced particularly by the introduction of catalytic converters on cars, and by the 1992 ban on straw and stubble burning.

Lead

This naturally occurring grey-bluish soft metal enters the atmosphere mostly (an estimated 90% of total emissions) as an emission from motor vehicles using fuels with alkyl lead additives, but also through lead manufacturing processes and the incineration of plastic packaging materials. (Lead from other sources contaminates land and water supplies.)

Lead inhaled from particles in the air (an estimated 40% of human exposure) is a serious health hazard. Its effects on the human body include:

- damage to the nervous system
- effects on blood pressure, possibly leading to hypertension and heart attacks in adult males

- effects on mental development.

It is a Class 3 (doubtful) carcinogen.

Nitrogen dioxide

Nitrogen oxide is oxidised in the atmosphere to the more toxic nitrogen dioxide (NO_2), which is also produced naturally by bacterial and volcanic action and by lightning. Its main man-made emission sources are power stations and road transport. There is also significant human exposure from cooking on unvented gas stoves and cigarette smoking.

Nitrogen dioxide and VOCs lead to the formation of ground-level ozone. Nitrogen dioxide can cause respiratory illness and reduced lung function, and make airways more sensitive to allergens such as the house dust mite, but is not regarded as a very serious health hazard.

Perhaps more seriously, nitrogen dioxide can readily be converted to nitric acid, one of the main ingredients of acid rain. This has a severe impact on lakes, soils and forests. Even short-term exposure can cause irreversible damage to plants, and long-term exposure causes reduced growth and crop yields, and damage to trees.

UNECE (see below) and UK standards for nitrogen dioxide in the air are regularly exceeded at present.

Ozone

Ozone is not emitted as such from industrial and similar sources, but is formed in the lower atmosphere by photochemical reactions involving carbon monoxide, volatile organic compounds and nitrogen oxides that are released from vehicle emissions, power stations and various industrial processes, becoming an ingredient of 'photochemical smog'. There is a high natural background level, particularly in the 'ozone layer' of the stratosphere, where it is formed in reactions triggered by ultraviolet light. Ozone levels in both the upper and lower atmosphere are highest in hot sunny weather, and because of the complex web of chemical reactions of which ozone forms a part, tend to be higher in rural than in urban areas.

The functions of the ozone layer are discussed in Chapter 4.

In the lower atmosphere, ozone is a pollutant with significant effects. A strong pungent blue gas, it is an irritant to the eyes, nose and throat, and can lead to respiratory and other health problems. It is also thought to increase sensitivity to allergens (for example, pollen) and to affect the immune system. It also damages plants, disrupting the membrane integrity of leaves and needles, and affecting their ability to photosynthesise.

Current levels of ground level ozone regularly exceed EC and UK targets.

Particulate matter or PM_{10}

'Particulates' is a general term for small particles of matter (including dusts, acid and other materials) that are found suspended in the air. For measuring pollution the general reference is to PM_{10} – that is, particles with a diameter less than 10 μm (0.01 mm).

There is limited understanding of the impact of particulates, but general agreement that at high concentrations they constitute a very significant and damaging pollutant. Among their effects are:

- to contribute to urban smog, which limits visibility and leads to respiratory problems
- to carry carcinogenic material into the organism
- to damage plants by reducing their rate of photosynthesis and blocking cell openings
- to damage structures by soiling and abrasion.

It has been estimated by Friends of the Earth that up to 10,000 people a year die prematurely in the UK as a result of particulate emissions, and in some parts of Europe such emissions are considered to be the main cause of plant damage.

Most particulate matter is emitted by road traffic, and particularly by diesel-powered vehicles, by other combustion sources, and by industrial processes. ('Black smoke' is another name for this matter.) Natural sources include sea salt spray and suspended soil dust, and some particulate matter is created by chemical reactions in the air.

Particulate levels, though falling steadily, still give some cause for concern.

Sulphur dioxide

A major ingredient of acid rain, sulphur dioxide can damage both agricultural crops and natural vegetation by affecting membranes and inhibiting photosynthesis. In humans it causes breathing problems which are particularly severe when it is combined with particulate and moisture inhalation and forms sulphuric acid in the lung.

The main pollution source is the combustion of sulphur-containing coal and oil. Some pollution comes from natural sources such as sulphur springs. Sulphur dioxide levels have fallen in the UK but still regularly exceed both EC and the more stringent WHO guidelines.

Sources of air pollution

Up to and through the first half of the last century, the main cause of air pollution was the burning of coal, particularly in domestic premises. Since the 1960s this has been overtaken by traffic. Sector by sector, the following are the main sources of air pollution.

Industrial processes

Many industrial processes give rise to some pollution problems. The chemical industry is particularly vulnerable, and it has been estimated that it contributes almost

50% of all air pollution, but even less obviously 'dirty' industries can contribute to the problem, for example in their use of solvents and cleaning materials. All industries, by using energy, are in part responsible for the pollution caused by power generation. Proportions of other pollutants from the industrial sector (as an end-user) in 1997 were:

sulphur dioxide	34%
carbon dioxide	27%
nitrogen oxides	19%
black smoke	10%
carbon monoxide	4%

SOURCE: VARIOUS UK GOVERNMENT STATISTICS

Power generation

Power stations were responsible for the following proportions of emissions in 1997:

sulphur dioxide:	65%
carbon dioxide:	28%
particulates (PM_{10})	16%
black smoke	6%
nitrous oxide	3%

SOURCE: VARIOUS UK GOVERNMENT STATISTICS

The quantity of sulphur pollution has fallen significantly, as power stations have tended to switch from sulphur-rich coal to low-sulphur coal and other low-sulphur forms of fuel such as oil and natural gas, and technological changes have also reduced power station emissions. (See Chapter 10.)

High chimney stacks mean that emissions from power stations and other industrial sources have less immediate impact than pollution sources close to the ground such as traffic. However, it is now recognised that higher stacks have served to displace the problem, with UK emissions creating severe problems as far afield as Scandinavia.

Mining and related activities

Coal mining, though much reduced in the UK, still contributes 9% of methane emissions.

Petrol refining

In 1996 motor spirit refining was responsible for 26%, and DERV of 4%, of estimated emissions of volatile organic compounds (VOCs) in the UK.

Road transport

Vehicles were responsible for the following proportions of emissions in 1996/7:

carbon monoxide	74%
1,3-butadiene	68%
lead	61%
black smoke	58%
nitrogen oxides	48%
VOCs	30%
particulates (PM_{10})	25%
carbon dioxide	22%

SOURCES: *DIGEST OF ENVIRONMENTAL STATISTICS 1998; AIR QUALITY STRATEGY 2000*

The increase in motorised traffic (discussed in Chapter 11) has vastly increased the quantities of exhaust gases entering the atmosphere. Improved vehicle emissions standards, although they have done much to limit the rise in pollution, have not succeeded in reversing it. Traffic pollution also enters the atmosphere at a much lower level than the stack emissions from power stations and other industrial sources, so it has a more immediate impact. It is possible to measure clearly the two daily peaks in air pollution that coincide with morning and evening rush hours.

Domestic fuel use

Domestic fuel may not seem polluting at the time of use, but its production gives rise to a large amount of pollution. Domestic fuel use (as an end-user application) accounted for the following proportions of pollutants in 1996 in the UK:

carbon dioxide	28%
sulphur dioxide	28%
black smoke	22%
nitrogen oxides	13%
carbon monoxide	9%
methane	9%

SOURCE: VARIOUS UK GOVERNMENT STATISTICS

Waste treatment processes

Landfill waste disposal sites generate an estimated 46% of all UK methane gas emissions. Waste incineration is also a significant cause of harmful emissions.

Levels of air pollution

This is an indication of levels and trends for emissions of some of the main pollutants mentioned above.

	1970	1990	1996
		thousand tonnes:	
sulphur dioxide	6,350	3,764	2,028
nitrogen oxides	2,374	2,752	2,060
carbon monoxide	7,652	6,687	4,645
lead (from road vehicles)		2.2	0.9
VOCs including benzene	2,243	2,632	2,111
PM_{10} (thousand tonnes)	538	314	213

SOURCE: *DIGEST OF ENVIRONMENTAL STATISTICS 1998*

Not all pollutants are measurable by the estimated quantity of emissions, since some are formed by chemical reactions in the air. Atmospheric levels vary from location to location, and depend on the life in the atmosphere of the substance.

Indoor air pollution

The types and levels of pollution inside buildings and vehicles are often different from – and sometimes considerably higher than – those outside. Many individuals spend a substantial part of their lives inside buildings, sometimes in highly polluted industrial atmospheres, and the pollution in these environments can have a significant impact on their health.

Among the common sources of indoor pollution, in addition to industrial processes, are:

- combustion of gas and solid fuels (for cooking, heating, etc.) which can give rise to emissions of carbon monoxide or nitrogen oxides, and of particulate matter
- people, who breathe out carbon dioxide, tobacco smoke (see below), emit organic compounds giving rise to body odours, and transmit bacteria
- building materials, which can give off formaldehyde, VOCs, radon, fibres and particulates. Newer homes are particularly vulnerable to pollution
- pest killers, timber treatments and the like. Buildings should always be properly ventilated after treatment
- furnishings and consumer products, sources of VOCs, formaldehyde, pesticides and bacteria
- office equipment, which can give off VOCs, and in operation generate ozone
- painting and decorating activities, whose formaldehyde and VOC-laden fumes can be particularly noxious
- natural radon gas from the underlying ground, which can become concentrated in buildings in areas prone to radon that are not designed to prevent its build-up
- integral garages, which are sources of exhaust fumes containing carbon monoxide, nitrogen dioxide and VOCs
- air-conditioning systems, which can provide an environment for mould spores and airborne bacteria to multiply.

Studies have shown that concentrations of nitrogen dioxide, carbon monoxide, respirable particulates, formaldehyde and radon are often higher indoors than outdoors. A Building Research Establishment study found, among other conclusions, that indoor concentrations of benzene were on average 1.3 times outdoor concentrations, and were particularly high in environments where smoking took place and in houses with attached garages.

Particular risks are posed by inadequately vented heaters, which give rise to around 100 fatalities in the UK each year.

Related information on environmentally friendly buildings is in Chapter 13.

Tobacco smoke

Tobacco smoke is a major pollutant of air, particularly inside buildings and vehicles. There is clear evidence that it is carcinogenic, leading to lung cancer and to cancers of the bladder, renal pelvis and pancreas. It also contributes to respiratory problems, and the smell is obnoxious to many people. Depositions from tobacco smoke also damage the decor in buildings.

Among populations where cigarette smoking has long been established at high levels, up to 90% of male lung cancers are attributable to it, with the female proportion rising to approach the same level.

For these reasons it is now becoming standard practice for responsible organisations to ban smoking in the workplace.

Monitoring UK air quality

Responsibility for air pollution control in the UK lies partly with the Environment Agency (which has absorbed the functions of Her Majesty's Inspectorate of Pollution) and partly with local authorities, but monitoring air quality is a function of the DETR. The National Environment Technology Centre (NETCEN) prepares a National Atmospheric Emissions Inventory for the DETR, which derives estimates of the quantities of emissions primarily from statistics and research.

Two types of monitoring of air quality are carried out, one designed to give instantaneous measurements of pollution concentrations, and one concentrating on average levels over longer (daily or monthly) periods. Monitoring is carried out at both urban and rural sites, including 'background locations' which are representative of the overall level of air pollution, and 'hotspots' such as areas with high traffic concentration and in the vicinity of large industrial plants. Pollutants monitored on a regular basis include:

- sodium dioxide
- oxides of nitrogen
- carbon dioxide
- ozone
- particulates (PM_{10})
- benzene

- 1,3 butadiene
- black smoke concentrations in urban areas
- toxic organic micropollutants (TOMPs)
- lead.

(More information on individual substances and their effects is in the Glossary, page 207.)

Air quality information is provided to the public via the mass media, on Teletext, on government web pages (where it includes archive information), and via a free air quality telephone line (0800 556677).

Improving the quality of the air

On the whole, strategies for improving air quality are those discussed in earlier chapters, and centre on:

- limiting polluting activities (such as the use of motorised transport, and of domestic and industrial energy)
- substituting less damaging substances for those that are particular causes of pollution
- improving production and emissions control technology.

Strategies and regulations

Agreements on the reduction of chemicals which impact global warming and destroy atmospheric ozone are covered in Chapter 4.

Different regulations intended to combat air pollution may be intended:

- to limit the emission from particular types of source (for example, combustion plants or motor vehicles)
- or to limit the emissions of particular pollutants.

There is a wide range of both European and UK regulations with these objectives, and only the major pieces of legislation can be mentioned here.

World Health Authority (WHO) Guidelines

In 1987 the WHO carried out a detailed assessment of various atmospheric pollutants, and developed guidelines on the maximum amount of pollutants in the air (using various different types of measurement) that should be permitted to avoid a risk to human health. These were revised and updated in 1994/5.

The Fifth Community Action Plan on the Environment

EC and international standards for many pollutants are set in this action plan, under which targets have been drawn up for a reduction in the levels of sulphur dioxide and nitrogen oxides emissions.

The UN Economic Commission for Europe (UNECE) Geneva Convention on Long Range Transboundary Air Pollution 1979

This was the first multilateral treaty concerning air pollution. It focuses on the problems of acidification and low-level ozone. It has led to the drawing up of a number of specific protocols:

- The first sulphur protocol (Helsinki) 1995.
- The second sulphur protocol (Oslo) 1994. This agreement, signed by the UK in December 1996, set targets for the reduction of sulphur dioxide emissions of 50% by 2000, 70% by 2005 and 80% by 2010, all from a baseline of 1980 levels – targets which the UK is so far exceeding.
- The first nitrogen oxides protocol (Sofia), 1988.
- The persistent organic pollutants protocol, 1998.
- The heavy metals protocol, 1998.

A new protocol to tackle acidification, eutrophication and ground level ozone was signed by the UK in December 1999. It set emission limits for 2010 for sulphur dioxide, nitrogen oxides, VOCs and ammonia.

EC Directive on Ambient Air Quality Assessment and Management 1996

This framework directive sets out a strategic plan for controlling air pollution, and a series of daughter directives have set out limit values to apply across Europe for twelve air pollutants including sulphur dioxide, nitrogen dioxide, particulate matter and lead. It came into force in 1999 and Member States are required to implement it by July 2001.

EC Large Combustion Plant Directive 1988

This directive, specifically concerned with controlling and reducing sulphur dioxide, oxides of nitrogen and particulate emissions from large power plants, was implemented in the UK within the Environmental Protection Act 1990. It introduced the concept of the 'bubble', the emission quota which each generator must not exceed. Specific limits are set annually for each power plant, and the total of individual plant limits represents the 'bubble'. This enables the generator to 'trade' emission limits between plants. It set standards for new plants and programmes of compliance for existing plants, and was amended and tightened in 1998.

Other EC Directives

Among the subjects of other EC directives have been:

- Emissions from petrol and diesel engines.
- Sulphur contents of fuels.
- VOC emissions from the storage of petrol.

- VOC emissions from certain industrial activities.
- Emission limits for new and existing incineration plants.
- Nitrogen dioxide.
- Ozone and ozone-depleting substances.
- Lead.
- Carbon dioxide emissions from transport.

The National Air Quality Strategy

The National Air Quality Strategy for England, Scotland, Wales and Northern Ireland – Working Together for Clean Air, was updated in 2000. Among the methods for improving air quality standards are:
Further development of the national air quality monitoring networks.

- **Local Air Quality Management** (LAQM) which requires local authorities to take responsibility for reviewing and assessing the current and future quality of air, and to designate an Air Quality Management Area wherever specific action is necessary. The Greater London Authority Act 1999 gave powers to the Mayor for London to prepare a London air quality strategy.
- **Integrated Pollution Prevention and Control,** discussed on page 68.
- **The Auto-Oil Programme,** aimed at progressively reducing emission limits for cars and the amount of benzene, sulphur and aromatics in petrol.
- Increases in, and changes in the structure of, road fuel duties, and other strategies to reduce the level of motorised transport (discussed further in Chapter 11).
- Energy-saving programmes (see Chapter 10).
- **Zones of Industrial Pollution Sources,** identified by the Environment Agency in major industrial areas, where it monitors, models and works to improve air quality.

Specific standards for Local Air Quality Management in the NAQS (which generally also represent objectives to be achieved by 2004 or 2005) include:

Sulphur dioxide	100 ppb measured as 15-minute mean, not to be exceeded more than 35 times a year
Particulate matter	50 $\mu g/m^3$ as a 24-hour mean, not to be exceeded more than 35 times a year
Nitrogen dioxide	105 ppb as a 1-hour mean, not to be exceeded more than 18 times a year
Carbon monoxide	10 ppm as a running 8-hour mean (by December 2003)
Lead	0.5 $\mu g/m^3$ as an annual mean
Benzene	5 ppb as a running annual mean (by December 2003)
1,3 Butadiene	1 ppb as a running annual mean (by December 2003)

National, but not local, objectives include:

Ozone	50 ppb as a running 8-hour mean, not to be exceeded more than 10 times a year
Nitrogen oxides	16 ppb as an annual mean
Sulphur dioxide	8 ppb as an annual mean and winter average

SOURCE: *THE AIR QUALITY STRATEGY FOR ENGLAND, SCOTLAND, WALES AND NORTHERN IRELAND*

Experts on air quality have assessed the improvements that can be expected as a result of current policies, and the areas where these fall short of the requirements and further action will be necessary. Levels of pollutants such as benzene, carbon monoxide and lead are expected to meet the targets. More concern exists about the levels of nitrogen oxides and particulate matter. These are heavily dependent on the level of motorised transport, and further action may be necessary to reduce the growth in transport in order to achieve the targets. Ozone too causes difficulties, not least because it is an international rather than a national problem. It has been estimated that nitrogen oxide and VOC emissions need to be reduced to around 50% to 70% of their current levels if the targets are to be met. To reach this level would require concerted action across Europe and beyond, at a level which (in spite of recent progress) is not yet apparent.

Lead in petrol

The general sale of leaded petrol has now been ended in the UK. The steady move away from leaded petrol has already had a significant effect on lead pollution. Recent surveys show that blood lead levels have decreased by approximately 50% since the mid-1980s, and concentrations of lead at sample sites have reduced drastically.

Clean Air Act 1993

A succession of Clean Air Acts (1956, 1968 and 1993) have provided a framework for the reduction of emissions from chimneys in the UK, leading to the introduction of smokeless domestic fuels, smokeless zones, and bringing the virtual elimination of wintertime smog. The latest is the 1993 Act which broadly prohibits emissions of dark and black smoke from chimneys serving boilers and industrial plant, and requires new non-domestic furnaces to be capable as far as practicable of operating continuously without emitting smoke when burning their designed fuel. It also sets controls for chimney heights, which are regulated by local authorities.

7 Water: quantity and quality

The control of water quality and water use in the UK (including both abstractions from water supplies, and discharges into them) is handled in a framework that is based on the type of water being considered and the functions it is perceived to have.

Water resources can be divided into:

- inland surface water: that is, rivers, streams and lakes
- groundwater: that is, supplies of freshwater held beneath the surface
- coastal and estuarine salt waters.

Among the major functions of water resources are:

- to provide a medium for ecosystems of plant and aquatic animal life
- to support wetland ecosystems
- to provide a medium for fishing, shellfish farming and similar activities
- to provide a medium for bathing
- to provide drinking water
- to act as a recreation and amenity resource
- to be a resource for general use domestically, in industry and in agriculture
- to be the medium for disposal of certain forms of waste (the sewage system).

Among the core issues concerned with water in the UK are:

- maintaining water quality so that it can fulfil the functions outlined above
- maintaining the distribution and supply of water so that it can fulfil the functions outlined above
- controlling land drainage
- prevention and control of flooding
- increasing the reuse of rainwater and greywater (waste water from, for example, washing facilities and cooling processes).

Water supply management

Most uses of water (apart from in-stream uses such as fishing and boating) operate on a cyclical basis. The water is abstracted from the natural supply, and used for a specific domestic, industrial or agricultural purpose. Waste water is then returned to the system, via one of two types of drain:

- surface water drains, including land drains and most road drains, which lead directly to rivers, streams or soakaways, and are designed to carry uncontaminated water only

- foul water drains, designed to carry contaminated waste water to a storage lagoon, treatment system or sewage works, after which the water is discharged once treatment is complete.

After treatment (where necessary), the returned water once more becomes part of the general supply. This man-made system complements the natural system of evaporation and precipitation.

Artificial abstractions from the supply, discharges to it, and treatments, are controlled with a view to ensuring that each body of water maintains or acquires a standard suitable for the purposes to which it is being put. (There are separate standards applicable, for example, to drinking water and to bathing waters.) Necessarily the regulatory bodies need to set a balance between the needs of the water system and the needs of water users, and sometimes abstractions and discharges are permitted at levels which have some damaging effects on water levels and water quality.

The freshwaters controlled in the UK ('controlled waters') include all watercourses and groundwater. Their quality is controlled by the Environment Agency and the Scottish Environmental Protection Agency. It is achieved largely by regulating consents for abstractions and discharges to water (which can set a number of criteria, for example, when and where a discharge can be made and what its composition should be), by making technology or technique-based requirements on dischargers, and by setting emission limits for discharges.

Over 110,000 discharges of waste water into the water system, many of them small, are regulated by consents in England and Wales. These range from major industrial and sewage effluent discharges to minor surface water outlets. (Consent is not necessary for domestic purposes.) Only discharges from point sources can be controlled in this way.

The compliance rates for discharge consents in 1996 were:

- 97% of consents to sewage treatment works operated by Water Companies.
- 74% of trade discharges.
- 53% of private sewage discharges.

SOURCE: *DIGEST OF ENVIRONMENTAL STATISTICS 1998*, TABLE 3.17

Other measures to control and improve quality include:

- improved treatment standards for sewage
- better management of activities which could give rise to accidental pollution
- growing more vegetation in close proximity to watercourses
- direct physical clean-up measures, for example, dredging polluted silt from watercourses.

Regulation of drinking water standards is handled by the Drinking Water Inspectorate, part of the DETR. Local authorities also have some powers and obligations over drinking water quality, and UK water suppliers have various duties including the duty to provide consumers with wholesome water (meeting various specific standards) for drinking and other purposes.

The quality of inland waters

Inland freshwaters are assessed both on their chemical composition, and on their capability to sustain life. Freshwater life varies greatly between healthy rivers and bodies of water, since it is affected by factors such as the climate, the geology and physical features. However it is possible to predict what the biology will be of a freshwater environment in an unpolluted state, and by comparing that with the actual situation, to arrive at an assessment of the state of the water.

Features which affect the quality include:

- The quantity of dissolved gases, particularly oxygen, but also nitrogen and carbon dioxide. These are generally beneficial, and dissolved oxygen in particular affects the ability of the water to sustain life.
- The proportion of ammoniacal nitrogen, which is often found in water as a result of the discharge of sewage effluent. High levels are inimical to fishes and other aquatic lifeforms.
- The concentration of phosphorus and nitrate-based fertilisers, which can pollute water by leaching from treated land. A high level can lead to excessive algal growth, or eutrophication.
- The concentration of pesticides and other chemical substances. Some of these are harmful to aquatic life, and to humans who use the water for bathing or for drinking; others are vital trace elements which add to the taste and nutritious value of 'mineral water'.
- The acidity of the water, which is affected by acid rain (see Chapter 5), by carbon dioxide dissolving to create weak carbonic acid, and by leaves and other vegetation decomposing to produce organic acids. This is measured as a pH factor. Low pH, acidic water can cause pipe corrosion and is less supportive of aquatic life. High pH, basic water is often created when the water percolates through chalk or limestone. It tastes caustic and furs pipes. The normal requirement for drinking waters is a pH between 6.5 and 8.5. (Below 7 rates as acidic.)
- The turbidity of the water: that is, the proportion of suspended particles, either inorganic (for example, mineral sediments) or organic (for example, algae).
- The quantity and variety of pathogenic micro-organisms which are spread particularly through sewage contaminated water, and can cause diseases such as leptospirosis or Legionnaire's disease.
- The presence of oil and grease, which have various negative effects that cause damage to aquatic plant and animal life.

The Environment Agency's methodology for classifying the water quality of rivers and canals is known as the General Quality Assessment (GQA) scheme. It is designed to provide an accurate and consistent assessment of the state of the water quality, and changes in it over time. Two samples, taken annually in spring and autumn, provide an overall judgement of the quality. A core principle is that the water environment should not be allowed to deteriorate.

The GQA has two elements:

- Chemical GQA, based on chemical measurement of the most common types of pollution. It includes standards for biochemical oxygen demand (BOD) and ammonia, which give an indication of the amount of pollution from sewage or from agricultural sources, and for dissolved oxygen (DO), since this is essential to aquatic life. Other measures taken are of the acidity of the water, and the presence of copper and zinc, which are toxic to much aquatic life. Stretches of water are graded A (the best) down to F.
- Biological GQA, a broader measure of quality based on the invertebrates found on the river bed, including insect larvae, snails, worms and many other groups of animals, which can be affected by infrequently-occurring pollutants not measured by the chemical GQA. Grades for biological GQA are a to f.

In future waters may also be graded on nutrients and on aesthetic quality.

The Environment Agency sets informal River Quality Objectives (RQOs) and works to achieve statutory Environment Quality Standards (EQSs) which establish the concentrations of specified substances.

In 1999 just under 92% of the rivers and canals by length in England were classed as of 'good' or 'fair' chemical quality. Many of the poorer-quality waters were in older industrial areas, but these have shown significant improvement, with about half of the rivers and canals in the Midlands and Northern England improving by a grade or more, often as a result of improvements in sewage works (for example, in Kidderminster, Stourbridge and Southam). In Wales nearly 99% of rivers were classed as 'good' or 'fair'. However, there remain a significant proportion of waters of poor quality. For example, in the Mersey Basin (the most polluted waters in the UK) there are residues of mercury, lead, cadmium and other heavy metals in the rivers and estuary. They remain in the sediment for many years and are slowly released into the water or absorbed by organisms on which fish feed, bringing them into the food chain.

Water quality in Scotland and Northern Ireland was generally better.

Biological measurements are taken every five years. In 1996 about 35% of river length in England and Wales was rated very good for biological quality, and over 30% good, with only 2% rating as bad. Over 25% of river length improved by one or more classes between 1990 and 1996. (Statistics from the Environment Agency website.)

In general smaller quantities of pesticides and other pollutants are found in groundwater than in surface waters, but levels are likely to continue to rise, owing both to delays in response to high levels of pollution in the past, and to a tendency for the pollutants to build up owing to lower discharge rates. Evidence from a number of sites shows a rising trend in nitrate levels.

Bacteria and viruses in water are not considered to be a major threat in the UK, but some harmful bacteria are endemic. It is generally difficult to test for their presence.

Drinking water

Market research published by the Drinking Water Inspectorate in 1998 indicated that in the UK:

- 75% of people drink water straight from the tap.
- 10% use a filter.
- 5% drink bottled water.
- 5% drink alternatives.
- 5% boil tap water before drinking it.

The research also indicated that 70% of people were satisfied with the quality of their tap water, but 20% were dissatisfied, because of either the taste, the cloudiness or discoloration.

The general guidelines for the drinking water supply are designed to minimise this type of customer resistance, by ensuring that the water:

- poses no threat to health
- is acceptable in colour and clarity
- is treated and distributed efficiently
- will not corrode the distribution system excessively.

In 1999, 99.82% of the 2.8 million (approx.) tests carried out on UK drinking water met the relevant standards. Between 1997 and 1999 there were reductions in the number of tests showing problems with coliforms, faecal coliforms, odour, iron, manganese, lead and individual pesticides. New regulations introduced in 1999 ensure that drinking water is now tested for the presence of Cryptosporidium, a micro-organism which can cause diarrhoea and vomiting. (Source: Drinking Water Inspectorate.)

Coastal and marine water quality

Marine water can be affected by, for example:

- sewage outfalls that discharge into the sea
- other dumping of materials from the shoreline
- deliberate dumping from ships of waste oil and other refuse
- incidents at sea that lead to oil spillage
- polluted precipitation.

It has been estimated that shipping is responsible for only 12% of marine pollution, with the main threat in EC-controlled waters coming from ships that do not fly the flag of a Member State. Pollution from ships tends to be worsened by poor port facilities which leaves ships with few alternative ways to dispose of refuse.

Action to improve the quality of marine waters is focused on:

- protecting species and habitats
- conserving fish stocks
- preventing eutrophication or excessive algal growth
- controlling shipping

- controlling pollution by hazardous substances.

In England and Wales in 1996 the quality of water in 92% of estuaries was classed as good or fair, judged by biological, chemical and aesthetic criteria, and 4% were classed as bad. In Scotland 98% was good or fair, and Northern Ireland 88%. (Source: *Digest of Environmental Statistics 1998*.)

Particular monitoring is devoted to the amounts of heavy metals, of pesticides and fertilisers, and of suspended particles, being discharged into the sea. The quantity of most dangerous pollutants, particularly lead and zinc, entering coastal waters has declined substantially during the 1990s, as a result of various measures being taken including the implementation of Integrated Pollution Control.

Regulations that have come into force in the 1990s have dramatically reduced the amount of land-based waste material that can legally be dumped at sea. The dumping of untreated sewage, sewage sludge, colliery waste and non-inert industrial wastes at sea ended in the 1990s. Dredged materials continue to be dumped (a total 51.2 million wet tonnes in 1996) but their dumping is controlled by licence. A global ban on the sea disposal of all radioactive wastes, under the London Convention 1972, was accepted by the UK in 1994. It superseded a ban which applied only to high level radioactive waste, but does not prevent authorised discharges of low level liquid radioactive waste into the sea, which are still made by various nuclear establishments in the UK.

Bathing waters

A limited number of sites are designated as bathing waters: 463 in England and Wales in 1999, including nine inland bathing waters. The waters at 91.5% of these locations now meet the overall bathing water standards, a considerable increase on the 56% which met them in 1987.

Water treatment

Natural processes contribute considerably to the cleansing of the water supply. Water that filters through clay, silt or sand into the groundwater supply is effectively cleansed of many impurities in the process, and micro-organisms in water bodies, rivers and streams and in the soil also have a role to play in breaking down organic contaminants. Sunlight too can kill bacteria and viruses.

Water requires artificial treatment, however:

- to render it fit for use as drinking water
- before the return of waste water and sewage to the general freshwater supply, to remove contaminants and ensure it does not pollute the environment unacceptably.

A number of methods are used to treat drinking water. Among them are:

- screening and straining, to remove larger objects
- coagulation and flocculation techniques to remove colour, turbidity and algae
- sedimentation: the slow settling out of impurities

- sand filtration
- disinfection, often with chlorine, sometimes by ultraviolet or ozone treatment
- fluoridation, with a view to protecting children's teeth.

More complex treatments are often required for contaminated water before it is discharged. Among these are:

- sedimentation, the settling-out of solid contaminants
- adsorption, to concentrate and remove impurities
- centrifuging, to separate out solid contaminants
- flotation, to separate out oil and grease
- ion exchange, which helps to remove metal impurities
- reverse osmosis, a membrane technology used to separate out dissolved solids such as salts
- solvent extraction
- and various biological testaments.

Improvements in water treatment techniques mean that levels of pesticides and other contaminants in treated water no longer mirror the levels in the environment.

Pollution problems

Factors that affect the quality of inland freshwaters also affect the quality of groundwater, estuarine and coastal waters.

The quality of water and of the ecosystem it supports is affected not only by abstractions and discharges but by rainfall, the amount of sunshine and rates of evaporation. When rainfall is lower than average and river flows are low, the quality is likely to be lower. Increased river flows tend to dilute the effect of particular point sources of pollution, but unusually high rainfall can cause problems such as the increased leaching of pollutants from the soil, and increased silt pollution.

Water pollution generally is caused by:

- the discharge or spilling of polluted material into the water supply
- run-off: that is, water crossing a polluted land surface before entering watercourses
- leaching: water percolating through polluted soil and joining the groundwater supply
- precipitation through polluted air, which can, for example, pick up pesticides, asbestos dust, lead, chlorinated hydrocarbons, carbon monoxide, sulphur dioxide, nitrous oxides and radioactive fallout
- in drinking water, by lead, iron or other substances from supply pipes.

Among the most significant pollutants are:

- pesticides
- fertilisers

- silt
- dangerous chemicals
- oil
- sewage.

Pesticides

Pesticides are a particular hazard when they contaminate water supplies, and in the UK all water supplies, including surface freshwaters, groundwater, and coastal and estuarine waters, are regularly monitored for pesticide content.

Because there are so many pesticides, there is concern not only about the level of individual substances, but also about the cumulative level. The statutory regulations governing water companies in the UK set down prescribed concentrations for individual pesticides in drinking water of 0.1 μg/l, and for total pesticides of 0.5 μg/l. Individual limits are also set down for some pesticides, some of which (for aldrin, for example) are lower than the standard limit.

In 1999 only about 0.01% of the drinking water samples tested exceeded the limits for the presence of pesticides.

The Environment Agency monitors non-drinking waters for the presence of pesticides, and of the 65 pesticides for which Environmental Quality Standards (EQSs) have been determined, 30 exceeded their EQS at least one site in 1997. 14% of freshwater sites monitored failed at least one EQS.

Nitrates and phosphates

Generally long lived compounds of phosphorus (phosphates) and nitrogen (nitrates) are widely used as agricultural fertilisers, as well as in detergents and for some other purposes. Run-off and leaching from agricultural land leads to raised phosphate and nitrate levels in fresh and marine waters. Some nitrate pollution also derives from treated sewage discharges.

High levels of fertilisers can lead in some weather conditions to eutrophication, or excessive algal growth. This depletes the oxygen supply in the water, affecting the aquatic ecosystem, and it can produce toxins (as in the blue-green algae which appeared in the UK in 1989) which are harmful to humans and other animals. In inland waters the main cause of eutrophication is organophosphorus fertilisers, while in coastal and estuarine waters it is caused primarily by nitrates. Eutrophication is a significant problem in the UK: for example, about 84% of wetland Sites of Special Scientific Interest are thought to show some symptoms. Since 1989 phosphorus levels have tended to fall, because fewer phosphates are used, for example in detergents, and the treatment for removing them has improved. In the UK nitrate levels in rivers have generally been constant since 1975, but nitrate levels in some groundwater sites are rising.

Some commentators also believe that high nitrate levels in drinking water may present a risk to human health, but there are few known effects. Friends of the Earth estimate that the drinking water for an estimated 850,000 people in the UK has nitrate concentrations above the permitted EC level. In England and Wales, 72 areas covering about 600,000 ha, are designated as Nitrate Vulnerable Zones, where concentration limits exceed, or risk exceeding, permitted levels, and Action Programmes are required to control the problem.

Annual average concentations of nitrates in Great Britain (in mg/litre):

1980	1990	1996
13.6	13.2	16.4

Annual average concentrations of orthophosphates in Great Britain (in mg/litre):

1980	1990	1996
0.28	0.40	0.38

SOURCE: *DIGEST OF ENVIRONMENTAL STATISTICS 1998*, TABLE 3.11A

Silt

Silt build-up is involved in 5% of all water pollution incidents. This major pollutant is even more of a hazard when it is contaminated with oil, sand or chemicals, or when it contains organic matter with a high biochemical oxygen demand. Silt pollution in waters is often related to construction activities, and caused by rainfall run-off from disturbed or stripped ground. Other sources are water pumped from excavations, stockpiles, plant and wheel washing, site roads and disturbance of the river bed or erosion of banks, especially when clean water is discharged straight into a river using a powerful pump.

Dangerous chemicals

Concerns raised by industrial chemicals, and the framework for monitoring their use and discharge, are outlined on pages 58–60. Individual substances and their effects are listed in the Glossary (page 203).

Among the substances which cause particular concern in water are heavy metals such as zinc, copper, lead, nickel, chromium and mercury, the levels of which are generally falling slowly.

Physical changes to the ecosystem around the water

As well as man-made changes to the water course itself, changes to the surrounding environment can have an effect on water quality. For example, the destruction of vegetation adjacent to a river or canal might increase fertiliser and pesticide run-off levels. Conversely, an increase in adjoining vegetation could have a positive protective effect.

Pollution incidents

In 1999 there were over 32,000 reports of water pollution, and nearly 14,500 were substantiated after investigation. (This is a decrease of 19% in substantiated incidents on the 1997 figure). Of these, 92 were classed in the most serious category, the lowest figure since records began.

Common sources of pollution incidents were the construction industry, incidents relating to landfill activities, sewage and agricultural incidents. Often incidents involving oils and fuels (accounting for around 3,750 of the substantiated incidents), hydrocarbons and other chemical contaminants were among the most severe and difficult to clean up.

Among those penalised recently was a Lancashire company which was fined £5,000 for allowing diesel oil to enter a brook.

The sewerage system

Water service companies in England and Wales, and sewerage undertakers in Scotland and Northern Ireland, are responsible for the sewage collection network and for the operation of treatment works and discharges. There are 320,000 km of sewers in the UK, which between them collect over 11,000 million litres of urban waste water every day. There are around 9,000 sewage treatment works.

Sewage is less than 0.1% solid material. The solids include biodegradable materials which, if untreated, can starve the receiving waters of oxygen, affecting their ability to sustain aquatic life. When separated out, this material forms sewage sludge, over 1 million tonnes of which are produced in the UK every year.

Producers of urban waste water (industrial effluents, domestic sewage, etc.) are not obliged to discharge it directly into the public sewerage system, although this is the most common option. The other option is to pre-treat it in a waste treatment plant, before discharging it either to the surface water system or to the sewage treatment system.

The quality of effluent from sewage works has improved steadily over recent years.

Under EC regulations dumping of sewage sludge at sea has ceased entirely. The sludge is now disposed of primarily by recycling to agriculture, although smaller quantities are sent to landfill and land reclamation sites, and incinerated. Sludge can provide a valuable source of agricultural nutrients, but it can also contain toxic elements, and the UK government is committed to amending the current regulations in 2000, with a view to ensuring that by the end of 2001 all sludge applied to land is treated to a new minimum standard. Other possibilities for reusing sludge include:

- using it as a peat replacement
- mixing it with gravel to form an artificial topsoil for landscaping
- using it as a fuel.

Among the substances that must not be discharged into surface water drains, but into the sewerage system, are:

- domestic sewage
- industrial effluent, including biodegradable waste water

- storm water
- detergents (in industrial use) including those described as biodegradable
- waste oil
- pesticides and veterinary medicines.

Silty water requires treatment before disposal. It should never be pumped into rivers, streams or surface water drains, and should if necessary be diverted from drains and watercourses with the use of sandbags. Activities that could give rise to silt pollution should be planned carefully. Settlement lagoons or grass plots on site can be used to separate out silt from waste water.

Water abstraction

The Environment Agency is responsible for ensuring effective management of English and Welsh water resources, mostly through a system of abstraction licensing. Under the **Water Resources Act 1991**, virtually anyone wishing to take water from a surface or underground source (except for small-scale domestic or agricultural uses, and some one-off purposes such as firefighting) must obtain an abstraction licence. The approximately 45,000 licensees pay an annual charge, which is based not on actual usage but on their maximum permitted usage. The abstraction licences generally contain conditions, for example to prevent waters being abstracted from rivers in drought conditions, and are fixed-term.

Of the total water abstracted:

- about 50% is abstracted by water companies
- 30% is used by power stations
- 6% is used for other industrial purposes
- less than 1% is used for spray irrigation of crops.

Only a very small proportion is used as drinking water. The UK as a whole uses approximately 8.4 billion litres of water per day. This breaks down into about 380 litres a day per domestic household, approximately 160 litres per person, of which only about 5 litres is for drinking and cooking.

Many users discharge back to the water supply system almost as much water as they abstract, so although this waste water often requires treatment, it does not deplete the overall water supply. Among the exceptions are spray irrigation and evaporative cooling processes, and water is also lost continually through evaporation, and by leakage from the water supply system, which can account for up to 40% of water supplied.

About one-third of UK public water demands are met from groundwater, with the remaining two-thirds being fulfilled by surface resources, including tidal water which is used by electricity generating stations for cooling purposes. Groundwater is held in limestone and sandstone aquifers which are found over much of England, although not in Wales or the West Country. It is replenished by rainfall, mostly in winter since the evaporation and absorption rates are much higher in summer. UK average annual rainfall is 1,050 mm/year, just above the global average, although it varies from around 500 mm/year in the Thames estuary to 2,400 mm/year in the Lake District.

In the UK over the last two decades the demand for water has tended to increase by just over 1% each year. Industrial and general agricultural demands have tended to fall, and demands for spray irrigation, fish farming, hydropower and domestic usage have risen.

It is important that water abstraction be maintained at a sustainable level. Over-abstraction can lead to:

- loss of wetland habitats
- loss of river and marine habitats
- navigation problems
- public health risks
- loss of public amenity value
- risks of soil drought
- building subsidence.

Overall, the UK has a plentiful natural supply of freshwater, but the supply pattern and the demand pattern are not well matched across the country. There is a surplus of water in Scotland, Northern Ireland, Wales and most of England, but a shortage in much of southern England. In the World Resources Institute rating scale, England and Wales have been categorized as 'low' in terms of water resources, and London as 'very low'. The Environment Agency makes drought orders when water supplies are threatened: a varying number are issued annually, with 1995, for example (a relatively dry year) seeing 53 issued.

General predictions for future water demand suggest further falls in industrial demand and an increase in domestic demand and the demand for spray irrigation purposes. The conclusion of *Climate Change and the Demand for Water,* a study issued by the DoE in 1996, was that without increased demand management overall public water supply demand might increase by between 12% and 38% over the 1991 demand by 2021. Climate change could add between 3% and 6% to that increase. Such an increase would undoubtedly put pressure on resources in some parts of the UK, hence the increasing emphasis on measures to control water usage. (The UK government strategy is discussed on page 597–8.)

Controlling water use

For organisations, the first step to water demand management is a water audit. This should be based around regular meter readings, and should compare consumption rates and patterns with those of comparable organisations.

Night flow tests can be particularly useful in helping to identify leaks and other unnecessary usage in premises that are occupied only during the day. For example, such audits have emphasised the large amount of water consumed by automatically flushing urinals, which can be turned off at night, or replaced by a waterless urinal system.

Draft DETR Guidelines were published in July 2000 on company control of, and reporting on, water usage. These are intended to help businesses save money, to conserve resources, and to ensure that current and future legislative demands are met. A six-step cycle is proposed, consisting of:

- identifying a water management champion
- reviewing water costs, use and discharge
- setting targets for improvement
- achieving these targets
- reporting the outcome
- and repeating the cycle again.

Domestically, water demand can be reduced by, for example:

- Reducing the volume of WC cisterns by installing a brick, a sand-filled bottle or similar object. (Flushing a toilet uses an average 9 litres of water.)
- Avoiding the usage of automatic sprinklers, in favour of targeted watering, using recycled water (bathwater or washing-up water) as much as possible, and ensuring that garden watering is done in the evenings and not in the mornings. (A garden sprinkler used for 10 minutes consumes 100 litres of water on average.)
- Purchasing domestic appliances which are water-efficient in their operation. (A dishwater can use 20/50 litres of water per cycle, and a washing machine 100 litres.)
- Taking showers rather than baths (average water usage, showers 30 litres and baths 90 litres).

The use of domestic water meters can help to encourage a reduction in demand.

The total water demand is also being tackled by a programme requiring water companies to reduce their water leakage levels. In 1997/8 leakage levels fell by 12% over the 1996/7 level, and mandatory targets set by Ofwat require water companies to continue reducing leakage levels.

Flooding

As global warming begins to take effect, floods are becoming more common, in the UK and in the rest of the world. For example, 7% of the landmass of England and Wales (6% of which is built-up) would be at risk of flooding at least once in every century were there no defences. In 1998 and 1999, 25 people died as a result of floods in the UK. The Environment Agency recently introduced a new system of flood action warnings, and a Floodline (tel: 0841 988 1888) has been set-up to give the public precise information in the event of a threatened flood.

Policies and legislation

International regulations

Pollution from ships is necessarily the subject of international rather than national regulation. The 1973/1978 **International Conventions on the Prevention of Pollution from Ships (MARPOL)** led to a number of regulations, not all of which have been ratified by sufficient nations to come into force. These cover:

- oil
- noxious liquid substances in bulk
- packaged goods
- sewage
- garbage.

Various UK legislation implements the MARPOL agreements, including regulations that forbid the dumping of plastics at sea. The sewage dumping regulations in MARPOL have not yet been ratified by sufficient nations to come into force. When they are implemented new ships will be given ten years to comply.

The earlier Paris and Oslo conventions which covered marine pollution from land-based sources, ships and aircraft have now been subsumed into the **OSPAR Convention** for the Protection of the Marine Environment of the North-East Atlantic, which entered into force in March 1998, and was extended in July 1998. This provides for signatories to draw up programmes for the prioritisation and control of hazardous substances, with the target of near-zero emissions by 2020.

EC legislation

EC legislation on the control of water pollution is set in the general framework outlined in Chapter 2 and Chapter 5. A sizeable number of directives have been issued, setting pollution limits for particular substances, or setting out the quality standards required for waters that are used for particular purposes. Among the significant directives which have given rise to UK legislation or regulations are:

Directive on the Quality of Surface Waters Intended for the Abstraction of Drinking Water, 1975

This initial directive on drinking water quality has since been amended as standards have been tightened.

Directive on Pollution caused by the Discharge of Certain Dangerous Substances into the Aquatic Environment 1976

This core legislation on control of dangerous substances is outlined on page 68. (Also relevant is the Directive on Integrated Pollution Prevention and Control - see page 68.)

Directive on the Quality of Bathing Waters 1976

EC legislation on bathing waters requires them to meet eleven physical, chemical and microbiological standards, including measures of their contamination by sewage. Both mandatory and guideline standards are given.

Directive on the Quality of Shellfish Waters 1979

This directive specifically sets out standards for shellfish waters, which are designed to protect them from pollution and thus ensure that the shellfish themselves do not carry pollutants. In England and Wales 119 shellfish waters are designated under the directive, and the water at each site has been monitored since 1999.

Directive on the Quality of Water for Human Consumption 1998

This directive (a revision of earlier directives) specifies parameters based on WHO guidelines, for monitoring and controlling the quality of drinking water and water used in food preparation.

Directive on Protection of Groundwater against Pollution caused by Certain Dangerous Substances, 1980

The 'groundwater directive' sets out measures intended to protect groundwater from pollution from various sources. It is implemented in the UK through a variety of legislation including the Environmental Protection Act 1990, with the most recent regulations, requiring many businesses to register their liquid disposal activities, coming into force in 1999.

Directive on Urban Waste Water Treatment, 1991

This directive is the source of recent and continuing UK regulations which control sewage disposal. In practice it will mean that 2,000 of the largest sewage works in the UK (together treating around 90% of UK sewage) will be required to provide additional treatment facilities by 2005. The regulations cover smaller sewage works but the requirements for them are less stringent. Sizeable discharges from food and drink industries are also regulated.

Directive on Water Pollution by Nitrates, 1991

This requires Member States to reduce nitrate pollution in waters that arise from agricultural inputs.

UK policies

UK policies to control the quality and supply of water also fit within the general framework of sustainable development policies that are outlined elsewhere in this book. Specific policies to deal with water only are considered here.

Water: Nature's Precious Resource

The NRA (now subsumed into the Environment Agency) published its strategy document, *Water: Nature's Precious Resource, an Environmentally Sustainable Water Resources Development Strategy for England and Wales*, in 1994. Concerned with the supply of water rather than its purity, the strategy set out plans for some resource development but for a more proactive programme of demand management, concluding:

> *'There is a good chance that demand can be managed to generally achieve future demand levels... meaning that... no strategic resources will need to be completed in England and Wales for perhaps 20 years or more.'*

A subsequent paper, **Water Resources and Supply: Agenda for Action 1996** updates this strategy, and provides a 32-point action plan for the government, regulators, water companies, manufacturers of water-using equipment and water consumers. It is further updated in the Environment Agency's *Environmental Strategy for the Millennium and Beyond,* which has among its key objectives:

- to demand reductions in leakage from water companies
- to encourage the public to view water usage differently and to use it more efficiently
- to promote the development and sale of low-water-usage domestic appliances
- to support the imposition of compulsory selective metering, and the voluntary acceptance of water meters
- to work to improve the quality and use of groundwaters
- to insist upon water saving measures in connection with new developments
- to alleviate the problems caused by low-flow rivers
- and to seek for further control of water abstraction licences.

A *Policy and Practice for the Protection of Groundwater for England and Wales* was issued by the Environment Agency in 1998.

UK legislation

The water supply industry was privatised in 1989, and the bulk of active legislation postdates privatisation. Among the core pieces of legislation controlling the supply and quality of water are:

The Water Act 1989 which set the framework for privatisation and also set up the Drinking Water Inspectorate and the industry regulator Ofwat (The Office of Water Services). It also transferred various regional water authority powers to the National Rivers Authority, which was later subsumed into the Environment Agency. It is almost entirely superseded by two later acts:

The Water Industry Act 1991 is concerned primarily with the regulatory framework for water supply. It places requirements on UK water suppliers to provide consumers with wholesome water, deals with the disposal of effluent, consolidates various earlier regulations, and includes statutory requirements for monitoring pesticides.

The Water Resources Act 1991 deals with the control of water quality and water abstraction. It made the NRA (and subsequently the EA) responsible for the protection of controlled waters from pollution, provided for establishing Water Quality Objectives (WQOs) for relevant territorial, coastal and inland fresh water, and made the NRA (and subsequently the EA) responsible for licensing water abstractions.

Various amendments to previous regulations were made in the **Environment Act 1995.**

The **Water Fittings Regulations 1999** specify standards for WC flushing, with a view to reducing the amount of water expended on each flush from the 13 litres or so used by older-style WCs down to as little as 4 litres (in a dual-flush system).

UK regulations to control levels of pollution in general follow the guidelines set by EC regulations.

The government consulted in 1998 on the question of water charging (particularly for domestic customers) and affirmed the policy that water meters should not be compulsorily extended to all customers. New charging arrangements were set out in the **Water Industry Act 1999**, which affirms the principle of customer choice and much reduces the ability of water companies to disconnect customers for non-payment.

8 Contaminated and derelict land

Contaminated land should be differentiated from derelict land. Derelict land is land that has been sufficiently damaged by industrial or other use that it is not capable of being put to beneficial use without treatment. Contaminated land is land that contains contaminants: that is, substances which are causing, or are likely to cause, water pollution or other significant harm. It has a statutory definition, since local authorities and others have obligations in respect of it. Contaminated land need not necessarily be derelict; derelict land need not necessarily be contaminated. The prime concern here however is with land that is both derelict and contaminated.

Soil composition varies naturally, and many soils across the country contain toxic substances such as heavy metals, some of which are naturally present and others present as the result of man's past activity. Because of this natural variation it is difficult or impossible to set specific standards that soils must reach. However, in many locations which are known to have been the sites of polluting activity it is clear that there is a particular problem with contamination.

Among the activities that lead to the dereliction and/or contamination of land are:

- landfill disposal of waste
- mineral excavation, except when it has been mined under planning conditions or other arrangements that oblige it to be restored once activities cease
- use by the armed services
- a wide range of industrial uses, including chemical and pharmaceutical manufacture, oil refining and storage, town gas production, metal treatment and finishing, iron and steel production, paint and dyestuffs manufacturing, and tanning
- railway usage (including sidings and depots)
- scrap handling, fly tipping, cable burning and similar activities
- sewage treatment
- the application of contaminated sewage sludge to agricultural land
- dockyards and filled dock basins.

Land may be contaminated not only by direct use but indirectly, for example by:

- chimney stack emissions
- contaminated groundwater
- migrating gases
- drain leaks.

The demolition of buildings containing asbestos is also a significant source of contamination.

Among the hazards created by land contamination are:

- Direct contact with toxic substances: for example, oils, tars, carcinogenic chemicals and asbestos.
- Inhalation of toxic gases generated within the land, such as hydrogen sulphide, or toxic particles blown up from the land.
- Ingestion of soil that contains contaminants.
- Eating produce grown on, and contaminated by, contaminated soil.
- Contamination of the water supply, by water leaching through contaminated land.
- Fire or explosion: from any combustible materials, and especially from landfill and other gases. This can be caused, for example, by explosive gases migrating into buildings.
- Damage to concrete, plastic pipes and other substances, for example by oils and acidic chemicals.

In 1993, it was estimated that across the UK there were 39,600 ha of derelict land. The main types of dereliction were:

- general industrial dereliction 25%
- spoil heaps 23%
- excavations and pits 15%
- derelict railway land 14%
- military dereliction 8%
- mining subsidence 2%
- other forms of dereliction 13%

SOURCE: ADAPTED FROM *DIGEST OF ENVIRONMENTAL STATISTICS 1998*

Accurate statistics are not available for contaminated land, which has not been surveyed on a systematic basis. The Environment Agency estimate is that more than 300,000 ha of land is affected, comprising between 5,000 and 20,000 sites.

The term for the treatment of contaminated land so that it can be put to beneficial use is 'remediation'. Among the advantages of this process are the following.

- It minimises the pressure for development on greenfield sites by encouraging 'brownfield' sites to be used in preference to them.
- It encourages the economic and social regeneration of run-down inner-city and former heavy-industrial areas.
- The introduction of new uses, whether agricultural, amenity-based, housing or industrial, leads to new employment opportunities.
- It enhances the environment, especially in inner-city areas where green open spaces are at a premium.
- The improved vegetation cover on areas reclaimed for use as open spaces can provide a wildlife habitat and help to counteract global warming.

However, many contaminants are extremely difficult and expensive to remove, and this limits the scope of what can be done.

Around 80% of the land currently being reclaimed and reused was formerly used for sand and gravel working, for open-cast coal workings or for dumping the spoils of deep coal mining. Over 50% of the land reclaimed is used for agriculture, with a further 30% being put to leisure and amenity uses.

Regulations and policies

EC regulation is less important in this sphere than in many other environmental areas. Conversely, common law is rather more important, and statutory provisions to deal with contaminated land derive largely from the common law tort of nuisance, bringing about the principle of a statutory nuisance.

From Victorian roots, this history of legislation led to statutory nuisance provisions in the **Environmental Protection Act 1990.** Part II of **The Environment Act 1995** also covers contaminated land and derelict mines, and once the provisions in both Acts are fully implemented there should exist a comprehensive framework for identifying contaminated land, analysing the threats it poses, and taking action to deal with the contamination and to bring the land back into beneficial use. Consultation on some aspects of implementing this legislation (in the form of Regulations under the authority of the parent Acts) is continuing, particularly regarding the application of the regulations to radioactively contaminated land.

The regulatory regime requires local authorities to identify contaminated land in their area and to maintain a register of contaminated sites, and certain information about their regulatory actions. They are obliged to determine if the land is a 'special site', a sub-category of contaminated sites which includes sites owned by the Ministry of Defence, those lying above important aquifiers, and other sites which, for various reasons, may best be served by becoming the responsibility of the Environment Agency. Other contaminated sites are handled by the local authority itself.

Once a site has been identified and registered, the regulatory body must decide and consult on the remediation that is needed, and take steps to ensure that it takes place. This involves notifying and consulting with owners, occupiers and other appropriate persons. The first responsibility for remediating the site lies with the person who caused or allowed the pollution to occur. However, if this person cannot be found then the current owner or occupier can be made responsible. If at the end of a three month consultation period no commitment to deal with the hazard has been reached, the local authority may issue a 'remediation notice' which obliges the recipient to assess the land, to clean up contamination and to monitor it thereafter.

The current government brought a new regime for contaminated land into operation in April 2000, in the **Contaminated Land (England) Regulations,** which integrate the various responsibilities for carrying out and funding the remediation of contaminated land.

New uses of land often require it to achieve different standards from those that were appropriate to the former use. The framework for dealing with this is the planning system: that is, planning permission is not granted for new uses unless the intending developer has demonstrated that the land has been – or is to be – rendered suitable for the proposed use.

The highest standards are generally required for housing use, which is likely to lead to both adults and children being in intimate contact with the soil. Lower standards are required for land that is to be left as an open space for agriculture, for amenity purposes or for nature conservation, and this in part accounts for the predominance of these uses among land that is put to beneficial use after remediation.

As well as proposals to deal with the contamination of land, there are policies and regulations intended to prevent the problem from continuing to arise in future. Environmental Impact Assessments help to ensure that any development proposal is considered on a 'cradle-to-grave' basis, taking account of clean-up requirements after the activity ceases as well as of the impact of construction activities. Conditions to planning applications are used to specify in detail the responsibility of the developer to carry out remediation measures.

For sites used for mineral extraction, 'aftercare' conditions, introduced in 1982, can require that the land be treated for up to five years following the replacement of soil after the extraction has ceased. Treatments include cultivation and the application of fertilisers, and they have been shown to improve greatly the quality of the resulting land.

Radioactively contaminated sites

A separate regime applies to nuclear processing facilities, but some sites which are radioactively contaminated as the result of other commercial activities – including the manufacture of gas mantles, of luminising items, the phosphate industry, gas works using uranium catalysts, and landfill sites where a certain amount of radioactive material was dumped before the **Radioactive Substances Act 1960** came into force in 1963 – fall under the general regime for contaminated land. The intention is that radioactively contaminated sites should be designated as 'special sites', and regulated by the Environment Agency.

Reclamation and remediation in practice

The reclamation of derelict land, and the remediation of contaminated land, has tended to proceed slowly in the UK, although it may be that the new regulatory regime, combined with a greater awareness of environmental issues, will lead to an improvement in the clean-up rate in future. In England, 9,500 ha were reclaimed for beneficial use between 1988 and 1993, when the last survey of derelict land was made. A number of new initiatives, and the influx of Millennium Fund funding, should mean that the rate of reclamation has increased over the last few years. However, increasingly high standards for the removal of contamination, and the technology required to achieve them, tend to make remediation an ever more expensive process.

Funding and partnerships for land reclamation

Grant aid has long been available for purposes such as land reclamation, but many programmes of grant aid have been wound down, and others initiated, in recent years. Some long-running projects have drawn funding from a succession of different sources of public funds. Most current funding requires a 'partnership' element, with businesses, local authorities and voluntary bodies combining to make use of local, national and EC funding. The National Heritage lottery fund and the Millennium Fund have also proved important sources of funding.

The Contaminated Land Supplementary Credit Approval programme provides finance for local authorities which have a responsibility to deal with contaminated land where they cannot recover the funding from other parties, for example:

- sites owned by local authorities
- sites where the contamination has been caused by local authorities, for example, private landfill sites contaminated by the dumping of municipal waste
- sites where no other responsible person can be traced.

This money is also used by the Environment Agency, to deal with water pollution caused by land contamination. The budget for the financial year 1998/9 is £15 million.

The Single Regeneration Budget

The Single Regeneration Budget provides funds for specific projects for economic, social and environmental regeneration that are carried out on a partnership basis. From 1994 to 1999 general funding for the reclamation of derelict land within the SRB was administered via English Partnerships, but from 1999 the Regional Development Agencies have administered the Single Regeneration Budget and assumed regional regeneration responsibilities. Reorientation of the SRB in 1998 was designed to ensure that it focused primarily on the most deprived areas and communities.

The Environmental Trust Tax Credit Scheme

This innovative feature of the Landfill Tax introduced in 1996 should help to increase the funds available for restoration of contaminated and derelict land. Landfill operators can choose to make a voluntary donation to an environmental body which could (as one option) use the finance to fund an environmental regeneration scheme. The landfill operators claim back a credit of 90% on their landfill tax liability. Reclamation of old landfill sites for community uses could prove to be fundable under this scheme. For example, the 160 sq km site of the Great North Forest in the north-east of England is to be used for recreation and nature conservation, and is being remediated with the help of a landfill contribution of £35,000.

The Coalfields Community Task Force is a newly established body intended to develop action programmes to regenerated blighted former mining areas. Another option still under discussion is the creation of an independent UK Trust for Derelict Land.

The Land Stabilisation Programme

This seven-year progamme, launched in 1999, is designed to stabilise and regenerate non-coal mine workings.

Groundwork

The Groundwork Trust, a community partnership organisation, is publicly funded on a sizeable scale (via the SRB, the EC and the Millennium Commission) to tackle environmental, social and economic regeneration through partnership schemes. Among the projects being carried out are:

- regenerating two East Manchester water corridors, the River Irk in Collyhirst and the Rochdale Canal in Miles Platting, to regenerate derelict and neglected urban environments
- regenerating the derelict mill site of Boarshaw Clough near Rochdale to create a community nature site, a recreational facility and an educational resource
- transforming the former Rothwell Colliery into a country park with multiple usage.

The Urban Task Force

The Urban Task Force is a DETR-led initiative to regenerate urban areas in decline. It is discussed further in Chapter 12.

Remediation methods

There are three core methods of remediating contaminated land:

- To cap the site, that is, encapsulate the contaminated material by covering it with an impervious coating of clay or other materials. The material itself is not treated, but the risk to health and to the environment is much reduced.
- To remove the contaminated material to landfill, and to remediate the site once it is no longer present.
- To treat the contaminated material on site, so as to remove or reduce the contamination.

The UK has tended to be slow in comparison with the US and much of Europe in adopting on-site treatment technologies, but interest in these is now growing.

Among the technologies that can be used to treat contaminated land are:

- ground stabilisation and microencapsulation: techniques to fill voids and add strength to the mass of material by introducing fillers
- bioremediation, a biotechnology technique which takes advantage of the natural ability of micro-organisms to degrade many organic contaminants
- soil flushing (the name for *insitu* treatment) or soil washing (for material that has been removed from the site)
- pumping and other techniques to remove contaminated gas
- electro-osmosis, an electrical technique which helps to improve soil consolidation and to extract contaminants
- and a variety of chemical treatments.

9 Waste management

> *'We must tackle the quantity of waste produced, breaking the link between economic growth and increased waste.'*
>
> *WASTE STRATEGY 2000 FOR ENGLAND AND WALES*

A recent Gallup survey commissioned by the Groundwork organisation indicated that 63% of small and medium-sized enterprises regarded waste and its management as a key business issue. Research in January 1998 by NOP for the environmental charity Waste Watch showed that 98% of people considered recycling an acceptable form of waste management, 60% considered incineration acceptable, and only 40% considered landfill acceptable.

Waste and its sources

The EC as a whole produces more than 2 billion tonnes of waste every year. The UK produces around 423 million tonnes, made up approximately as follows:

- 74 million tonnes of mining and quarrying waste
- 80 million tonnes of agricultural waste (including animal excreta, unusable carcasses, straw etc.)
- 70 million tonnes of waste from demolition and construction activities
- 69 million tonnes of industrial waste
- 35 million tonnes of sewage sludge
- 51 million tonnes of dredged spoils
- 28 million tonnes of municipal waste including 26 million tonnes of household waste, and all other types of waste handled by local authorities such as street litter and civic amenity site waste
- 15 million tonnes of commercial waste.

The UK also imported approximately 76 million tonnes of hazardous waste in 1996, an increase from 40 million tonnes in 1988/9. (Waste is imported for treatment but not for disposal without treatment.) In 1996 it was estimated that the UK exported 12,072 tonnes of waste. (Source: *Digest of Environmental Statistics 1998.*)

It is estimated that for every tonne of manufactured goods produced, 11 tonnes of resources are employed. The ten original partners in the Leicestershire Waste Minimisation Initiative calculated that on average waste accounted for 4.5% of their turnover.

In 1995/6, each household in the UK produced an estimated 22 kg of waste. Packaging makes up approximately 35% of the weight and 50% of the volume of household waste. The overall amount of household waste has tended to increase more slowly than consumer expenditure over the last ten years (about 30% increase in consumer expenditure, compared to 2–3% increase in household waste), largely because packaging is tending to become more lightweight.

Waste not only adds to the costs of the organisations and households which produce it: it also wastes valuable natural resources. Its disposal presents problems including:

- the risk of pollution of air, land and water supplies
- unpleasant smells
- loss of land to landfill sites
- aesthetically unattractive landfill sites and incineration facilities.

Special waste

Special waste is industrial or commercial waste consisting of, or contaminated with, substances that make it dangerous to life. These include, for example, by-products of industrial processes and spent or out-of-date chemicals. The definition of special waste was amended by regulation in 1996, to include further types such as waste oils. In 1997/8 the total amount of special waste produced in England and Wales was around 5 million tonnes.

The definition of special waste, and the requirements covering it, do not include household waste, but a number of hazardous items can arise in household waste. The following, for example, should be treated as hazardous and disposed of accordingly:

- mineral and synthetic oils and greases
- asbestos
- clinical waste
- battery acids
- some household cleaners.

Current patterns for the disposal of waste

The most common methods for dealing with waste are:

- disposal to landfill sites
- incineration
- recycling.

Trade waste (that is, non-hazardous industrial and commercial waste) is normally compacted before being transported to landfill. Most municipal waste (about 85% in total in 1997/8) is also disposed of to landfill. In 1999 there were 1,512 licensed landfill sites in England and Wales, a fall from around 3,400 in 1994. In 1997/8, 14% of municipal waste had some value extracted from it by either materials recycling, centralised composting, or energy from waste schemes.

Special waste should be disposed of by controlled methods, and there are arguments for pre-treating all of it, but in practice about 126 million tonnes of special waste is sent directly to landfill without prior treatment each year. It is also common for hazardous liquids to be disposed of via the sewers.

Until recently, a considerable amount of waste (including industrial wastes, construction waste, untreated sewage and sewage sludge) was disposed of by dumping it at sea. Recent changes in regulations have eliminated this method of disposal for all but limited classes of inert wastes of natural origin which would cause no harm to the marine environment.

Waste management and reduction

Organisations should establish a waste management strategy as part of their overall environmental strategy. This not only enables an organisation to act in an environmentally friendly manner, it also leads in most cases to real cost benefits.

The practice of waste management does not begin with methods for disposing of waste: it begins instead with methods for ensuring that a minimum of waste arises. Waste management professionals work with a hierarchy of options for handling waste. From the most to the least desirable, these include:

- waste reduction techniques
- pre-consumer recycling, that is, recycling offcuts and other surplus material arising within manufacturing facilities
- primary recovery, that is, recovering and reusing waste materials
- secondary recovery, that is, obtaining other forms of value from waste, for example, by using it as a fuel or by composting
- segregation and disposal in the hope that value can later be recovered
- disposal without recovery of value, by incineration or landfill.

By developing a strategy, organisations can expect to:

- improve efficiency and move towards cleaner technology
- reduce not only waste disposal costs, but also energy and water costs
- minimise long-term environmental liability and insurance costs
- reduce the risk of accidents including spills, minimising lost resources, downtime and lost production
- improve employee safety
- improve their overall company image.

A waste management strategy

The strategy should take a holistic approach, considering not only solid waste but also gases and liquid waste. It should consider not only the internal costs of waste, but also external costs, including those that fall on the waste producer now (such as landfill taxes) and those that may do so in future, as the polluter-pays principle is extended in practice.

It should begin with a fact-finding phase that reviews operations, and identifies the waste stream: that is, how the pattern of waste generation (including waste water, solvent evaporation and other losses) relates to the production pattern.

The strategy should identify clearly what waste is generated – by material as well as by quantity – and discover where, how and why it is created.

It is good practice to allocate the costs of dealing with waste to the process that generates the waste. All staff should also be made aware of the costs of the materials they handle.

The strategy should aim to involve all members of workforce, while ensuring that responsibility for achieving targets is clearly allocated, and that senior management is fully involved and committed. Staff should be fully informed and where appropriate, formally trained.

A brainstorming session can help to generate ideas for further investigation. Where potential changes to processes, equipment or procedures are identified, they should be assessed to discover what potential they hold for reducing waste, for improving efficiency, and for saving money. Those proposals that score highly can then be selected for further investigation in more depth in the initial phase of the project, with lower-scoring proposals being investigated subsequently.

Quantified and prioritised targets should be set, for example, for a percentage reduction in the quantity of waste generated, or in the amount disposed of to landfill. Conveying these targets to staff in cash terms can help to emphasise the importance of the strategy. Results should be monitored, and the process kept under continual review, since new opportunities for improving waste management may continually arise. A staff suggestion scheme should also be a feature.

A 'cradle-to-grave' waste management strategy will include:

Review of product design: to ensure that the product has an optimum lifespan, that it is cheap and simple to repair (if appropriate), that its design facilitates materials reuse at the end of its life, and that it is efficient to produce.

Review of raw materials sourcing and use: to consider whether use of different materials, different grades or different sizes, might reduce the amount of waste arising. This should also include a review of packaging requirements, for example, to avoid purchasing many heavily-packed small items when bulk deliveries requiring less packaging would be more efficient. Delivery of liquids by tanker and storage in a bulk tank is not only cheaper in many cases than buying in drums, it also saves the cost of disposing of the drums after use. Where appropriate, preference should be given to suppliers who provide reusable packaging, for example, plastic-lined drums where only the liner need be disposed of, or returnable plastic crates instead of cardboard crates.

For assembly operations, the purchasing function should be tied in with Bill-of-Materials (BOM) requirements, to ensure that the correct quantity of components to the correct specification are obtained. Inaccuracies in purchasing can lead to assembly-line imbalances and to quality problems which increase the proportion of rejects.

Review of stock handling procedures, ensuring that excess stock holding and poor handling procedures do not generate outdated and redundant stock. The stock control system should check the lifetime of all items, and the FIFO (First In – First Out) system be used to rotate stock. Ordering to take advantage of bulk offers should be carefully controlled to ensure that no more is ordered than can be used within the product lifetime.

Bulk storage arrangements should be reviewed, for example to ensure that all containers are completely emptied before disposal. Arrangements and tools for opening packaging should also be considered, since careless opening can damage contents.

Review of production procedures. For example, the replacement of multi-purpose piping systems with dedicated piping for different types of liquid ingredient can pay for itself in saved time, reduced material waste and reduced requirement for cleaning materials. Poor tool design, or the use of inappropriate tools, can increase the proportion of waste material and rejects. Practices in replacing or reusing solvents and other materials should be reviewed: filtering can give solvents a longer life, and they can continue to be effective when they appear dirty. Procedures that facilitate the separation of different waste materials contribute to the viability of recycling, and the strict separation of contaminated materials that class as special wastes will reduce disposal costs.

Review of waste disposal procedures. The review should ensure that all waste disposal is in full accordance with legal requirements. The following substances, for example, should not be disposed of via sewers or as part of general trade waste, and can often be recovered and reused:

- paints, inks, thinners and cleaners
- degreasing agents
- dry cleaning solvents
- glycols used in antifreeze
- other pharmaceutical and chemical products.

There are also legal requirements covering the interim storage of waste, to minimise hazards and prevent littering. In some circumstances a waste management licence may be required. Materials subject to leakage should be stored in properly designed, designated areas well away from surface water drains and water courses. Used oil should be stored in a bunded area for collection, and oil and fuel filters should also be stored in a designated bin in a bunded area. (See also Chapter 5.) Sufficient skips or other receptacles should be provided for waste to be optimally separated. Skips and refuse compactors should be covered or netted to prevent litter being blown out, and emptied or replaced before they are full. Emergency plans and equipment should be in place, to deal with spillages, fires, etc.

The review should consider whether materials can be recovered, recycled or reused, researching possible markets and the best available technology. It should consider the degree of waste treatment that should be carried out on site.

Waste minimisation clubs

The joint DTI and DETR Environmental Technology Best Practice Programme promotes the establishment of waste minimisation clubs throughout the UK. Approximately 50 clubs are now established or proposed, and at least 300 companies, small and large, have joined club projects. The aim is to share information on best practice, and thus to generate environmental improvements and cost savings through waste minimisation. A six-monthly newsletter, *Club News*, keeps members abreast of developments. Many companies who use the scheme to help initiate a waste management programme discover that a small outlay can result in significant cost savings.

Companies were asked about their waste minimisation strategies by the Environment Agency in 1998/9, and it was found that of the businesses surveyed:

- 16% claimed to have achieved some waste reduction
- 40% claimed to monitor waste expenditure
- 30% claimed to have a published environmental policy, and 80% of those policies covered waste issues.

Packaging waste

In 2000 it was estimated that a total of around 9,200,000 tonnes of packaging waste flowed into the UK waste stream. There has been a trend since the 1980s for such waste to include combinations of materials – such as mixed plastics, plastic lamination on paper and cardboard cartons, and flexographic inks – which made it difficult to recycle, and hazardous to incinerate. (The US Environmental Protection Agency has estimated that 71% of the lead emissions and 88% of the cadmium emissions from incinerating municipal solid waste come from plastics packaging materials.) Although there were also positive trends, such as the move towards more lightweight packaging, and the substitution of plastic for glass bottles, packaging was seen by the early 1990s as presenting a significant problem.

The EC has tackled this problem by making it specifically the responsibility of the producer to deal with the problems. A 1994 EC **Directive on Packaging and Packaging Waste** gave all Member States until 2001 to:

- recover between 50% and 65% of packaging waste
- recycle between 25% and 45% of the waste, including a minimum of 15% of each of the main packaging materials.

Recovery is a wider concept than recycling, and also encompasses energy recovery, composting, and spreading waste on agricultural land.

These EC regulations have now been incorporated into UK law as the **Producer Responsibility Obligations (Packaging Waste) Regulations 1997**, and affect all organisations which handle 50 tonnes or more of packaging materials a year, and have an annual turnover above £1 million. The overall UK target is for industry to recover 52% of its packaging waste, with at least 16% achieved through recycling, by 2001. Material-specific recycling targets issued for consultation in August 2000 require businesses to recycle at least:

- 578,250 tonnes of paper
- 323,250 tonnes of glass
- 16,497 tonnes of aluminium

- 112,500 tonnes of steel
- and 240,000 tonnes of plastics.

(Source: DETR, *Consultation Paper on Recovery and Recycling Targets for Packaging Waste in 2001*)

The regulations apply to:

- manufacturers of packaging materials, including glass, aluminium, steel, cardboard and plastics
- converters of material, that is, bottle, can and box makers
- packer/fillers
- retailers.

Each of these activities carries a percentage obligation. Although small firms are excluded, the regulations apply to wholesalers who supply small shops. Organisations which are covered by the regulations are obliged to register with the Environment Agency or to join a collective 'compliance scheme', and to meet the percentage requirements for recovery of their packaging materials. Among the compliance schemes so far established are Valpak, Biffpack, Wastepack, Difpack (for the dairy industry), Jempac (in South Wales) and Wespack.

The DETR produces detailed free guidance to assist organisations in complying with the regulations.

Recycling

As noted above, recycling is an important element in a waste management strategy, although it is a less desirable technique than waste minimisation.

Recycling is appropriate when:

- there exists a reliable supply of suitable waste material
- it is feasible and economically viable to collect the material and transport it to a reprocessing site
- it is technologically possible and economically viable to reprocess the waste into raw materials and products
- markets exist for the raw materials and products produced by the recycling process.

Recycling can be expensive, with much of the cost residing not in the technological process but in the materials-collecting operation. The costs are frequently underestimated, and many recycling schemes prove less economically viable than schemes such as incineration of waste with energy recovery. Contractors will often pay to obtain materials of significant intrinsic value (such as scrap metal), but organisations may have to pay the contractor to dispose of bulky, low-value waste such as cardboard. In many cases however the cost will be less than the cost of disposal to landfill.

Although about half of all household waste could be recycled, it is estimated that only around 5% in the UK is recycled or composed.

Other problems include the following.

- Bulk waste-disposal contracts can militate against increased recycling, particularly if penalties are imposed when the volume of waste falls.
- Industry standards and legal requirements can limit the use of relatively low-grade recycled material. For example, high quality steel in the UK may contain only a limited proportion of ferrous scrap, and as a result much ferrous scrap is exported to countries which specialise in producing lower grade iron and steel.
- Space and other practical limitations make it difficult to separate out materials which could be recycled.

Pre-consumer recycling (of factory waste) tends to be particularly viable, because the waste material is often available in quantity, it is readily separated from other waste, and there is often a market close at hand for the end product.

Statistics on the amounts of materials recycled are difficult to interpret, because they frequently use different definitions and assemble data in differing ways. They are given here for general guidance only.

A glossary of recyclables

aerosols

CFC gases and their replacement HFCs and HCFCs, all used extensively as aerosol propellants, can damage the ozone layer and contribute to the greenhouse effect. It is therefore important that aerosols are recycled and the gases recovered.

agricultural waste

Most agricultural waste is returned to the land as fertiliser or soil conditioner.

aluminium

The extraction of bauxite, the raw material from which aluminium is obtained, often takes place in areas of high biodiversity such as tropical rainforests, and its processing into aluminium requires vast amounts of energy. Recycling aluminium saves up to 95% of the energy needed to make aluminium from bauxite ore, and helps to conserve important habitats, so it is of particular environmental importance.

An estimated 4 billion aluminium cans (predominantly for drinks) are sold in the UK each year. Used cans are worth almost 1p each. In 1998 over 36% of cans were recycled, earning recyclers nearly £10 milion. (Steel cans have minimal value in comparison.) Cans are easy to collect, relatively clean, and can be crushed to minimise their space requirement.

The Aluminium Can Recycling Association promotes the recycling of aluminium drink cans. They can be collected at can banks and civic amenity sites, through doorstep schemes, and in workplaces.

ash

Power station ash is widely used as an aggregate.

batteries

A well-established scheme exists in the UK for the recycling of lead acid batteries, with at least 90% now being collected and recycled. For nickel cadmium batteries the industry has a target of recycling 200 tonnes for 1997/8, rising to 600 tonnes in 2000/1. (The

ReBat scheme for recycling these was launched in 1997.) The recycling of other types of battery, particularly small batteries, is environmentally desirable, because they contain environmentally damaging heavy metals and other substances. However, although it is technically possible to recycle almost all the major constituents, there are a number of significant difficulties.

- Post-use battery collection schemes are difficult and expensive to set up.
- There is a shortage of cheap and efficient plants for sorting mixtures of batteries into concentrates suitable for existing recycling processes.
- There is as yet no proven technology for recycling mixtures of different types of battery.
- The most widely used battery systems (alkaline-manganese and zinc-carbon) have a low intrinsic value.

An EC directive requires schemes to be set up to recycle batteries containing heavy metals, and the standards were tightened sharply under a further directive, the implementation of which the DTI was consulting on in Autumn 2000.

building aggregates

A variety of building materials can be reused as aggregates after crushing. About 50-55% of construction and demolition waste is believed to be used in this way, as is ash from power stations.

building materials

Other building materials can be salvaged and reused, and there is a thriving market for the salvage of wood, marble, slates, old bricks, and items of architectural interest.

cardboard

Cardboard from commercial activities is recycled by specialist firms, and cardboard is accepted by some civic amenity recycling schemes. Used cardboard can also be reused directly in many organisations where it arises, for example as a packaging filler.

CFCs and HCFCs

These potentially harmful gases are recycled from aerosols, from fridges and from other uses.

compost

Most biodegradable waste can be composted down and used as fertiliser, on either a domestic or a commercial scale. The target in the government's waste strategy is for 1 million tonnes of organic household waste per year to be composted by 2001, and for a total of 25% of household waste to be recycled or composted by 2005. Almost 105,000 tonnes of putrescible waste was collected from households for composting in 1995/6, but this does not take allowance of households composting their own waste in gardens and allotments.

computers

Computers account for nearly 14% of the 900,000 tonnes of annual waste arisings of electrical and electronic equipment in the UK. There are a number of outlets for refurbished computer equipment, among educational organisations, charities and small businesses, and in the developing world. The DTI issues a guide on reuse opportunities.

computer discs

Used discs can be remanufactured, and discs made from recycled materials.

electrical appliances

These can be recycled by:

- donating equipment that is in working order but no longer required to charities, schools and similar potential users, or selling it to second-hand dealers
- donating or selling equipment beyond economic repair to repair shops so that functioning parts can be reutilised
- recovering the metal and/or plastic content.

The DTI produces a guide on recycling white goods, of which almost 75% are currently recycled.

fluorescent tubes

These contain rare metals, and although few schemes are currently in operation, there are plans in hand to extend the schemes for their recovery.

furniture

Unwanted furniture can be sold to second-hand dealers, or passed to charities, particularly those which help households in need of domestic items. (There are restrictions however which prevent the reuse of foam-filled furniture.) Wood furniture that is no longer usable can be turned into wood chippings or sawdust. (See wood waste below.)

garage waste

Among the items which should be handled by specialist firms are antifreeze, oil, oil filters, lead acid batteries, brake fluid and thinners, all of which have some reuse value and are potentially environmentally damaging.

gases

Best available technology ensures that most gases used in industrial processes can be recovered and recycled for reuse.

glass

In the UK in 1998, approximately 22% as much glass packing was recycled as glass packaging was produced, while the total proportion of glass recycled was 26%. It is not always necessary to melt down glass bottles in order to reuse the glass: bottle return schemes (for washing and reuse) are still more environmentally friendly.

For every 1 tonne of cullet (waste glass) used in glass manufacture, 1.1 tonnes of virgin raw material is saved. There are also significant energy savings, since making glass from cullet requires only about 65% as much energy as making it from raw materials, and few noxious gases are emitted.

Glass is collected in door-to-door schemes, in bottle banks, at municipal collection facilities, and by commercial contractors. The recycling process successfully removes most metal contaminants, such as aluminium bottle caps and neck rings, paper labels, plastic labels, cardboard and some other foreign matter. However, it cannot always remove unexpected contaminants such as brick, stones, ceramics, broken china and dirt. Most mixed cullet is suitable for green glass, a limited market as it makes up only approximately 15% of the container glass market, but all cullet collected is used in the UK, and there is a world-wide shortage of cullet. Heavily contaminated glass waste can potentially be used in composite roof-covering materials, in glass-fibre making, reflective beading, as a stone substitute in road making, and for underground drainage tubes.

metals

The scrap metal industry is very long established, and it has been estimated that more ferrous metal is recovered and recycled in the UK than all other materials combined. The metals recovered range from iron girders to small amounts of precious metals found in fluorescent light tubes and thermometers, and include sizeable recoveries from vehicles, domestic white goods and domestic brown goods. The British Metals Federation estimated that their members handle approximately 2 million scrapped vehicles and 15.5 million units of white goods each year, and that 42% of steel, 39% of aluminium, 32% of copper and 20% of zinc is recycled. Many heavy metals are toxic, so recycling helps to avoid pollution, and in most cases it is financially viable.

nuclear fuel

The plutonium and uranium in spent nuclear fuel can be recovered by reprocessing. The current expectation is that between 25% and 30% of the used fuel produced world-wide will ultimately be reprocessed.

oil

Waste oil can be either laundered or re-refined. Oil laundering is used mostly for industrial lubricants, which are treated to remove water, sludges and split emulsions, then blended with virgin oils, after which they may be suitable for the same or a slightly downgraded use. Re-refining produces lube oil of adequate quality for reuse, but at present it is generally not economic in the UK. Tighter controls on emissions from combustion plants contribute to the difficulties of reusing waste oil as a fuel. Garages and industrial users collect waste oil as a matter of course, and it is estimated that most 'lost' oil is from DIY mechanics. They should never dispose of waste oil down drains or sewers, but should always take it to a used oil bank. (Tel. 0800 663366 to find the location of the nearest one.) There is general agreement that better public awareness, plus better reception facilities at garages and/or more facilities for waste oil at civic amenity sites, would reduce the amount of pollution from this source and increase recycling rates.

organic wastes

Composting (see above) is the most usual method of recycling these.

packaging material

Cardboard, plastic and wooden packing cases are among the packaging materials capable of being recycled. Producer responsibility regulations affect the handling of these materials. Among the recyclable materials that can be used as packaging fillers are scrap cardboard, shredded waste paper, and crumbled polystyrene.

pallets

Pallets are commonly reused, with a network of commercial suppliers handling them, and when they are too damaged to be capable of further use, wood pallets can be turned into wood chippings or sawdust. (See wood waste below.)

paper

As with glass, it is not always necessary to pulp paper in order to reuse it. In offices much paper that has been used on one side only can be recycled for use in scrap pads, and often stationery supplies can be increased by holding 'stationery amnesties' encouraging individuals to empty their desks and cupboards of unwanted supplies. Environmental benefits also come from reducing paper usage: for example, by sending emails instead of hard copy messages wherever possible.

Almost all paper is capable of being recycled. However modern contaminants – including wire, staples, latex adhesives, plastics, inks, particularly flexographic inks which are not removed by current flotation de-inking technologies, and water-resistant coatings which hinder the pulping process – add to the difficulty of recycling successfully and obtaining a good grade of end product.

In the UK in 1997 about 5 million tonnes of paper was recovered from the waste stream, and 4.6 million tonnes was recycled (the remainder was exported).

Recycled paper is graded A, B, C or D depending on its quality. Lower-quality paper waste, including most household waste paper, is not used for paper but for low-grade board products, test liners, and industrial paper towels. The higher grades of recycled paper are made from factory offcuts, while lower grades derive from sources such as office waste, 85% of which is made up of mostly relatively high-grade white paper.

Very poor quality paper, or paper which has been in contact with food, may be unsuitable for further recycling, in which case it can be composted.

Recycling of newsprint is subject to new regulations: see pages 123–4.

The paper-making process is a heavy user of water, and making paper from recycled fibres uses 70% less energy than making paper from virgin fibres.

Paper is collected for recycling in doorstep schemes, in neighbourhood paper banks, at civic amenity sites, and by commercial contractors. The average office worker generates more than half a kilo of scrap paper every day. Offices in organisations with environmental action plans should have well-planned paper recycling schemes, with either waste-paper boxes for each individual if space permits, or central collection points, which are best sited at places where paper is used heavily such as in the vicinity of photocopiers or printers.

Those wishing to increase their use of recycled paper for environmental reasons should check the markings carefully, to ascertain what proportion of recycled material a paper product contains, and of what quality. The National Association of Paper Merchants has a marking system for recycled papers, and among the other schemes in common use is the German blue angel mark, which is given to paper that is 100% recycled and contains at least 51% C/D low grade waste paper.

It can also be beneficial to shred waste paper (particularly confidential waste, where this is a requirement in any case) and use the shreddings as a packaging material.

plastics

Plastics are separated out for collection in some municipal schemes, but it is difficult to process plastics from household wastes economically, as they usually consist of a mixture of different polymer types that require separation out before processing, and are contaminated with, for example, dirt, paper labels, printing inks and food residues.

Recycling of plastics used in industry is more cost-efficient. In total, approximately 265,000 tonnes of plastics a year is recycled in the UK, with post-use recycling accounting for about 100,000 tonnes a year.

A sizeable proportion of plastics for recycling are exported to developing countries where environmental regulations are more lax and labour costs are lower.

The recycling process normally produces low-grade heavily pigmented plastic, and because of the difficulty in ensuring that the material is sterile and has no chemical contaminants, this material is not normally used for applications which would bring it into contact with food or beverages.

Among the products made from recycled plastics are knitting yarn and fibre for (for example) filling duvets and sleeping bags.

plastic cups

Because of the volume of these used in many organisations, they justify separate collection. Once washed and granulated, they are recycled for uses such as video cassette cases.

refrigerators

Refrigerators which contain CFCs and similar gases should have these gases recovered before the core recycling process (for recovering metals, etc.) gets under way.

rubber

Most rubber recycling is of vehicle tyres, although other products suitable for recycling include rubber belting, hoses, life-rafts, carpet underlay, footwear components and seals. (See tyres below.)

sewage sludge

This is discussed on page 92.

silver

Silver is used in photographic processes from which it can be extracted for reuse.

solvents, oils and chemicals

Many of these are environmentally damaging and they should be recycled not least to avoid the harmful effects of disposal.

steel

Domestically, food, pet food and beverage cans can be retrieved for recycling through can bank schemes and by magnetic extraction. The current recycling rate for all steel used in the UK is 42%, although the proportion of steel cans recycled is lower. Steel is also recovered from industrial and commercial sources, and from white goods and brown goods. (See metals above.)

textiles

Textiles have long been recovered and recycled in the UK, but this is a labour-intensive operation which is marginally economic at best. The decline in the UK textile industry has affected the market, and in order to increase the proportion of textile recycling it will be necessary to develop new outlets for textile waste. On a small scale, textiles can be reused domestically, for example as floor cloths and dusters, and there is a flourishing second-hand clothes market, including both commercial and charitable enterprises.

toner cartridges

The cartridges from laser, ink-jet and bubblejet printers, from some laser fax machines, and the toner and drum cartridges from some photocopiers, can be recycled, primarily in manufacturer-sponsored schemes, for retooling or recovery of materials. These contain toxic materials and recycling is necessary to prevent disposal causing pollution problems.

tools

Some charities collect unwanted hand and electrical tools for reuse, often in the developing world.

tyres

About 28 million used tyres per year generate between 400,000 and 468,000 tonnes of scrap. A joint industry/government working group is monitoring progress in recycling tyres in the UK, and the recovery/recycling rate now stands at around 75%. An estimated 42% of the value of scrap tyres was recovered in 1996, compared with 20% in 1992. A proposed EC Directive will ban the landfilling of whole tyres from about 2003 and shredded tyres from 2006.

About 35% of scrap car tyres are suitable for retreading, the most economical form of recovery. It has been calculated that if the tyre market is to remain steady, retreads should have an optimum market share of 26%.
Rubber can be devulcanized so that it can replace a proportion of virgin rubber in new rubber products, but this is not an economic process when (as at present) virgin rubber prices are low, and there is little activity at present in the UK. It is hard to achieve a high quality through devulcanizing, so it is used in applications where low-quality rubber is acceptable, such as doormats.
Rubber crumb has applications in brake linings, landscaping mulch, as an absorbent for oil spills, as carpet backing, and for sports surfaces. It can also be used as an additive for asphalt in road surfaces, an application that has been promoted through law in the US to help reduce the landfill demand. Finally, scrap rubber can be burned as a good energy source.

vehicles
See separate section below.

wood waste, shavings and sawdust
These are used particularly for animal bedding and pet litter.

End of life vehicle recycling

About 1.9 million motor vehicles reached the end of their lives in 1997 in the UK. The volume of imports and exports (of the 60 vehicle manufacturers selling in the UK, only about 20 manufacture their goods here, and 48% of the total UK output goes to export) has contributed to the fact that recovery of material is generally not treated as a manufacturer problem, although there is an increasing onus on manufacturers to make their vehicles more readily recyclable.

The EC is currently consulting on a proposed Directive on End of Life Vehicles, with a view to increasing the proportion of material recovered. This currently runs at approximately 75% (although some industry projects have achieved 80%), and the proposal is to increase it to 85% by 2005 and to 95% by 2015. One suggestion is that a Certificate of Destruction could be required at the end of a vehicle's life, to ensure that it is captured by an approved dismantling organisation. There is concern that this will be difficult to enforce if the vehicle does not have a positive scrap value, and the last owner and/or holder is obliged to pay for its dismantling, leading to the US suggestion of a 'cash for clunkers' incentive scheme.

There are an estimated 40 vehicle shredders in the UK, and approximately 4,700 vehicle dismantlers (typically a much smaller-scale operation), of whom it is estimated that up to one-third are either operating illegally or have an outstanding application for a license.

Cars typically contain hazardous components (for example, in fluids, tyres, batteries, air-conditioning systems and air bags) and there is concern that these should not enter the waste chain. PVC too – commonly used for car upholstery – can cause environmental problems. Changes in vehicle design can make it simpler to strip out these hazardous items when the car is being dismantled or before shredding, and most major car manufacturers are now reviewing designs with this in mind. The Ford Motor Company has a strategy for recycling which focuses not only on this, but also on the use of recycled materials within new cars. For example, they are considering using:

- recycled plastic bumpers to make new rear lights
- recycled soda bottles to make door padding and luggage rack side rails
- recycled battery containers to make splash shields
- recycled rubber from tyres to make brake-pedal pads.

Incineration

Waste is incinerated for two reasons:

- to reduce the amount of space required to dispose of it (down to that required by the residual ash)
- and to generate energy.

The two are not exclusive, but not all waste burning is used for power-generation purposes, although this is a feature of most recent facilities. The generation of energy from refuse is discussed further in Chapter 10.

The ash from incinerated waste occupies only about 10% of the volume of uncompacted waste, but the space gain is less (40–50%) when unburned waste is compacted before disposal. The ash can be a concentrated source of heavy metals and other pollutants, and particular care needs to be taken in its disposal. It is normally treated as a special waste.

Although incineration is now widely used as a method of waste disposal, there are still serious differences of opinion about its acceptability. There are several important objections.

- The emissions from the incineration process may contain highly toxic substances such as dioxins and furans, produced when chlorine-containing compounds such as plastics and bleached paper are burned.
- Incinerating organic wastes generates nitrous oxides which lead to acid rain.
- Incinerating organic wastes releases carbon dioxide, a greenhouse gas.
- Incineration wastes valuable resources, which although they might currently go instead to landfill, could perhaps later be recovered and recycled.
- Once a capital investment has been made in incineration facilities, there is less incentive for waste producers to invest in waste minimisation.

One recent report for the EC suggested that every tonne of municipal waste burned caused between £21 and £126 worth (depending on the location of the incinerator) of damage to the environment and/or to human health.

Increasingly strict regulations governing incineration processes (introduced in December 1996) should help to reduce the potential health hazard, but Friends of the Earth, for instance, remain opposed to all waste incineration.

Landfill

Landfill sites in the UK handle the disposal of roughly 85% of controlled wastes and 70% of special wastes, including those that are treated before disposal. As well as being unattractive, and a non-productive use of land resources, landfill gives rise to two particular hazards:

- Rainwater passing through the site can leach away pollutants which will then enter the groundwater supply.
- Chemical reactions within the landfill mass generate quantities of landfill gas, which can be noxious and which contains a large proportion of methane, a powerful greenhouse gas.

Until recently, the general assumption in the UK was that any contaminants contained in leachate (that is, contaminated water leaching out of the site) would be sufficiently dilute that they could be ignored. Aquifers in the UK – unlike, for example, in the Netherlands, where the water table is very close to the surface – tend to lie deep in the ground, and the strata above them serve to filter water before it reaches them. However, it is apparent now that groundwater can become contaminated in some circumstances, and more stringent regulations (derived from EC legislation) have been introduced to reduce the risk of pollution.

As a result of the new regulations:

- Clinical wastes (that is, biological and chemical wastes from hospitals, clinics and so on) are banned from landfill.
- Leachate and groundwater is monitored at least twice a year, for thirty years after waste disposal on the site ceases.
- Collection and drainage systems are required, to ensure that no liquid accumulates at the bottom of the site.
- The risk from landfill gas must be assessed, and unless it is apparent that it is not necessary, arrangements must be made to collect and treat it.

These regulations have increased the cost of landfill disposal, and together with landfill tax, have helped to increase the financial incentive for organisations to explore waste minimisation and recycling options.

The landfill tax was introduced in October 1996, and has increased steadily till it now stands at £11 per tonne per tonne for standard waste (to be increased by £1 per tonne for at least five years from 2000) has helped to remove the cost advantage of this method of waste disposal.

A 1988 survey of mineral workings in England showed that about 9,500 ha had permissions or requirements for restoration, with waste-filling a common solution. It is not thought that there will be a shortage of sites for landfill operations in the foreseeable future, although the sites are not all well located in relation to the pattern of refuse production.

Two different management philosophies have developed about the best way of dealing with the potential hazards from landfall material.

- Treatment by engineering methods, primarily entombment (that is, the enclosing of the landfill material within an impermeable casing, for instance, of clay) to ensure that no hazardous materials can leach out.

- Active treatment of the landfill material to remove or reduce the risk, for example, using enhancement materials to speed the physical and chemical degradation of the waste.

Treatment of existing landfill material is proving a difficult option, and entombment is commonly chosen in the UK at present as a method for dealing with the risks posed by landfill. It seems probable that in future the trend will be to pre-treat materials more thoroughly before dumping them.

The concept of 'sustainable landfill' implies that the material in the landfill will reach its 'final storage quality' (in which no further chemical reactions can be expected) within thirty years. The ultimate aim is to restore landfill sites to other productive uses, and many sites have already been restored, largely by encapsulating the landfill material. This is discussed further in Chapter 8.

Landfills are now seen as a significant potential source of energy, and in particular several recent schemes make use of landfill gas. This is discussed further in Chapter 10.

Fly tipping

The increased cost of landfill disposal has increased the risk of illegal dumping of waste, or fly tipping. Under the Environmental Protection Act 1990, fines for fly tipping can be up to £20,000 or six months in prison. However, enforcement is not easy, and a 1997/8 survey found that 60% of local authorities felt fly tipping had increased since the introduction of the landfill tax, with 44% considering it to be a significant problem.

Radioactive waste

Radioactive waste is divided into three classes:

- High-level waste, for example, spent nuclear fuel, a highly hazardous material which requires reprocessing and treatment before disposal. The quantity produced has risen by 38% since 1987, owing to the higher amount of nuclear power generation.
- Intermediate-level waste, for example, nuclear reactor components and the irradiated metal cladding for nuclear reactor fuel. This is typically stored awaiting disposal. The quantity produced has increased by 43% since 1997.
- Low level waste, items with a small degree of contamination such as workers' clothing and worn out or damaged equipment from nuclear facilities. Normally this is stored for a short period then disposed of in special landfill sites, which are subject to biannual monitoring.

Waste of all levels declines in its degree of radioactivity over time, since some of its unstable radioactive elements have short half-lives. However, other atoms will have long half-lives, so some degree of risk remains for a considerable time.

High-level waste generates heat as it absorbs some of the radiation that is generated by nuclear activity, and as well as requiring shielding to remove the risk of atmospheric contamination, it needs to be cooled. (Lower-level wastes do not generate sufficient heat to require cooling.) In time the amount of heat generated also decreases. Typically, used fuel is stored in water-filled pools (wet storage) or in metal or concrete structures filled with inert gas or air (dry storage). It may be stored either at the originating nuclear installation, or at a dedicated storage facility. This form of storage demands continuing maintenance, monitoring and security measures, and should eventually be supplanted by a more permanent disposal method.

Among the methods that have been actively considered for permanent storage of high-level waste are:

- Transporting the waste into space.
- Transmutation, that is, inducing chemical changes (through nuclear activity) to reduce the long-term radiotoxicity of the waste.
- Geological disposal: burying the material deep (for instance, 500–1,000 m below the surface) in an ice-sheet, or in sediment or rock beneath the deep seabed, or in sediment or rock on land. Land-based geological disposal has now generally been agreed to be the most practicable method of disposal.

No permanent disposal facilities of this kind are yet in operation in the UK.

The government now publishes on a regular basis details of all civil high enriched uranium and plutonium held in the UK.

See also page 66, for information on other sources of radioactive waste.

Policies and regulations

EC policies and regulations

EC policy on waste management has five guiding aims:

- to avoid waste by promoting environmentally-friendly and less waste-intensive technologies and processes, and the production of environmentally sound and recyclable products
- to promote reprocessing, in particular the recovery and reuse of waste
- to improve methods of waste disposal, introducing stringent environmental standards
- to tighten the provisions on the transport of dangerous substances
- and to reclaim contaminated land.

A general principle is that waste should be disposed of where it is produced, and should not be transported across boundaries without good reason. The **Basel Convention** sets guidelines for the transboundary movement of hazardous waste, and was signed by the EC in 1989.

A number of specific directives deal with individual hazardous substances, and for reasons of space are not be summarised here. Among the more general EC regulations are:

The Directive on Waste of 1975 lays down general principles for the collection, disposal, recycling and processing of waste, and is supplemented by the **Directive on Toxic and Dangerous Waste 1978** which lists toxic and dangerous substances that require special treatment, and the **Directive on the Landfill of Waste 1999** which sets down procedures for the acceptance of waste and the management of landfill sites.

The Directive on the Supervision and Control within the Community of the Transfrontier Shipment of Hazardous Waste 1984 implements the policy outlined above. It has been supplemented by regulations in 1993 and 1995 controlling the shipment of waste into and out of the EC.

A **1986 Directive on Sewage Sludge in Agriculture** sets out measures to control the spreading of sewage sludge (which may contain heavy metals and other contaminants) on agricultural land.

Two 1989 **Directives on New and Existing Incineration Plants for Municipal Waste** lay down emissions standards to ensure that atmospheric contamination from incineration is reduced to a minimum. The standards are stricter for large plants than for small, and existing plants are to be brought into line with the standards for new plants in two stages. Another directive in 1994 specifically covered the incineration of dangerous waste.

Finally, the **Directive on Packaging and Packaging Waste 1994** is now being brought into operation in the UK as described on pages 110–111.

UK policies

Waste management policies have long been a part of the UK government's environmental strategy. The Labour Government produced an updated *Waste Strategy 2000 for England and Wales* in 2000, with key measures including:

- statutory local authority recycling targets and action plans
- a new Waste and Resources Action Programme to develop new markets for recycled wastes
- increased use of the landfill tax credit scheme
- the introduction of tradable permits for those producing biodegradable waste
- an extension of the obligation for producers to recover waste matter, applying for example to senders of junk mail and newspaper publishers.

Targets include:

- reducing the amount of industrial and commercial waste that goes to landfill to 85% of 1998 levels by 2005
- recycling or composting at least 25% of household waste by 2005, rising to 30% by 2010 and 33% by 2015.

UK legislation

Much recent UK legislation derives from the EC measures briefly outlined above. More generally, the **Environment Protection Act 1990** set the current framework for waste management, imposing a statutory duty of care on those with the following involvements with waste:

- producers
- importers
- holders
- carriers
- treaters.

All the above are obliged to ensure that controlled waste is handled in accordance with the regulations, that it does not escape from control, that it is transferred only to authorised people or organisations, and that it is adequately described and clearly labelled to enable proper handling and treatment.

The Radioactive Substances Act 1993 (which replaces very similar earlier legislation), as well as providing for the registration of premises where radioactive substances are handled, deals with authorisations for the handling and disposal of radioactive waste.

The **Recycled Content of Newsprint Bill 2000** requires publishers of newspaper and magazines to ensure that an increasing proportion of newsprint is collected and recycled, and that an increasing proportion of recycled fibre is used in newspaper production.

10 Energy

> *'Although the environment is seen as part of the problem and part of the solution, what is missing is an incentive to move towards a more sustainable approach.'*
>
> *PROGRESS REPORT ON THE EC 5TH COMMUNITY ACTION PROGRAMME ON THE ENVIRONMENT,* 1997

Energy usage is important to the environment primarily because of the damage caused by the mining of fossil fuels and by the processes that generate energy, including combustion and nuclear fusion. Of particular concern is the impact of energy production on climate change.

Non-renewable fuels are a finite resource, and the rate at which they are being consumed is also a source of some concern, but there is no immediately foreseeable danger of a fuel shortage in the UK.

This chapter looks first at the current energy situation in the UK, the trends that are shaping it, and the problems it causes. It then looks at individual sources of energy, with the emphasis on renewable, more environmentally friendly energy sources. Finally it considers strategies for reducing energy consumption, and briefly reviews UK and EC energy policy and legislation primarily from this perspective.

Strategies to reduce the energy requirement of motorised transport are covered in Chapter 11 and not in this chapter.

Energy supply and consumption

Energy statistics can be difficult to decipher. It is important to distinguish between the amount of energy generated in the UK and the amount consumed. The latter includes the consumption of imported energy: for example, electricity from the French grid. A distinction must also be made between primary energy consumption and secondary energy consumption. Prime users are those who make direct use of fuels, including electricity generating plants, which account for about 32% of prime energy use. (The remainder includes industrial prime energy usage and transport.) Secondary users include those who make use of the electricity that is generated by the generating plants.

Energy supply

The pattern of fuels used in the primary energy sector has changed significantly over recent years:

	1990	**1998**
Oil	37%	33%
Solid fuels	31%	19%
Gas	24%	38%
Nuclear, hydro, electricity imports	8%	11%

'SOURCE: *DIGEST OF ENERGY STATISTICS 1999*'

This is the result largely of changes in the fuels used for electricity generation. In 1990 coal made up 67% of the fuel for this purpose; by 1999 this had fallen to 28%. Nuclear power stations accounted for 24.5% of generating capacity, and renewable energy sources for less than 4%.

In the UK and the EC as a whole, the share of the market taken by coal is expected to continue to fall over the next ten years, while natural gas, already the dominant fuel outside the transport sector, increases its market share.

The UK's proven and probable reserves of oil are being consumed at a rate of 8% a year (although the probability of new reserves being discovered means it is most unlikely the UK will run out of oil in just over ten years), while natural gas reserves are being consumed at 4% a year. The EC as a whole imports just under half of its fuel requirements.

Energy consumption

The total consumption of energy in the UK is rising steadily, although now not rapidly. (For example, for the period March to May 1998 DTI figures show that it was 2.9% up on the same period in 1997.) In million tonnes of oil equivalent, temperature corrected, UK consumption has been:

1950	143.5
1972	212.6
1998	235.2

'SOURCE: *DIGEST OF ENERGY STATISTICS 1999*'

This rise is much slower than the rise in GDP: energy consumption per unit of GDP in 1996 stood at 54% of the 1950 level.

Generally the demand for energy in the industrial sector has fallen, reflecting both a decline in manufacturing industry and greater fuel efficiency. There have also been significant improvements in fuel efficiency in other sectors, but these have been counterbalanced by increasing demand factors: for example, the greater number of vehicles, albeit they tend to be more fuel efficient. The amount of electricity supplied to end users has risen substantially: domestic electricity rose from 77.0 TWh in 1970 to 110.4 TWh in 1999. So has the demand for fuel for transport purposes, which now accounts for 34% of total final energy consumption (with the domestic sector accounting for 28%, and industry for 24% approximately).

The domestic energy requirement has increased largely because of a rise in the number of households, by approximately 17% since 1970. A quarter of all electricity consumed in the UK is for domestic purposes other than space heating.

Lighting takes up about 20% of UK electricity use, and the EC estimates that between 25% and 50% of the electricity consumption of the average office is taken up by lighting.

The pollution problem

In 1996 electricity power stations in the UK accounted for:

- 65% of sulphur dioxide emissions
- 28% of carbon dioxide emissions
- 22% of emissions of nitrogen oxides
- 16% of particulate matter (PM_{10}) emissions
- 3% of nitrous oxide emissions

SOURCE: *DIGEST OF ENERGY STATISTICS 1999*

Friends of the Earth estimate that producing and consuming one unit of electricity causes 0.3 kg of carbon dioxide to be released into the atmosphere.

Other primary users of energy also accounted for a substantial amount of pollution, so that altogether energy usage (and particularly the usage of fossil fuels) is a major cause of global warming, of acid rain and of a range of other pollution problems.

If the UK is to meet the targets for reductions of emissions outlined in Chapter 4, it is essential that the use of fossil fuels be reduced.

Fossil fuels

The main fossil fuel are:

- oil
- natural gas
- coal.

Their prime advantages of using these fuels are that:

- fuel-using processes (including transport and electricity generation) are to a large degree designed around these fuels at present
- they are relatively compact, compared for example with renewable biomass fuels
- they are comparatively transportable, and oil in particular is used in the transport sector for this reason
- the technology to make use of them is well developed and continuing to improve.

Their prime disadvantages are that:

- Finite resources exist and at the current rate of utilisation many known resources will become exhausted. Replacement resources, where they can be located, are often more expensive to exploit.
- Mining fossil fuels is directly damaging to the environment, adversely affecting landscapes and destroying ecosystems.
- Combustion of fossil fuels is a dirty process which leads to a considerable amount of atmospheric pollution.

Coal

The UK's coal production, and particularly the production from deep pits, has fallen dramatically over the last twenty years. In thousands of tonnes, the UK produced:

	Deep mined	Open cast
1960	189,039	7,674
1972	109,086	10,438
1998	25,014	15,033

SOURCE: *DIGEST OF ENERGY STATISTICS 1999*

The UK now imports about a third of its coal requirement, while it imported next to no coal prior to 1960. Major power producers account for approximately 71% of the coal used in the UK.

Gas

The manufacturing of 'town gas' in the UK declined at the end of the 1960s until by today none is produced. At much the same time came a surge in natural gas production, which has continued unabated.

UK production in GWh:

	town gas	natural gas
1960	66,615	791
1972	17,848	291,078
1998	–	1,048,827

SOURCE: *DIGEST OF ENERGY STATISTICS 1999*

In particular the use of natural gas as a fuel by electricity generating plants has increased. Although industrial demand fell during the 1980s and early 1990s, it has been rising since the mid-1990s.

The consumers of natural gas in 1998 were:

Domestic	36%
Industrial	19%
Electricity generators	26%
Services	12%
Other	8%

SOURCE: *DIGEST OF ENVIRONMENTAL STATISTICS 1999*

Oil

Oil remains the prime fuel for motorised transport, which accounts for the bulk of oil usage in the UK. Both oil refining and the combustion of oil are significant sources of pollution. Land-based oil extraction is also a 'dirty' process with negative impacts on its immediate environment, and offshore oil extraction poses problems for the marine environment. Oil spills, particularly at sea, are among the most serious of environmental accidents, causing considerable damage to marine life, and the evaporation of petroleum and other fuel oils also releases pollutants (including benzene, a known carcinogen) to the atmosphere.

UK oil production increased by 3.25% in 1999, reching a record level of 137 million tonnes, and nine new UK oil fields started production in the year.

Nuclear power

Nuclear power generation also uses non-renewable resources, although it presents quite different environmental problems from those caused by fossil fuels. This non-combustion process does not produce greenhouse gases. However, it does generate nuclear waste, the treatment and disposal of which is difficult and expensive, and there is a risk of radioactive contamination both from power plant operation and from waste disposal.

Nuclear power supplied 59 TWh of electricity in 1990, and 91 TWh in 1999. The amount of high-level nuclear waste has increased proportionately, but there have been less than proportionate increases in intermediate-level wastes, and the amount of low-level waste produced and disposed of almost halved between 1986 and 1994, reflecting technological improvements.

There are currently no plans to build new nuclear generating capacity in the UK.

Radioactive pollution is discussed in Chapter 5, and the handling of radioactive waste in Chapter 9.

Renewable energy

Renewable sources provided less than 1.2% of UK energy in 1998, accounting for about 1.7 million tonnes of oil equivalent. In general, electricity generation from renewable sources involves a high initial investment, although subsequent operating and maintenance costs are lower than for conventional power generation. Current accounting systems and taxation policies still make it difficult to justify the initial investment, but renewable energy is generally cost-effective:

- where an exceptional fuel source is available: for example, an outstanding wind turbine site, some hydroelectric power sites, major landfill deposits providing large sources of methane
- in areas beyond the reach of the national grid, including island communities
- where side-benefits help to justify the cost of the project, or the project is itself a side-benefit: for example, where it is necessary to dispose of landfill gas and it can be used as a fuel, or where passive solar design is employed in new buildings.

Changes in fiscal policies to take fuller account of the environmental costs of fossil fuel usage could release the very considerable unrealised potential for developing many renewable energy sources. This is likely to occur at an increasing rate as part of the drive to achieve UK and EC targets to reduce emissions of greenhouse, ozone-depleting and other harmful substances. Friends of the Earth, for example, estimate that if renewable sources were to meet 14% of the EC's primary energy demand by

2020 (less than half of the estimated EC potential for these forms of energy) then carbon dioxide emissions would be reduced by 16.2%, and there would be a net increase of 515,000 jobs.

Already the amount of energy generated by some renewable methods (including wind power and biofuels) is increasing at a very rapid rate.

The spread of renewable fuel usage in 1996 in the UK was:

Refuse combustion	21.4%
Industrial wood	19.1%
Large scale hydro power	16.3%
Landfill gas	15.1%
Domestic wood	7.7%
Biofuels (other than those mentioned separately)	6.9%
Sewage gas	6.9%
Wind power	2.9%
Straw combustion	2.7%
Small scale hydro power	0.6%
Active solar energy	0.4%

SOURCE: *DIGEST OF ENERGY STATISTICS 1999*

The DTI has had a Renewable Energy Programme, managed by the Energy Technology Support Unit (ETSU), since 1974, and has spent over £330 million on research, development, joint ventures, and on working to establish an institutional framework that takes account of the environmental and other benefits of renewable energy sources in assessing projects.

Wind energy

The generation of energy by wind turbines is a completely renewable and completely clean form of electricity generation. Although the technology is fast developing, the principle of wind power dates back to the start of recorded history. Modern wind power is also very flexible, offering opportunities at every scale from small wind turbines to serve a single building or site, to major wind farms making a significant contribution to national energy requirements. Wind power can also be used directly, for example to drive pumps, but the perceived potential here is much smaller.

Wind turbines function best on exposed sites away from obstructions, and there are many potential sites in the UK, especially on the treeless hills of Northern England, Scotland, Wales and Cornwall. They are not effective in built-up areas where there is too much turbulence. Offshore sites are also a real possibility, with the European continental shelf providing the environment for winds steadier and higher than any to be found onshore, and some commentators predict that in the long term a large proportion of EC wind farming will take place offshore.

Wind turbines are cheap to run, but capital costs tend to be high, especially for offshore developments. Other negative aspects of this form of energy include:

- The visual impact of sometimes very tall turbines. Many promising sites are in areas of high landscape value.

- Noise from the turbines.
- Loss of habitats in building wind farms, and possible wider disturbance to wildlife.
- Possible interference with radio signals, although there are technical solutions to this problem.

The installed capacity of wind turbines in Europe has been increasing by about 40% per year over the last six years, and by the end of 1999 there was over 3,600 MW of wind energy capacity in Europe, of which 273 MW was in the UK. In 1998 there were 58 wind generation projects in the UK, 52 of which were new schemes. The electricity produced by these wind farms has increased by a factor of 26 since 1992. This still seems small in comparison, for example, with Denmark, where 8% of energy is provided from this source, and the Danish government's target is to generate 40% of the electricity requirement from offshore wind farms by 2030. Greenpeace estimate that the same proportion could be met in the UK, while the ETSU's prediction is that at least 20% of UK electricity demand could be met by land-based wind turbines, and a further 16% by off-shore installations.

A growth in wind farming would also create jobs, primarily in construction and maintenance: by Greenpeace's estimate, up to 36,000 over the next twelve years.

Biofuels

'Biofuels' is the general term given to biological materials that are used for fuel purposes. (This generally excludes fossil fuels, although they too derive from biological sources.) 'Biomass' is the more specific term for solid biofuels. There are also liquid biofuels, and biomass can be processed to produce gaseous fuels.

Biofuels too are not new – wood is a typical biofuel – but much of the technology that enables the range of biofuels and their uses to be extended is comparatively new. Some of these technologies – for example, chipping, consolidation into briquettes, drying, pressing to extract oil, fermentation, thermochemical gasification, and anaerobic digestion processes that generate gas – are used to produce more compact and efficient fuel than the original biomass, that can be burned in a convention steam-raising plant. Others are alternatives to combustion technology, generating heat directly through thermochemical reactions such as pyrolysis or digestion.

Among the most common biofuels are:

- mature timber, including wood waste (which can be up to 50% of the total timber crop)
- coppiced wood shoots
- waste paper and other biological components of municipal waste
- vegetable oil crops such as sunflower, soya, rape, linseed, maize and olives
- slurry (animal waste) and sewage sludge
- chicken litter
- waste material from processing food or fibre crops
- straw.

Some of these are waste materials that arise in any event, and their use as biofuels is one solution to their disposal. For example, digestion plants for slurry and sewage sludge may operate mostly as a treatment process, but they generate heat as an useful side effect. However it is also economic to grow some crops specifically for use as biofuels, particularly on EC set-aside land that cannot be used for food crops.

Among these are coppiced woods. Modern short-rotation or arable coppice techniques involve growing specially selected fast-growing varieties, typically of willow and poplar. They are harvested after three to five years, with the shoots being chipped into woodchip fuel. In the UK currently about 5,000 ha are being planted for this purpose, to supply new wood-fired power station projects.

The use of crop waste as biofuels can also make it economic to grow different varieties, which lead to a higher quantity of residue.

Wood waste can be collected either by changing the point at which branches and tops are stripped from timber crops, or from sawmills.

Among the biofuels currently being utilised in the UK are coppice as noted above, chicken litter, already used to fuel two small power stations in the UK with more planned, and scrap tyres. The UK's first large-scale straw-fired power station (a fuel that is more desirable now that stubble burning in fields is banned) is in operation in Cambridgeshire. There has also been active (government-funded) commercial research into digesting farm slurries to generate biogas. On a small scale it is difficult to make this cost-effective, but it is thought there is more potential (and less risk of environmental impact) in larger-scale plants allied to centralised slurry handling facilities, and this continues to be the focus of development work.

On the whole biomass-fired power stations have a relatively low electrical efficiency, not least because many of them are small-sized. (It is not practicable or economic to transport the more bulky biofuels over long distances.) Fuel efficiency can be increased by pre-processing the fuel. Biofuels are not emission-free, although (apart from mixed wastes where the biological matter is contaminated by other substances) they tend to be relatively low in emissions, and in particular low in sulphur compared to fossil fuels. Enthusiasts argue that the repeated growing and burning of a fuel crop should not contribute to global warming, although this is difficult to quantify. Clean-up technologies (and intrinsically clean, non-combustion technologies) improve the environmental performance of biofuel-powered facilities.

Solar energy

As much energy reaches the earth from the sun each hour as the population of the earth uses in one year. Technologies now exist to take advantage of this energy, and to use it directly for purposes such as:

- space heating and water heating
- lighting
- pumping water
- refrigeration
- and indirectly through electricity generation.

There are three basic ways of using solar energy:
Passive solar heating and lighting: that is, designing buildings to make the best use of the sun as a source of heat and light.
Active solar heating, using collectors to capture the sun's heat and a transfer system such as water or oil to carry the heat to where it is needed. This can directly produce hot water, be used for space heating, or the heat can be stored for later use.
Photovoltaic technology, generating electricity from the action of sunlight on certain materials such as silicon.

The advantages of solar power are that it is a clean technology, causing little or no noise, pollution or other environmental damage, and that in some circumstances it is very cost-effective. At least a degree of passive solar design is cost-justified in new building, and photovoltaic technology is competitive particularly in remote locations where grid electricity is not available. (It is widely used, for example, to provide lights for navigation buoys and lighthouses, and to provide power for communities and leisure sites in remote places.) It is also used for gadgets such as electronic calculators and radios. Active solar heating is cost-effective in hot countries with a reliable supply of sunlight.

The problems of solar power are that the achievable power density is low, particularly in less hot countries, that it is difficult to harness diffuse sunlight as a power source (though it is easy to channel direct radiation through mirrors or lenses) and that the availability is not well matched to the peak demand. As with other forms of renewable technology, the capital cost is relatively high although running costs are low.

Solar power is not used on a large scale in the UK, but it is used on a small scale, with active solar collectors being used primarily for domestic heating (about 70% of total usage) and for heating swimming pools (about 30% of total usage). World-wide, the trend is for the use of photovoltaic batteries as a source of energy to increase by around 16% each year.

Geothermal sources

The heat held under the ground, either in 'hot rocks' (or 'HDR' – hot dry rocks) or in geothermal aquifers, is another potential source of power. In some parts of the world this is seen as being a promising power source, but UK experience to date has been limited and mixed. Most UK potential is in the West Country, but a hot-rock experiment in Cornwall, which ran from 1977 to 1990, was abandoned since it appeared unlikely to show useful results. Geothermal aquifers present opportunities for heating purposes, although the water available is not hot enough for electricity generation. They have been used successfully to power an experimental district heating scheme in Southampton, but there is very limited potential to expand the proportion of UK energy deriving from this source. There are now more than 30 countries utilising geothermal energy, approimately 12,000 MW are used as heat and 8,000 MW are transformed into electricity. Internationally, the use of geothermal energy increased over the period 1990–98 by about 4% each year.

Hydropower

There is limited potential in the UK for sizeable dam-based hydroelectric schemes, and most of this has already been realised. However, there is some scope for small-scale projects, and these were encouraged by the 1989 Water Act which exempts them from water abstraction charges.

Tidal power and wave power have been seen as promising potential energy sources, but these have proved difficult to realise. It is only practicable to exploit tidal power at specific estuary sites (for example, on the Severn) where tides are large and the geography is suitable for constructing a power generation facility. The UK is thought to have more potential sites than the remainder of Europe, but none have as yet been exploited. Wave power is still at the experimental stage.

Energy from waste

A large number of waste materials can be used to generate power, including both biological materials (see Biofuels above) and non-biological materials. In addition, the methane gas that is generated by decomposition processes in landfill sites can be harnessed as a fuel. The technologies to make use of these fuel sources are available, and the importance of waste materials as a fuel is growth fast, with much unrealised potential still perceived. One recent estimate was that the energy equivalent of 26 million tonnes of coal per year could be derived from waste in the UK.

The amount of municipal solid waste used to generate electricity has risen from 160,00 tonnes of oil equivalent in 1992 to 580.2 tonnes in 1999. Overall the following waste products were used to generate energy in 1999 (in thousand tonnes of oil equivalent):

wood	710.3
municipal solid waste	580.2
straw	71.7

SOURCE: *UK ENERGY IN BRIEF, 2000*

Because solid waste is a low-energy fuel (the calorific value of municipal waste is about a third of that of coal) it is most appropriate for local facilities that combine energy-generation with heat utilisation. Although refuse-burning is not always cost-effective purely in terms of power generation, it is justifiable as a method of retrieving value from waste disposal, particularly where incineration is in any event the preferred disposal option.

Incineration of mixed waste is a process that gives rise to some concerns about the emission of hazardous materials. This is discussed further in Chapters 5 and 9.

The first UK plant to use municipal waste, SELCHP, opened in south-east London in 1995. It was followed by plants in Tyseley, Birmingham in 1997 and Cleveland in 1998, and others including the Sheffield 'Green Heat' district heating network and the City of Dundee Energy from Waste facility. At Tyseley the unit incinerates 350,000 tonnes a year of municipal solid waste, to generate 25 MW net of electricity, enough for 25,000 households.

The UK's first tyres-to-energy plant, opened in 1993, deals with 94,000 tonnes of scrap tyres (21% of the UK total), generating 30 MW of electricity that is both used on site and sold. It also recovers about 27,000 tonnes per year of solid by-products for recycling. Kingsbridge, Devon is an example of a plant which uses sewage sludge to generate electricity.

Methane gas

Methane that can be used as a fuel is produced both by sewage works and in many landfill sites. When sewage sludge is digested – as is done in most large UK sewage works – the gas is often used for generating electricity, either for use on-site or for general sale.

The exploitation of landfill methane is also now commonplace. The gas is collected, typically in a network of interconnected 'wells', and channelled to a nearby power generating facility. The first schemes were developed in the US in the 1970s, and there are now several hundred operating world wide. Although this method of recovering value from wastes rates below recycling and similar techniques in the waste management hierarchy, it is a worthwhile solution where there are existing landfill sites to be exploited.

There are now about 50 landfill gas facilities in the UK, for example, at the Middletown Broom landfill site in West Yorkshire. UK capacity increased 44% between 1998 and 1999.

Improving the efficiency of power generation

In the medium term, the move to less polluting forms of power generation will much reduce the amount of pollution caused by this activity. There is also a role to be played, however, by improving the efficiency of power generation processes using fossil fuels.

Traditional forms of power generation are not efficient in converting fuel to transmissible energy. The efficiency of an average coal-fired electricity generating station is only about 38%, although gas-fired plants achieve an average 55% efficiency. Combined Heat and Power (CHP) plants, in contrast, can reach conversion efficiencies of 70% to 90%.

Combined Heat and Power (CHP)

Combined heat and power technology takes advantage of the heat that is generated, particularly when using lower-efficiency fuels, and uses this directly as a heat supply for buildings, industrial or agricultural processes in the immediate neighbourhood of the CHP plant. CHP is particularly associated with neighbourhood heating schemes, but recent plants have provided heat, for example:

- to the pasteuriser unit in a brewery
- to swimming pools

- to greenhouses, using recovered carbon dioxide to boost plant growth
- to dry biomass fuels before they are used.

Combining the electricity generation with the heat production enables CHP plants to achieve very high energy conversion efficiencies. CHP tends to work best as a small-scale technology since there is normally a limit to the amount of heat that can productively be used in the vicinity of the plant. CHP plants are often used to meet heat and power requirements on single industrial sites, with any excess energy generated being fed into the national grid.

The CHP capacity in the UK more than doubled between 1990 and 2000, and there is thought to be the cost-effective potential for it to be doubled again. A study for the DETR by the Energy Technology Support Unit (ETSU) has suggested that up to 17 GW of CHP plants could economically be justified by 2010.

Since GHP is a more efficient method of using fuels, it contributes less proportionally to atmospheric pollution. The CHP Association estimate that the increased use of CHP schemes could achieve up to 20% of the UK's carbon dioxide emissions reduction target. A move to CHP would also benefit employment prospects: Friends of the Earth have suggested that CHP could create up to 34,000 jobs over the next fifteen years.

CHP technology is not dependent on a particular type of fuel, and CHP plants have been powered by both conventional fossil fuels and newer renewable fuels. CHP plants have been built to use waste fuel, and are particularly suitable for low-efficiency fuels such as biomass, because the 'waste' heat generated is put to productive use. At present, natural gas is the most common fuel for CHP facilities.

Reduced pollution from fossil fuels

The volume of pollution from the combustion of fossil fuels is tending to decrease in the developed world (although this is not true of the developing world). There are two major reasons:

- The shift from small multiple sources of combustion to large power stations, which have better pollution prevention technology, and which disperse their pollutants at higher altitudes (although this spreads the pollution rather than reducing it).
- The shift from sulphur-rich coal to low-sulphur coal and other low-sulphur forms of fuel such as oil and natural gas.

Among significant technological developments is the Integrated Gasification and Combined Cycle (IGCC) System for generating power from coal. Where conventional coal-burning power stations create sulphur dioxide because of the sulphur content of the fuel, which they then remove from the flue gas (leaving a solid waste product), the IGCC method removes the sulphur before combustion. This cleaner technology results in lower emissions not only of sulphur dioxide but also of nitrogen oxides, and it also results in greater fuel efficiency. Several demonstration plants are being planned or built, and it looks as if the IGCC process will be the norm for coal-fired power generation in the early part of the next century.

Energy efficiency for end users

Although the move to less environmentally damaging fuels and more efficient power generation techniques will do a considerable amount to reduce the current level of environmental damage attributable to the energy sector, a further major contribution must come from end users. Therefore there is a major initiative, at all levels from the international to the local, to ensure that users:

- do not use energy unnecessarily (for example, not taking unnecessary journeys by motorised transport, and switching off electrical equipment when it is not needed)
- ensure that buildings are energy efficient, improving the insulation of existing buildings and designing new buildings with energy saving in mind
- ensure that processes are energy-efficient
- ensure that both commercial and domestic equipment is energy efficient.

The DETR estimated in June 1998 that 10 million tonnes of carbon emissions would be avoided if all business sectors adopted energy-saving measures which are:

- current best practice
- known to be cost-effective.

This would take the UK a quarter of the way to achieving its carbon dioxide reduction target for 2010.

A further 2 million tonnes could be saved by the use of more fuel-efficient domestic appliances, cutting domestic electricity consumption by up to a third, and according to ETSU estimates, up to 1.4 million tonnes could be saved by energy efficiency measures in offices.

Energy-efficient working practices

Simple methods by which energy efficiency can be improved, at home and in the workplace, include:

- Improving building insulation: for example, by physically insulating water tanks, roofs and cavity walls, by double glazing windows, by using blinds and drapes to reduce heat loss through windows, and by draughtproofing doors. (See also Chapter 13.)
- Reviewing the use of heating and air conditioning systems to ensure that they are used only when necessary. Time clocks can be used to restrict their use to hours when the building is occupied, and natural heating and ventilation (open windows, sunlight, etc.) should be preferred to artificial heating and cooling methods whenever possible. Operating hours for heating systems can often be shorter in spring and autumn than in winter. Systems should not be left on over weekends if the building is unoccupied.
- Reviewing thermostat settings. A 1°C reduction might have no noticeable impact on comfort, but it would reduce energy consumption by as much as 10%. Individual thermostats for radiators can help to avoid the overheating of little-used areas.

- Ensuring that doors and windows are kept closed when heating or air conditioning appliances are being used.
- Ensuring that vents and radiators are not blocked and are operating correctly.
- Ensuring that electrical and electronic equipment is switched on only when it is needed, and that it is switched off when not required. 'Standby' modes should be avoided when the equipment will be out of use for a long period, since these consume energy. For example, leaving a computer on standby consumes about a third as much power as leaving it on full. A computer monitor left on overnight wastes enough energy to laser print 800 A4 pages, and a photocopier left on overnight wastes enough energy to make 5,300 A4 copies.

Energy-efficient appliances

The use of more energy-efficient electrical appliances, particularly domestically, but also in industry and commerce, can be encouraged by:

- incentive schemes, such as differential taxation or trade-in schemes to end the life of old, inefficient appliances
- endorsement schemes and information campaigns to ensure that purchasers are fully informed
- support for research and development
- public and private procurement initiatives, to help provide an initial market for environmentally friendly new products.

Use of appropriate, correctly sized, and energy-efficient equipment can make dramatic energy savings. For example, combi-convection ovens require only about 50% as much energy as other types of oven suitable for similar uses.

Energy-efficiency labels for domestic white goods were introduced under EC regulations and are now mandatory for domestic fridges and freezers, washing machines, tumble dryers and washer-dryers, with other types of appliance due to be added to the scheme. They are discussed further on page 192.

The design of environmentally friendly products is discussed further on pages 188–90.

Disposable batteries

All batteries are less energy-efficient than mains electricity, and their disposal causes environmental problems. (See page 113.) Use of all batteries, even the 'button' batteries used in watches and some calculators, should be avoided as much as possible.

Portable disposable batteries are particularly poor transformers of energy: they consume 50 times more energy in their production than they provide. Using rechargeable batteries (only when mains electricity is not available as an option) is more environmentally friendly, and saves money in the long run.

Energy efficient lighting

As noted above, lighting accounts for about 20% of the total electricity demand, so an improvement in the efficiency of lighting can make a very significant contribution to overall energy efficiency. This can be achieved by:

- designing new buildings, and planning workspaces, to minimise their requirement for artificial lighting
- ensuring that lights are only switched on when they are needed, for example using time switches, or movement sensors to switch on lights in rarely-used areas
- ensuring that light sources are kept clean
- ensuring that no more light is generated than is required in the area
- using energy-efficient lamps.

Physical controls such as presence detectors, dimmers, time controls and daylight sensors can save typically 30-35%, and on occasion up to 60%, of the energy spend in non-domestic buildings.

On 1 January 2000 the mandatory energy labelling system was extended to lighting. This shows the energy efficiency (rated A to L), light output (in lumens), power consumption (in watts) and the life of the bulb in hours of each lighting device.

Because of factors such as the design of the optics and the quality of materials, lamps that look very similar can vary in their efficiency by up to 40%. The Building Research Energy Conservation Support Unit (BRECSU) estimate an average 10% could be saved by replacing poor performing luminaires for incandescent and fluorescent lamps with the highest performing ones of the same general type.

The common GLS (general lighting service) tungsten filament incandescent bulbs are an extremely inefficient method of producing light. Only 10% of the electrical energy they consume is converted to light, and the rest wasted as heat.

Fluorescent tube lamps are coated with a thin layer of phosphorus powder which absorbs ultraviolet radiation when a small amount of mercury reacts to an electrical charge. They use 75-80% less energy than incandescent bulbs, and last from eight to ten times as long, so there is less manufacturing and raw materials requirement. They should be preferred to GLS bulbs in most situations, although they are not suitable for use in locations where the lamps are frequently turned on and off.

Compact fluorescent lamps (CFLs) can be used to replace GLS bulbs in existing lighting fitments. Although more bulky, and unable to produce perfectly spherical illumination, they work satisfactorily in most circumstances. Although they are more expensive to buy, they pay for themselves after about 2,000 hours of use. The Environment Change Unit has estimated that it is economical to replace any lamp in use for more than 250 hours a year.

Fluorescent tubes themselves vary considerably in their energy efficiency. The old type of fittings with starter-controls are less efficient than newer ones with electronic 'ballasts', and the thinner 26 mm diameter tubes (which fit most modern tube fittings) use only 16.5% as much energy as a normal tube.

Friends of the Earth Scotland suggest the following priorities for investing in lighting upgrades:

- Replacing GLS bulbs used for more than four hours a day with the most appropriate and efficient form of fluorescent lamp.
- Replacing 38 mm diameter argon lamps in fittings with switch starters with 26 mm triphosphor lamps.
- Replacing filament spotlights with low-voltage tungsten halogen spots or compact fluorescent lamps.
- Reviewing the wattage of tungsten halogen lamps, beginning with high-wattage lamps used, for example, for external security or floodlights, continuing with lower-voltage lamps, and replacing them with lower-rated versions where appropriate.

Energy efficiency monitoring in businesses

Monitoring of an organisation's energy efficiency should be an integral part of an environmental management policy and strategy. As with other aspects of the corporate environmental strategy, it should be made a board-level responsibility, and given a high profile.

The DETR launched an energy Best Practice programme, 'Making a Corporate Commitment' in 1991 (now in its second phase, MCC2). This calls on organisations to reassess their energy efficiency strategy, develop plans to improve energy efficiency, and keep these plans under continual review. The scheme now has more than 2,000 members.

Policies, strategies, regulations

EC and UK strategies and regulations both cover the entire span of environmental aspects of energy management, from the mix of fuels used for primary energy purposes, to the encouragement of energy efficiency in the home and workplace.

EC policies

Environmental issues have come to play an increasingly large part in EC energy policy, and the White Paper, **An Energy Policy for the European Union**, published in 1995, identified environmental protection as one of three key objectives, along with overall competitiveness and security of energy supply. The Commission's view is that:

> *'The main thrust of a sustainable development policy for energy should be to ensure that prices more fully reflect the environmental impact of the various forms of energy. A major step in this direction could be changes in the balance of taxation from labour to natural resources... it may be difficult for Member States to shift their fiscal systems in this direction if major industrial competitors are not prepared to follow suit.' (The Union's Energy Policy,* EC online document.*)*

Among other aspects of energy policy arising from this are the development of Trans-European energy networks, and research and development into the supply, conversion and utilisation of energy.

A 1996 **Green Paper** and subsequent **White Paper on** *Renewable Sources of Energy* specifically developed the EC's policy on more environmentally friendly power generation, and set the objective of doubling the contribution of renewable sources to 12% by 2010, a move which the EC projected would generate between 500,000 and 900,000 jobs, save fuel costs, reduce fuel imports and reduce carbon dioxide emissions by 402 million tonnes a year. This led to a five-year programme beginning in 1998 to support renewable energy sources, including the financial support programme ALTENER II, and research and development programmes.

A series of EC directives have tackled the issue of emissions from large and small power plants, most notably the **Directive on Limitation of Emissions of Certain Pollutants into the Air from Large Combustion Plants, 1988.**

Also relevant are regulations to enforce the energy labelling of domestic equipment (see page 192), and to set minimum energy standards for equipment. Regulations covering boilers came into effect in 1998, and for fridges and freezers came into effect in mid-1999.

The UK government strategy

Current government policy on energy and the environment is focused on achieving the emissions targets to which the UK is committed, using a combination of the methods outlined above. Recent significant policy documents include *The Review of Energy Sources for Power Generation*, 1998, and *New and Renewable Energy: Prospects for the 21st Century*, 1999.

Targets include:

- obliging electricity suppliers to increase the proportion of electricity provided by renewable sources to 10% by 2010, subject to the cost to consumers being acceptable
- doubling the capacity of combined heat and power by 2010.

The policy is also concerned to protect the UK coal mining industry at a time of policy transition:

> *'The Government believes that it is of primary importance to act now to prevent the scope for diversity and security of supply being pre-emptively destroyed, while reforms are yet to feed through.' (Review of Energy Sources for Power Generation.)*

With this in mind it is working to limit the degree of further switch from coal to natural gas as a fuel particularly for power stations, while at the same time encouraging CHP, renewable energy, and clean coal technology initiatives.

The regulatory framework for energy in the UK is largely provided by the **Energy Act 1976** and the **Electricity Act 1989.** The **Utilities Act 2000** includes provisions to:

- promote efficiency in the supply of gas and electricity
- oblige suppliers to generate an agreed proportion of electricity from renewable sources (within a trading system)

- set and promote energy efficiency targets for consumers.

The **Renewable Energy Bill 2000** specifies that by 2010 at least 15% of electricity consumed in the UK should be produced from renewable resources.

The Climate Change Levy

This carbon tax will be introduced in April 2001, and applies to most energy (electricity, gas, coal, and secondary fuel sources such as LPG) used by industrial and commercial enterprises and in the public sector. The proposals which have not yet been finalised exempt energy-saving technology such as CHP schemes, and the use of renewable energy sources. It should also be possible for companies operating IPPC processes to agree energy efficiency targets and, on meeting them, receive a discount of up to 80% on their levy charges.

In 2001 a **Carbon Trust** will be created in the UK, to bring together an integrated programme of incentives to provide research, advice, and to encourage businesses, and especially SMEs, to invest in energy-efficient technologies.

The Non-Fossil Fuel Obligation (NFFO) and the Fossil Fuel Levy

In recent years the NFFO Renewables Orders, complex regulations which require regional electricity companies to buy a proportion of electricity from specified non-fossil fuel sources, have had a significant impact on the development of renewable sources of energy, by providing a reliable market for it. The Fossil Fuel Levy is a tax placed on non-renewable energy and nuclear energy, to help subsidise renewable energy developments. The government's current target is that 10% of UK electricity should be supplied from renewable sources.

Energy efficiency

The government's energy efficiency campaign has been developed by the Energy Saving Trust in partnership with industry. Its funding is being increased, from £19 million in 1998/9 to £25 million by 2000/1. Home Energy Efficiency Schemes also have a major part to play in achieving the energy efficiency savings that are required, and they too are supported by a budget which has recently been increased: from £75.1 million in 1998/9, it will rise to £125.1 million in 2000/1.

11 Environmental aspects of transport

> *'This country needs better transport – less congested roads and modern, affordable and reliable public transport. Our transport system and services have suffered from decades of under-investment. The result is overcrowding, congestion, delays, pollution and a lack of choice of how to travel.'*
>
> DETR, *TRANSPORT 2010: THE 10 YEAR PLAN*

Transport and trends in the UK today

Overall traffic volume and forecasts

At the end of 1998 there were 27.5 million licensed vehicles in Great Britain, 11% more than in 1990. Of these 22.1 million were cars and taxis. Nearly 70% of households in England and Wales now have at least one car, while 4% have three or more.

The average total distance travelled per person per year in the UK has increased significantly in recent years. In 1975/6 the average person travelled 5,147 km by car and 410 km on foot; in 1996/8 they travelled 8,514 km by car and only 270 km on foot. People travel farther than before to take children to and from school (up 40% to an average 4.5 km), to get to work (up 32% in the past 10 years), and to go shopping (up 24% in the past ten years).

On average people make eleven journeys over 1.6 km long by car each week, and only one by other forms of transport.

People spend no longer travelling – about an hour a day – but they tend to travel faster. Many drivers exceed the speed limit. The survey Vehicle Speeds in Great Britain 1998 found that in free-flowing motorway traffic 55% of cars were driven at over 112 kph, and 19% at over 128 kph. On urban roads too, when traffic conditions permitted 69% of car drivers exceeded 48 kph limits at the test locations.

National road traffic is forecast under present policies to grow by between 36% and 57% over the next 20 years. By 2025 road traffic will on current forecasts be nearly doubled from the 1990 level. Road freight is expected to rise by nearly two-thirds by 2025. Air traffic is set to rise at even more rapid levels into the next century: EC predictions are of a 182% rise from 1990 to 2010.

Car ownership and company cars

Almost nine out of ten workers have personal use of a car, and a quarter of these drive company cars. Most are individuals living in the one in four households with two or more cars: they are four times more likely than others to have a company car. About 10% of all cars are company cars (accounting for a disproportionate 20% of all car travel by distance), and more than half of new cars are first registered by companies.

Car ownership levels in the UK, although high, remain below the EC average.

Recent trends have shown a rise in the proportion of mini (up 20% from 1999 to 2000) and supermini cars sold, and a decrease in the sale of luxury and executive models, perhaps in response to the rise in fuel prices.

Cycling

The Bicycle Association estimates there are 21 million bicycles in Britain, with 50% of houses having more than one bike. However, cycling as a proportion of all road traffic fell from 37% in 1949 to 1% in 1998, although the trend may now have bottomed out.

More than 90% of children have bikes, yet fewer than 2% are allowed to cycle to school. By 2005 the National Cycle Network will have about 24,000 km of officially recognised, signposted, safe cycle routes all across the UK. It is hoped that this will increase the number of people using bikes and reduce congestion in certain areas.

Motorcycles

The number of licensed motorcycles in Great Britain in 1998 was 684,000; this figure is down from a peak of 1,577,000 in 1961. Only 1% of the distance travelled is by motorcycle.

Walking

Journeys by foot are short: an average length of 0.95 km, a figure which has been constant since 1975/6. On average people make just over 300 trips a year, totalling less than 322 km per year. (This includes the on-foot portion of journeys taken mostly by car or public transport.)

Men who are the main drivers of company cars walk less than a third of the average distance walked by men in households without cars.

Air travel

The number of passengers passing through UK airports has trebled in the past twenty years. In 1980 the British travelled around 1,089 billion passenger km, and in 1998 this had increased to around 2,621 billion passenger km. The volume of cargo handled at UK airports, though small in comparison with that carried by other modes of transport, has more than doubled over the last ten years, to 20.4 million tonnes in 1998.

Bus and coach journeys

A declining number of passenger journeys are made on local bus services: 4,191 million of them in 1997/8. Where buses have been deregulated (that is, not in London) the number of passenger journeys has fallen by 29% since 1986; it has risen 5% in London. The level of bus usage is now 24% lower than in 1982, with most of the fall coming outside London.

Freight transport

The amount of freight moved by heavy goods vehicles (HGVs) in the UK has increased 6% over the 1982 figure, to 152 billion tonne km in 1998. Articulated vehicles over 33 tonnes gvw were responsible for 66% of this road freight. A larger proportion of freight (over 80%) was moved by road in the UK than in the EC on average.

Lorries break the speed limit even more than cars do. *Vehicle Speeds in Great Britain* 1998 found that at sample dual carriageway sites 91% of articulated HGVs exceeded their 80 kph limit, and at its sample single carriageway sites 72% exceeded their 64 kph limit.

Purposes of journeys

In autumn 1998, 71% of workers in Great Britain travelled to work by car. Of these 13% used public transport, 11% walked and 3% cycled.

On average people travel over 4,180 km per year for leisure purposes.

The cost of motorised transport

The average British household spends about 16% of its total expenditure on transport, but these internalised costs are only part of the overall social and environmental costs of transport.

Transport plays a vital part in a thriving society. A good transport system can help:

- people (including the disabled) in towns, cities and rural areas to meet their practical, social and leisure needs
- promote new industrial and commercial investment, and sustain existing enterprises
- enhance the vitality of town and city centres.

However, there are many externalised costs of motorised modes of transport.

Consumption of non-renewable energy resources

In 1996 the transport sector took up more than 25% of the world's primary energy use, a proportion that is growing faster than any other sector. It accounted for 54% of the world's oil consumption.

Land requirements

The road system takes up 1.3% of the total EC land area, and the overall transport infrastructure occupies about 20% of the land in UK urban areas. Britain's three main airports, Heathrow, Gatwick and Stansted, alone account for 3,000 ha of land. The transport infrastructure has a generally poor effect on the aesthetics of the landscape, and transport requirements can lead to the demolition of buildings, the destruction of ecosystems, and the severance of existing communities.

Accidents

Road traffic accidents kill people, they use up health service resources, they cost time off work, and they cause physical damage.

Noise and vibration

This has an effect both on human (and animal) health and quality of life, and on buildings.

Waste

Although improvements have been made in the recyclability of vehicles, at the end of their lives they still generate sizeable amounts of waste. Waste oil for motor vehicles is also a significant environmental hazard.

Pollution

Perhaps the major environmental effect of motorised transport, however, is its contribution to pollution – particularly of the air, but also of land and water. The table below shows some of the major pollutants generated by motor transport, and percentages showing the pollution that the transport sector contributed in 1997. (The impact of each pollutant is described in more depth in the Glossary, page 203.)

carbon monoxide	74%
1,3 butadiene	68%
benzene	64%
lead	61%
nitrogen oxides	48%
particulates	23%

Although car engines are becoming more fuel-efficient, the growth in the quantity of auxiliary equipment (particularly air conditioning) tends to reduce the emission gains. Higher safety standards also lead to the production of heavier, more fuel-greedy cars, and congestion on the ever more crowded roads also increases the level of emissions in relation to length of journey.

Transport pollution is a particular problem in congested urban areas, where it can become a significant health hazard. (See Chapter 6.)

Reasons for the trends

Increasing affluence and the resulting private car ownership is clearly a major factor in the transport trends noted above. However, a number of other factors have been identified. Among the major ones are the following.

Changes in business practices

- Shifts in retail distribution patterns, from manufacturer-controlled to retailer-controlled distribution, with the increasing use of centralised distribution centres by major retailers.
- Growth in market areas, particularly for food and drink products, and a significant switch from local to nationwide marketing and distribution.
- The increased contracting-out of non-core activities, tending to add extra links and extra transport requirements to the supply chain.
- Tightening health and safety restrictions on the height of palletised loads, leading to a greater number of loads to be delivered.
- Just-in-Time manufacturing patterns, which if not designed with care can lead to an increase in the number of supplier deliveries.
- New types of shift working, particularly for office workers: for example, 12-hour and 24-hour telephone call centres.

Changes in land-use patterns

- The growth in out-of-town retailing in the 1980s and early 1990s. (Policies encouraging this have now been changed.)
- The move towards greenfield business parks.

Social changes

- The increasing number of small households.
- The steady reduction in the proportion of children making unaccompanied journeys to school.

Transport infrastructure changes

- Bus deregulation (outside London) leading in many cases to fewer and more expensive services, exacerbating the move from public to private transport.
- Rail deregulation, leading to fragmentation of the network and fare rises, and again to a switch to other forms of transport.
- Disproportionate investment in the road infrastructure (compared with rail). Road spending claimed the largest proportion of transport infrastructure investment from the early 1980s to the mid-1990s.
- Reductions in subsidy for public transport, making journeys by private transport more economical than bus, coach or train journeys for car owners.

Reversing the trend

It is increasingly widely accepted that the current trends in transport growth are unsustainable, and that sustainable development policies involve a major effort to reverse them. However, it is not yet clear that commercial enterprises or the general public are prepared to accept constraints that would affect their current patterns of behaviour, or that politicians are prepared to force them to do so.

Public attitudes

Undoubtedly there is increasing awareness of the environmental costs of motorised transport, but public attitude surveys suggest that although many people are prepared to accept 'carrot' policies to encourage them to change, they are highly resistant to 'stick' policies that could price them out of private car ownership and usage, and resist enforced changes in their lifestyles.

British Social Attitudes and other surveys throughout the 1990s revealed high levels of public concern about traffic congestion, pollution, and the impact on the countryside of major new road schemes. In a 1999 survey 72% rated exhaust fumes as a serious problem, 67% rated traffic congestion in towns, and 51% were troubled by traffic noise. A sizeable 93% of those surveyed thought that improving public transport was either very or fairly important (interestingly, a slight fall from 95% of respondents in 1996). Although 33% of respondents agreed that driving one's car was too convenient to give up for the sake of the environment, 28% disagreed and by implication were prepared to drive less because of environmental concerns.

Particular concern is sometimes expressed about the use of 'stick' measures in rural areas, where it is argued that many residents are forced to rely on private cars. However, the majority of traffic in rural areas is not generated by residents, but by the through traffic of visitors. It has been estimated that only around 5% of rural residents would genuinely find it difficult to adapt to the level of measures that have been suggested.

Measures that can be taken

World-wide, most policies aimed at generating a more sustainable pattern of transport usage employ some combination of the following elements.

Measures to stabilise or reduce the total volume of traffic, by:

- making some journeys unnecessary by changing land-use and other factors that determine travel patterns
- increasing the density of occupation of vehicles (by car-sharing, demographic change, or a switch from private to public transport)
- discouraging people from making journeys by increasing the cost
- discouraging people from making private car journeys by restricting parking at destinations.

Measures to encourage people to switch to less environmentally harmful forms of transport, for example:

- from road to rail
- from large cars to smaller cars

- from highly polluting cars to more environmentally friendly cars
- from cars to motorcycles (in certain circumstances: see pages 152–3)
- from motorised vehicles to bicycles
- from motorised vehicles to foot.

Measures to encourage technological improvements that will make vehicles less environmentally damaging.

Measures to discourage travel in areas and at times when congestion causes particularly serious environmental problems.

Technological improvements

A large number of technological improvements, some of them incremental and some more revolutionary, have improved fuel consumption rates and reduced the amount of pollution emitted by vehicles. Over the last decade, for example, emissions by heavy lorries have been reduced by between 60–80%. By 2010 carbon monoxide emission levels should be less than 50% of the 1990 levels and other pollutants will be reduced broadly in proportion. Recent EC directives have reduced the allowable carbon dioxide emissions from new cars, and the Auto-Oil Programme specifies stricter emission limits for cars and light goods vehicles.

Average fuel consumption rates for new cars improved from about 11 kg/litre in 1978 to 13.5 kg/litre in 1987, but have stayed in the 12.5–13.5 kg/litre range since 1987.

It is generally agreed that further improvements are unlikely alone to account for all the reduction in pollution that is necessary. Some commentators argue, however, that because current patterns of transport use are so well entrenched in our society, there is relatively little scope to achieve the necessary changes through altering them. In that case, it can be argued that a major concentration on technological improvement offers the best hope of a more sustainable transport pattern in future.

Lead-free petrol

Unleaded petrol was introduced in the UK in 1988, and by 1998 accounted for 77.2% of UK deliveries (up from 70.6% in 1997). Leaded petrol was banned from general sale in the UK from 1 January 2000, although Lead Replacement Petrol (LRP) is available for vehicles that cannot run on unleaded petrol, as are anti-wear additives which fulfil the same function.

Catalytic converters

Over 95% of new petrol-fuelled cars now have catalytic converters. However, catalysts do not work well until they have warmed up, so they are not effective for short journeys, although advances in technology should reduce this disadvantage. They also reduce fuel efficiency, and significant amounts of rare metals (which cause environmental problems) are used in their manufacture.

Electric vehicles

The market for electric vehicles is still very small: in 1996 there were about 7,500 electric cars in use world-wide. A major initiative in California to increase usage was abandoned in 1995 after it encountered numerous difficulties. Electric cars have a short range, and although many car journeys are short, the California experience brought home the message that drivers put a great deal of value on being able to meet their maximum needs as well as their average needs. The vehicles are dependent on a recharging infrastructure which it is expensive to put in place (and which is not yet available in most places), and although their performance has been much improved, it still tends to fall short of the performance of conventional cars.

Gas powered vehicles

Much emphasis has been placed by the government recently on encouraging gas-powered vehicles, but research by the Environmental Management Unit of the Environment Agency suggests that their emissions are little different from those from city diesel and city petrol vehicles using the latest vehicle engine technology. However, they are quieter, and by the end of 2001 there should be around 500 outlets for LPG motor fuel.

Planning and infrastructure policies

Road building

There is a superficial attraction in building new roads to relieve areas where congestion is particularly acute, but the evidence shows that new roads contribute to an increase in traffic, rather than to a reduction in congestion. Some surveys have suggested that road improvements in urban areas can lead to up to 40% more 'induced traffic'. In some cases traffic also increased on routes that were intended to be relieved by the new road, and the trend was greater in the long term than in the short term. It is now generally accepted that where new roads are built, they should be of relatively limited capacity and should be accompanied by traffic reduction measures on the roads that they are intended to relieve.

Land-use planning

The available evidence suggests that a trend to living in compact settlements leads to a reduction in the overall amount of travelling. Travel demand tends to rise sharply when the population density falls below 15 persons per ha, and to fall when it rises above 50 persons per ha.

People tend to make as many journeys in larger settlements, but they make fewer of them by car. However in the largest cities they tend also to make longer journeys. It also appears that journeys from individuals in smaller settlements are less emissions-efficient, but it is difficult to interpret this evidence since a number of other factors (for example, differences in household income in densely-populated and less densely populated areas) complicate the picture.

Overall, however, it seems clear that the planning policies which lead to the most environmentally-friendly traffic patterns involve:

- focusing development in urban areas
- concentrating on maintaining and revitalising existing neighbourhood, town and city centres, and restricting the development of out-of-town shopping centres and business parks
- limiting the development of small settlements, particularly villages within the commuter belts of cities
- requiring environmental assessments of new proposals which take full account of their transport implications, and ensuring that their designs are modified to be as environmentally friendly as possible.

More information on land-use issues is in Chapter 12.

Traffic management

Environmentally friendly traffic management includes:

- Channelling traffic along the routes best able to cope with it. Through traffic needs to be discouraged from entering congested areas such as city centres.
- Physically restricting access (by all vehicles, or for example by larger goods vehicles) to sensitive areas which are particularly vulnerable to damage or pollution, including noise pollution.
- Introducing permit systems where appropriate, to ensure that only residents and essential vehicles enter certain areas. These could be city centres, but they could also, for example, be tourist centres and private housing developments.
- Introducing congestion charging to reduce the amount of traffic at peak hours.
- Improving road signage to ensure that drivers use the best route. Research has shown that many drivers do not select the optimum route for their journey, adding significantly to their journey time and distance.

Permit systems are already in use in a number of cities world-wide, including Rome, Milan, Bologna, Athens and Barcelona. The technology is available to make them self-enforcing, for example by the use of smartcard-controlled barriers or transponders. Restricted areas can also be policed by the use of cameras to check permit usage, and by checking the permits on parked cars. Congestion and similar schemes can have high start-up costs, but research projects (based on traffic patterns in London, Cambridge and Bristol) suggest they could be highly effective.

Most surveys of towns where traffic management policies have reduced the amount of traffic suggest that these policies are advantageous to businesses in the controlled areas.

In 1999 the UK government consulted on traffic management measures including road user charging and charging on motorways and trunk roads in *Breaking the Logjam*, and this now seems likely to be brought into legislation as the **Transport Act 2000.**

Parking policies

Environmentally conscious parking policies include:

- reduced or high-priced parking provision in overcrowded areas (for example, city centres and popular tourist destinations)
- restriction of commuter parking, through pricing policies that discriminate against long-term and early-arriving parkers, a reduction n the amount of contract parking in public car parks, and a reduction in the amount of parking allowed in new commercial developments
- park and ride schemes to encourage commuters and shoppers to take public transport from the edges of towns and cities.

Local authorities have powers to control on-street and municipal off-street parking, and some limited powers over private parking provisions (including, but not limited to, planning powers for new developments). Powers for them to levy charges on workplace parking were proposed in ***Breaking the Logjam***, the government's consultation paper (1999) and should become law in the **Transport Act 2000**. Withdrawal of parking provision can however be counter-productive if it leads to drivers circling town and city centres in search of scarce spaces.

The evidence from park and ride schemes is ambiguous. Surveys suggest that some people travel farther as a result, and others travel more often, while a sizeable proportion (between 5% and 40% of users) switch to cars for their journey to the park and ride site when they would otherwise have made the entire journey by public transport.

Walking and cycling

Walking and cycling not only reduce pollution of the environment, they also contribute to good health. Friends of the Earth estimate that a 10% increase in the number of people cycling regularly would lead to a 4% reduction in the current amount of heart disease. Experiments by the Transport Research Laboratory have shown that the benefits of regular cycling are apparent in as little as six weeks.

Although cycle use remains at a low level, cycling campaigners argue that there is a great deal of suppressed demand. In the town of Houten in the Netherlands, which was designed to be friendly to cyclists, around 80% of all local journeys are made by cycle, showing what can be achieved.

Especially in the 9–14 age group, many more children would cycle to school if safe routes were available. Sustrans, the engineering charity which campaigns on behalf of cyclists, is currently working on a demo project to improve cycle routes to schools, and over 50 UK local authorities now have, or are planning, safe routes to school programmes.

A still more significant difference should be made by the **National Cycle Network**, again co-ordinated by Sustrans, which opened in June 2000. It provides 8,000 km of continuous traffic free routes to link schools, houses, shops and workplaces with each other and with the countryside, including at least one high-quality route through the centre of most major towns and cities. The national network has links with a large number of local networks, and further extensions to it are anticipated.

The network, made up of 42% minor roads, 7% town roads, 32% railway, canal, river and special paths, 7% promenades and footpaths, and 12% forest roads and tracks, is intended to be shared by cyclists (an estimated 45% of users), walkers (55%) and wheelchair users, and is planned to carry over 100 million journeys each year: 60% of them for work, school and shopping, and 40% for leisure purposes. Many of the cycle trips will be for journeys that had previously been made by other forms of transport.

As well as helping the environment, the National Cycle Network should contribute to sustainable employment, with an estimated 600 construction jobs being made available for each of ten years, plus 500 person/years of work for associated professionals. It is estimated that 5,000 new permanent leisure, tourism and retail jobs will be generated, and there will be 100 permanent jobs for rangers and maintenance workers.

Motorcycles

Although not as environmentally friendly as non-motorised forms of transport, the motorcycle can be more environmentally friendly than a car. Small-engined motorbikes can be built with only about one seventh of the resources and energy needed to build a car and are often more corrosion-resistant and have a longer useful life. However, as the British Motorcyclists Federation admits, 'modern motorcycles tend to be designed for performance rather than economy', and 1,000 cc superbikes normally have a fuel consumption rate of around 10.6 kg/litre, which is poorer than many small cars. Motorcycles do not at present have to conform to EC emissions regulations, and are not required to have catalytic converters fitted as standard equipment, although this may be changed by future legislation. Noise pollution is also a problem with many motorbikes.

Where smaller bikes are concerned, there is generally an environmental advantage if a single driver rides a bike rather than driving in a car, but when more than three people travel in a car it would add to the overall pollution if they were all to ride bikes instead.

'Cash for clunkers'

The point at which vehicles are scrapped is determined in large part by the market for second-hand cars, and the costs of vehicle maintenance. These in turn are influenced by the prices of new cars, and the overall costs of running a car. One policy option, which has been the subject of serious discussion in the US, is to encourage owners of older, highly polluting and inefficient vehicles, to scrap them early by paying a bonus: the so-called 'cash for clunkers'.

The developing policy and regulatory framework

EC transport policy

EC transport policy, as with its environmental policy, has elements that are the subject of community policy and law as well as elements that are devolved to the governments of Member States under the principle of subsidiarity. Article 74 of the Treaty of Rome provides for a common transport policy, and progress has taken place in developing one particularly since the mid-1980s.

High-level infrastructure requirements are the province of the EC, and centre on the trans-European network (TEN), which includes a transport network and also embraces energy, telecommunications and other aspects of the EC infrastructure. From a transport angle, the TEN includes roads, rail, inland waterways, airports, and various information management and control aspects. Developing the network will involve creating new links as well as adapting existing provision, but environmental aspects are an integral part of the planning. The European Commission comments,

> *'Since the present Commission took office in January 1995, it has put special emphasis on the need to create a better balance between road and other means of transport so as to reduce pollution and congestion and increase safety.'* (European Commission, *The Union's Policies – Transport,* online document.)

The incompatibilities in the present international transport network militate against efficiency, and ironing them out should *'embody the concept of sustainable mobility'*. The original aim was to realise the basic TEN design by 2010, but progress has been relatively slow to date (2000) because of a lack of public funding. Altogether the proposals include 70,000 km of rail track, including 22,000 km of new and upgraded track designed for high-speed trains, and 15,000 km of new roads to complete a 58,000 km road network.

Much other legislative action has focused on achieving a single market in transport and removing barriers to free competition.

The EC action programme for the period 2000–2004 focuses on **Sustainable Mobility**, and among its objectives are improving the interoperability of transport systems and deploying intelligent transport systems and finding less environmentally damaging energy alternatives. Other proposals include developing a **Citizen's Network**, a door-to-door integrated transport system which focuses on sustainability and a need to move away from dependence on private cars, and a strategy published in 1996 for **Revitalising the Community's Railways.**

Pollution control measures

Measures to improve the fuel-efficiency of vehicles, to improve the environmental performance of fuels themselves, and to reduce the volume of emissions, are regularly introduced by the EC. Those mentioned below are among the measures recently agreed or now in discussions.

The EC's **Auto-Oil Programme** provides for improvements in vehicle technology and fuel quality through higher standards. The aim is for both to be steadily improved to 2006 and beyond, and for a reduction to be achieved in carbon dioxide emissions from new cars of one third on current levels by 2010. EC level agreements with car manufacturers aim to improve the average fuel efficiency of new cars by at least 25% by 2008-9.

New EC proposals for revised vehicle and fuel standards, to take effect from 2000, should achieve overall emission reductions of around 50% on 1995 levels by 2005. Tighter emissions standards for new cars and light vans will apply from 2001, which will be between 2% and 50% more stringent than those currently in force. Emissions standards for new lorries are also proposed.

UK government policy

The UK government is constrained to act within the framework of the EC policy, but it continues to have a dominant influence over, for example, the level of road building, taxation, and policies such as road charging. Local authorities also have extensive powers, for example through planning policy, and via the capability to introduce lorry bans and restrictions on access. Under Section 63 of the **Transport Act 1963** they can take measures to promote the availability and use of public transport.

An integrated transport policy

In order to develop an integrated transport policy it is necessary to consider a wide range of issues, including the cumulative impacts of measures taken, the amount of new traffic that could be generated by transport measures and other developments, alternative modes of transport, and environmental impacts. The technique of strategic environmental assessment (SEA) has been developed to help achieve this.

However, now that substantial parts of the transport sector are privatised – including the rail network and most of the bus network – the government's powers of strategic decision-making are limited.

A White Paper, *A New Deal for Transport: Better for Everyone,* was published in July 1998, setting out the government's integrated transport policy, by which is meant:

- integration within and between different types of transport
- integration of transport with the environment
- integration with land-use planning
- integration with other government policies, for education, health and wealth creation
- promoting environmental objectives
- promoting economic development across all parts of the country
- achieving greater efficiency in the use of scarce resources, including road and rail capacity

- enhancing the vitality of town and city centres
- meeting the needs of rural areas
- reducing social exclusion and taking account of the basic accessibility needs of all sectors of society, including disabled people
- ensuring a high standard of safety
- and increasing awareness of transport and environmental issues.

The overall aims of the policy are to:

- reduce road traffic growth
- reduce emissions so as to minimise climate change
- minimise transport's land demand, protect habitats and maintain biodiversity
- limit the visual intrusion of transport
- reduce the use of non-renewable materials and energy sources
- ensure that environmental impacts are taken fully into account in investment decisions and in transport pricing
- enhance public awareness of transport and environmental issues.

A Commission for Integrated Transport is planned to provide independent advice to the government, and a Strategic Rail Authority to help to limit and reverse some of the adverse effects of rail privatisation, and improve the integration of the system, is specified in the **Transport Bill 2000** (before Parliament at the time of writing). The new Greater London Authority has responsibility for an integrated transport strategy for London, which is implemented through Transport for London.

In 2000 a long-term strategy, *Transport 2010*, was published to build on this basis. It stresses the roles of partnership with the private sector and local government, and sets out the framework for up to £180 billion of investment into the UK's transport system. Among the targets are:

- an 80% growth in rail freight in a decade
- completion of the Channel Tunnel Rail Link
- speeding up the introduction of cleaner fuels and cleaner vehicles
- up to 25 new light rail or tram systems in major cities
- up to 100 new park and ride services
- significant improvements in rural bus services.

Bus policies were also the core of a 1999 policy document, **From Workhorse to Thoroughbred: A Better Role for Bus Travel**, which outlined plans including improved local authority influence over bus services, measures to promote stability in bus provision, and provisions to encourage the incorporation of bus services into integrated transport networks. (Again, these are broadly implemented in the Transport Bill 2000.)

Legislation is planned to allow local authorities to charge road users, and to enable toll schemes to be introduced on trunk roads and motorways. Further legislation will enable local authorities to tax workplace parking spaces.

Current traffic forecasts are based on the assumption that the 1996 road network will remain broadly unchanged, apart from 'do minimum' measures such as junction improvements and parking restrictions.

Other recent policy documents include the ***National Cycling Strategy*** in 1996, with a target of doubling the number of cycle trips from 1996 levels by 2002 and doubling them again by 2012, a ***Transport Strategy for London,*** also published in 1996, ***British Shipping: Charting a New Course*** (1998), which sets out a strategy for reviving Britain's shipping industry while having regard for environmental issues, and ***Tomorrow's Roads: Safer for Everyone*** (2000), which sets challenging targets to reduce road accidents by 2010. The Scottish Executive also produced a paper on road user charging and workplace parking, **Tackling Congestion**, in 1999.

Much recent planning guidance has concentrated on improving the environmental impact of developments. Particularly notable are *Planning Policy Guidance Note (PPG) 13,* which encourages local authorities to try to ensure new development is either in existing centres, or in other places which are served by public transport, and to make associated measures to encourage a change in transport choices, and *PPG 6,* which is concerned particularly with parking policies to support town centres and retail developments. The Draft National Planning Policy Guideline, ***Transport and Planning for Scotland***, focuses particularly on taking a co-ordinated view of transport and land-use planning, adapting land uses over time to reduce travel needs, and relating development to transport arteries.

Significant legislation

The **Transport Act 1980** included measures to make it simpler to run car-sharing schemes, without needing PSV licences or infringing domestic car insurance policies. The **Traffic Calming Act 1992** increased the range of traffic-calming measures, which could be used by transport authorities.

The **Road Traffic Reduction Act 1997** is concerned with traffic on roads controlled by local traffic authorities (not trunk roads and motorways). Local traffic authorities have to assess levels of existing traffic and likely growth, and set targets of reducing either the total amount of traffic, or the anticipated rate of growth. Various targets can be set, for example:

- single targets covering all traffic at all times across the area
- specific targets for types of vehicles, for example, cars or HGVs
- targets for peak times
- targets for specific sub-areas
- targets relating to, for example, commuter traffic or journeys to school
- seasonal targets.

The Act also gave local traffic authorities additional controls over the type, location and price of parking facilities.

The **Road Traffic Reduction (National Targets) Act 1998** builds on this, specifying what environmental considerations must be taken into account in setting targets.

A sizeable proportion of recently announced government spending on transport (a ten-year programme totalling £180 billion was announced in July 2000) applies to public transport, but new road-widening schemes accounted for £21 million of the total.

The **Transport Bill 2000** has been mentioned above. It includes provisions on the liberalisation of air transport (following EC requirements), bus services, a workplace parking levy, and sets up the Strategic Rail Authority.

The Greener Vehicles Campaign

In 1997 regulations were introduced to allow local authorities in seven pilot areas to test vehicle emissions at the roadside and fine the drivers of particularly badly polluting vehicles. The Greener Vehicles Campaign was set up in conjunction with these, to offer free emission testing and advice on vehicle maintenance to drivers. Its first results showed that almost one in five of all vehicles tested were exceeding the legal emission limits, with diesel cars, vans and taxis proving to be especially poor performers.

What enterprises can do

Transport considerations will of course be an important part of any organisation's environmental assessment, policy and audit system. It will rarely be realistic for an organisation and its employees to cease entirely to use private transport, but much can be done nevertheless to reduce the overall environmental impact of the organisation's, and its employees', transport usage.

The types of measures that can be taken fall into the broad classes that were outlined above. They will include proposals to reduce the number of journeys made as far as is practicable, by ensuring that:

- the organisational infrastructure minimises its transport demands
- unnecessary journeys are avoided, and necessary journeys are made as efficiently as possible
- local suppliers are preferred to more distant suppliers wherever it is practicable.

The findings of research into freight transport growth suggest that enterprises' production and distribution systems are a more significant factor in their transport usage than either the quantity of their supply and delivery requirement, or their choice of transport mode.

Delivery systems can often be rationalised to reduce the number of vehicle-km per tonne of supplies. 'Flexing' of depot boundaries to improve transport efficiency, carrying third-party goods, and scheduling an increased number of drops per trip, can make a noticeable difference. Another possibility is integrated logistics assessment, a process which involves buyers and suppliers combining to see how their transport assets can most efficiently be used. Sainsbury's is among the retailers looking seriously at backloading vehicles belonging to other enterprises so as to reduce empty running.

Just-in-Time and other stock control systems should be planned carefully to ensure they do not lead to an increased delivery demand. More space-efficient handling equipment in warehouses can also make a contribution.

The use of larger vehicles (where the transport system can handle them without strain) or of compartmentalised vehicles carrying composite loads, can reduce the total number of vehicle-km required. Computer-assisted vehicle routing can enable drivers to increase the efficiency of their route selection.

Producer responsibility for unwanted packaging or life-expired products is an increasing legal requirement (see Chapter 9) and this can lead to heavy transport demand which should be minimised by careful planning.

Office staff may be able to reduce their transport use by making increased use of teleconferencing and other remote communications methods. On occasion home working may be a viable possibility, reducing the need for commuting, and dealing with subcontractors and freelances too can be planned so that face to face meetings are minimised and remote communication used as much as possible. Customers too should be considered. Telephone sales, internet sales, and delivery services can do much to limit the need for customer travel, and care should also be taken to ensure that journeys do not have to be made unnecessarily to make payments (for example of rents, regular bills or hire purchase instalments).

Another set of policies is concerned with ensuring that journeys are made by the least damaging form of appropriate transport. Measures here could include:

- auditing the current vehicle fleet and planning a programme to replace environmentally damaging vehicles by more environmentally friendly models
- reviewing the usage of public transport to see where it can viably replace private car usage
- reviewing car parking requirements and employee transport subsidies (for example, car loans) to ensure that they do not encourage environmentally damaging transport use and do encourage environmentally friendly transport
- specific measures to encourage cycle usage.

Possible concrete measures include the sponsoring of car sharing or car pooling schemes, season ticket loans for public transport, and negotiations with local bus and coach operators to ensure that services are well adapted to employee requirements, or to arrange for subsidised fare deals.

Parking policies should be reviewed to ensure that they do not encourage unnecessary car usage. Employees who pay for parking spaces on a period basis may choose to drive to work on fine days, for instance, where a more flexible charging system might encourage them to drive only when bad weather or work requirements make it desirable, and walk or cycle on other occasions. 'Essential car user' policies should be reassessed, to ensure that staff are not obliged to have cars available when the requirement for them is sufficiently occasional that it could adequately be solved by the use of pool cars, taxis or public transport.

Although train travel may be superficially more expensive than car travel, it frees employee time during the journey, while time spent driving tends to be 'dead time' for other purposes. A half-dozen phonecalls made or a paper written during a train journey can more than pay for the additional upfront cost.

Cycling can be encouraged by organisations offering:

- loans for cycle purchase
- a mileage allowance for cyclists
- free or subsidised cycle helmets as incentives
- secure cycle parking
- lockers for cyclists to hold a change of clothes and removable equipment such as lights and panniers
- shower and changing facilities for cyclists
- battery or light rechargers on the organisation's premises
- an office bike, purchased and maintained by the organisation, to be used for short trips off the premises (or within larger sites).

Environmentally conscious organisations may also choose to support cycle- rather than motorcycle-based courier services.

Specific targets are an essential feature of an effective policy. For example, DHL International (UK) Ltd has as part of its environmental policy a target to improve the fuel efficiency of its fleet by 15% over three years. It plans to achieve this through education, purchasing more fuel efficient vehicles, improved reporting and monitoring procedures, and driver training. It has produced a Fuel Efficient Driving Leaflet for staff, explaining how they can drive so as to minimise the environmental impact.

Nottinghamshire City Council's 'Green Commuter Plan' aims to cut employees' car travel by 30% over three years. Among the measures they are employing are flexible car parking permits, sponsorship of a car sharing scheme, discounted travel cards, and loans for staff buying bicycles. Boots also have a Green Commuter Plan, aimed at reducing the amount of car commuting to their Beeston site. Introduced (as many schemes are) to tackle congestion problems on the site, it also has a green payback.

Organisations have a responsibility to encourage their staff to drive in a manner which minimises fuel consumption and thus the environmental cost. This can be achieved through education, but must also be supported by fleet-handling and scheduling policies which ensure that there is no undue pressure on drivers to exceed reasonable speeds or drive aggressively. Signs on goods vehicles inviting public feedback on driver performance can also play a useful part.

Finally, both organisations and individuals might wish to consider supporting the Environmental Transport Association, a breakdown organisation which is specifically aimed at 'green' transport users, and which eschews the car-lobbyist policies of many other motoring and breakdown services. Aimed at transport users in general, not just car owners, its services include a conventional car breakdown and recovery service, but also include, for instance, a cycle rescue service, through which cyclists who break down can call out an ETA recovery vehicle to take them to the nearest cycle shop or railway station.

Driving techniques to minimise fuel consumption

The right driving style can significantly reduce fuel consumption, thereby saving natural resources and minimising pollution from exhaust fumes. All drivers should:

- consider their choice of vehicle carefully, and avoid buying unnecessary optional equipment such as power steering: it adds weight and consumes power
- make sure their vehicle's engine is properly tuned to maximise performance
- remove roof racks when they are not being used
- check tyre pressures regularly: underpressurised tyres reduce fuel efficiency
- not switch on the engine before they are ready to move off, and switch it off promptly when they stop
- try to park so as to drive off forwards, and avoid using electrical equipment (fan, radio, lights) when starting their car
- avoid carrying unnecessary material in their car
- minimise heavy acceleration and braking, aiming at a smooth driving style
- use the highest gear appropriate to their speed and driving conditions
- maintain a moderate speed, and always drive within the speed limit.

12 Land-use and planning

> *'A large increase in households is projected to form in England over the next twenty years. This means that, even with ...reuse, creating patterns of development that are more sustainable is a major challenge.'*
>
> *A BETTER QUALITY OF LIFE*, 1999
>
> *'A new vision for urban regeneration founded on the principles of design excellence, social well-being and environmental responsibility within a viable economic and legislative framework.'*
>
> *TOWARDS AN URBAN RENAISSANCE*, 1999

This chapter considers land-use aspects of sustainable development. It considers the current pattern of land-use, the degree to which it reflects a sustainable pattern of life, and the problems which it reveals. It reviews pressures for development and other changes, the EC and UK policies which determine the shape of allowable developments, and the regulatory system that controls changes. It also looks briefly at different patterns of land-use and their positive and negative impacts on the environment, and it outlines the system of Environmental Impact Assessments.

Although this chapter is by no means exclusively concerned with the rural environment, it looks briefly at biodiversity and at policies and at actions to conserve and enhance the natural environment. It does not deal in depth with the problem of derelict and contaminated land, which is covered in Chapter 8.

Land use and population

The UK's land was taken up in 1996 by:

	UK as a whole	England
Agricultural grassland and rough grazing	51%	37%
Agricultural crops and bare fallow	20%	31%
Urban and other unspecified land	15%	19%
Forest and woodland	10%	8%
Other uses	3%	5%

SOURCE: *DIGEST OF ENVIRONMENTAL STATISTICS 1998*

There is no accurate information on the amount of built-up land included in the figure for 'urban and other unspecified land', although recent research has suggested that it may comprise around 10–11% of the UK total.

The amount of land used for arable farming has fallen significantly in recent years, from around 5,013,000 ha in 1990 to 4,721,000 ha in 1996. In 1999, 572,000 ha consisted of set-aside land under the Common Agricultural Policy (CAP).

Inland water accounts for about 1.3% of the total area of the UK. (Source for figures above and below: *Digest of Environmental Statistics 1998*.)

The proportion of forest and woodland in the UK has doubled over the last 70 years. During the 1980s an average 24,600 ha of forests were established in the UK each year.

Surface mineral workings or deposits from mineral workings accounted for 60,000 ha of land sites in England in 1994.

The population of the UK was estimated to be 59.5 million in mid-1999, and is projected to rise to 61 million in 2012 and stabilise at about 62 million, around the year 2030. The number of households is projected (by the DETR) to increase at a faster rate than the population, reflecting the trend to smaller household sizes. In England it is expected to grow by 23% from 19.2 million in 1991 to 23.6 million in 2016. This implies an extra 176,000 households per year. (Projections suggest an extra 9,000 households per year over the same period in Wales.) Additional housing will be required to cope with the demand this will generate, and even if policies encourage the use of brownfield sites for housing (as they do), there will be a greater demand for housing development than suitable brownfield sites can accommodate. This could mean that 1.3% of the area of England will change from rural to urban uses between 1991 and 2016.

The pressure for more housing is likely to be the greatest single pressure for development in the UK over the next 20 years.

Although the amount of agricultural land in the UK changed little in recent years, there has been a decline of about 9% in the area used for growing crops, which is attributable in part to the EC set-aside scheme. In 1995 about 597,00 ha (2.5% of the total area) of land was set aside in the UK, of which about 15% was in productive use growing non-food crops, but the proportion of land required to be set aside has decreased steadily, down to 5% in 1997.

Protected land and buildings

The ten National Parks cover 7% of the land area of England, and 20% of Wales. (The Norfolk and Suffolk Broads, though not a National Park, also have statutory protection.) The 41 Areas of Outstanding Natural Beauty (AONBs) cover 16% of England and 4% of Wales. Collectively, 44 Heritage Coasts account for around 33% of the coastline of England and Wales, and 4,940 Sites of Special Scientific Interest (SSSIs), which are especailly important because of their animal or plant life, their geology or some other special feature, cover 1,192,554 ha (about 7.5% of the area) of England and Wales. These SSSIs include 478,631 ha of Special Protection Areas for the conservation of birds, and 91,391 ha of National Nature Reserves. Local Nature Reserves take up another 33,287 ha. Green belts now cover about 12% of the area of England, a proportion that doubled between 1979 and 1993. Some areas fall into more than one of these categories. All of these areas receive special protection to help to conserve their environmental quality.

In addition, 43 Environmentally Sensitive Areas cover 3,377,000 ha of England and Wales. In these areas, farming practices to help conserve environmental features are either maintained or adopted on a voluntary basis.

At the end of 1996, English Heritage had listed 450,351 buildings and scheduled 16,757 ancient monuments, affording these too additional protection, and there is protection particularly against demolition without prior consultation for buildings in the 8,592 designated conservation areas.

Other forms of special protection are provided by tree preservation orders and by the regulations concerning bats and other protected species, which ensure that conservation bodies are consulted before any work is done that affects their habitats.

Outside the statutory system, but also protected in various ways, are for example:

- the 272,659 ha owned by the National Trust in England and Wales
- 103,000 ha of reserves managed by the Royal Society for the Protection of Birds
- 36,000 ha of reserves owned or managed by the Royal Society for Nature Conservation
- 391,800 ha of woodland managed by Forest Enterprise, including 145,400 ha of Forest Parks.

The UK's biodiversity

The UK hosts:

- an estimated 30,000 species of animals, excluding marine and microscopic animals and less known groups such as mites and roundworms
- about 2,300 species of higher plants
- about 1,000 species of liverworts and mosses
- about 1,700 species of lichens
- about 20,000 species of fungi
- about 15,000 species of algae
- about 38 species of native freshwater fish
- about 220 species of birds.

(SOURCE: ENVIRONMENT AGENCY WEB PAGES)

The quality of the land

It is difficult to quantify the quality of either rural or urban areas, or to assess changes in their quality. Among the aspects of land use which affect its overall quality are:

- its natural history, and the variety of flora and fauna it sustains
- the maturity of its plant life and particularly of trees
- the presence and quality of landscape features such as field boundaries
- the intensity and nature of its current usages
- the visual impact of its natural and man-made features
- the accessibility of the area as a whole, and of specific parts of it, for different categories of individual and by different modes of transport
- the scope for improvement it offers: to improve its visual appeal, increase its nature conservation value, exploit its potential uses.

Measures which provide an indicator of quality include:

- the amount of atmospheric pollution
- biodiversity indicators
- levels of vandalism.

A few figures might help to round out the picture.

A recent MORI poll for the Groundwork organisation found that:

- 1 in 4 people felt there was nowhere for their children to play.
- 1 in 8 young people felt the area they lived in was attractive.
- 1 in 4 people felt that their area was 'cared for'.
- more than 1 in 6 people felt their area suffered high levels of crime.

The total length of hedgerows in England and Wales fell by 33% from 1984 to 1993.

The proportion of forest trees in Great Britain with crown density reductions of over 10% and over 60% (compared to a perfect tree) in 1997 were:

	over 10% CD reduction	over 60%
Sitka spruce	87.2%	2.7%
Norway spruce	88.6%	4.5%
Scots pine	94.6%	1.6%
Oak	98.8%	6.6%
Beech	97.3%	2.2%

SOURCE: *DIGEST OF ENVIRONMENTAL STATISTICS 1998,* TABLE 8.10

Between 1978 and 1990 the percentage changes in the numbers of plant species found in different types of plots in Great Britain were:

Crops/weeds	-6.2%
Tall grass/herb	3.8%
Fertile grassland	-0.0%
Infertile grassland	-12.4%
Lowland wooded	2.1%
Upland woodland	-20.7%
Moorland grass	-6.2%
Heath/bog	5.8%

SOURCE: *DIGEST OF ENVIRONMENTAL STATISTICS 1998,* TABLE 9.14.B

Control of land use and development

The UK has a three-tier planning system, in which national planning policies, regional plans and local plans are all developed at different levels of elected government. Most planning applications are dealt with by local authorities on a district level, but certain matters are handled on a county level.

The planning system is the most obvious method for controlling land use and development in the UK, but it is by no means the only method. EC and UK government policies of many kinds affect the demand for development and the pattern of farming. For example:

- economic policies affect the rate of business growth and the proportion of business failures
- energy policies affect the demand for fossil fuels
- transport policies at both national and local levels determine the land-use requirement for road building and other transport uses
- social and healthcare policies affect household sizes.

The quality of the landscape is affected not only by development but by, for example:

- land drainage patterns
- the intensity of agricultural use
- changes in production processes and in their level of emissions
- policies and practices regarding the decommissioning of redundant plant and restoring sites.

Planning applications

DETR statistics show that in the second quarter of 2000, district planning authorities in England received 143,000 applications for planning permission and other related consents, 10% more than in the same period of 1997. They made 125,100 planning decisions. Of these, 48% related to householder developments and 10% to new dwellings. The authorities granted 88% of applications, although in many cases this will have been after negotiation and with conditions attached.

County planning authorities (county councils and unitary authorities) received 432 applications relating to 'county matters' in the second quarter of 2000, and made 342 decisions. Of the decisions, 61% involved waste developments and 31% involved mineral extraction.

Environmentally positive development

Sustainable development does not mean no development. The principles of sustainable development are intended rather to ensure that the development which does take place sets a balance between the demands of the economy, society as a whole, and the environment, and takes into account the need to plan for future as well as present needs.

Any development has an impact which extends well beyond the actual site on which it is to take place. The following are examples.

- The requirement for raw materials will have an impact, for example on mineral extraction requirements and/or on the growth and supply of timber.
- The requirement for manufactured components will affect production activities and their associated levels of pollution.

- Development of a site may have an impact on drainage, affecting vegetation and wildlife habitats both within and beyond the site boundary.
- The site will have infrastructure requirements (for power supplies, telecommunications, water supply and sewerage, etc.) which may require off-site developments (cables, pipelines, electricity substations and so on). Its demands may affect services to the existing community.
- Construction will generate traffic, noise, and possibly chemical pollution and other impacts that affect the surrounding area.
- Operation of the facility will generate traffic, noise, and possibly other impacts that affect the surrounding area.
- As well as a landscape impact (on the character and quality of the landscape), the development will have a visual impact.
- Construction, operation or both may necessitate changes to road or other transport networks. New signage will also have an impact.
- The development will alter patterns of human activity, bringing about a wider effect on transport requirements, and possibly generating demands for housing, shopping, leisure and other supporting facilities.
- The development is liable to generate waste which will require disposal.
- The development may physically affect the cohesion of human communities and wildlife habitats.
- The development may have economic effects – for example, a new shopping development will draw trade from nearby shopping areas and possibly affect their continuing viability, leading to wider changes in land-use and activity patterns.
- Decommissioning or demolition will have an impact similar to that of construction.
- The development may have permanent effects on the site, which cannot be reversed by remediation conditions.

Environmentally sensitive development policies aim to:

- apply the precautionary principle, avoiding developments of uncertain environmental value
- take into account the full impact of the development, on- and off-site, including all the aspects outlined above, maximising positive and minimising negative impacts
- take into account the cumulative effect of demands for developments, as well as the impact of each individual proposal
- consider the entire lifecycle of the proposal, from site preparation and construction through to decommissioning or demolition
- ensure that improvements to the natural and/or built environment are brought about, particularly in areas that are currently of poor environmental quality
- ensure that areas of high value (in terms of either natural or built environment) are conserved

- ensure that every possible measure is taken to mitigate any adverse impacts of the development
- conserve habitats, particularly of rare species
- conserve natural resources
- ensure that capacities and thresholds are identified and respected.

More generally, these policies aim to ensure that developments take place on the most appropriate sites, and that on the chosen site, the development that is approved is the 'best environmental fit'. This involves, for example, selecting the best positioning for structures within the site, in order to preserve existing trees and other landscape features, to minimise the visual impact, and to take account of structural and circulation requirements. It involves choosing an appropriate design and appropriate materials for buildings, and planning ground modelling and appropriate planting to screen unattractive buildings, make the most of visually attractive features, and generally enhance the natural and built environment. It also involves considering the after-use potential, particularly of limited-life activities (such as mineral extraction) and setting appropriate conditions to ensure that this potential is realised.

Environmental analysis and Environmental Impact Assessment

'Environmental analysis' is the technique of analysing the environmental impact of a proposed development, and adapting the design so as to minimise its adverse impact (and maximise its positive impact). 'Environmental Impact Assessment' is a formal application of this technique, which in some circumstances is required by law. (See below.)

The environmentally sensitive landscape planning process begins with a 'baseline study' of the existing landscape and visual resource. This should focus on its sensitivity and its ability to accommodate change, identifying thresholds which may, if breached, bring about species losses. All relevant data should be identified and mapped.

It is then possible to prepare land-use and landscape strategies, mapping out in outline development alternatives that work to avoid constraints, mitigate the impact of the development, and take advantage of positive environmental opportunities. These can be worked up into outline proposals which can then be compared to ensure that the most desirable option is the one taken forward.

Whether it is required by law or not, it is good practice to produce a report which:

- outlines the likely environmental impacts of the proposed development
- specifically notes any unavoidable adverse effects
- explains where the Best Practicable Environmental Option has been employed to mitigate adverse effects wherever possible
- indicates what alternatives have been considered, as well as outlining the selected proposal
- considers the resource requirements of the development
- balances short-term human requirements with the long-term environmental requirement.

Planning gain

The concept of 'planning gain' was introduced into legislation by the **Town and Country Planning Act 1990**, although it has long been recognised as a part of the discipline of environmentally sensitive planning. The argument is that where a development (generally, a major development) is perceived to bring disbenefits to its neighbourhood, these should be balanced by introducing benefits additional to those which are integral to the development. In the planning regulations the intention is that the developer should offer to provide these as part of the overall 'package' that is submitted for planning approval, but the planning gain is equally real when they are funded from another source. The benefits might be either on-site or off-site, and could include, for example:

- park and ride schemes
- improvements to the transport network – for example, improved junctions or underpasses
- enhancement to road and/or river frontages
- waste recycling facilities
- 'shopmobility': loan of wheelchairs, subsidised transport and similar schemes to assist the disabled
- leisure facilities such as parks, swimming pools or leisure centres.

Planning and developing better rural and urban environments

The best sites for development

Planning policies are concerned not only with the impact of an individual proposed development, but also with planning land-use patterns on a wider scale. The pattern and density of land use has a major impact particularly on traffic, and (as was explained in Chapter 11) this is particularly significant because of the need to limit the amount of motorised traffic in order to reduce emission levels. It has been suggested that planning policy can affect up to 70% of UK energy usage overall.

In general, it is clear that the best policies for sustainable development are those that encourage new development to take place within existing settlements, and in particular within larger settlements. (The transport implications of this are discussed further in Chapter 11.) Relatively compact development is more environmentally friendly (in global terms) than lower-density development, but it requires careful planning if it is to provide a good quality of environment for those living and working within it. Policies to improve the quality of urban life, including protecting existing green spaces and creating new green spaces in urban environments, help to limit the pressure for development in rural areas.

The government's current target is that by 2008, 60% of new housing should be provided by building on previously developed land or by converting existing buildings, thus enhancing the density of development and protecting undeveloped land from unnecessary development. (In 1998 the actual proportion was 57%.) On average, dwellings on previously-developed land are more dense (28 per ha) than those built on greenfield sites (22 per ha).

Locating workplaces and amenities such as schools, shops and leisure facilities in or near housing areas helps to reduce the need for travel, and to enhance the quality of life for people in those communities. This is now the drift of public policy, and it also now receives general public approval. For example, in a 1995 British Social Attitudes survey the response of respondents to the suggestion that shops and offices should be encouraged to move out of town and city centres was:

- strongly agree/agree: 21%
- neither: 17%
- strongly disagree/disagree: 55%.

Greening cities

Many large and small schemes under various government and partnership initiatives aim to make cities more attractive environments not only for people but for birds and animals as well. Linking green spaces by developing 'wildlife corridors' helps to enable cities to become viable habitats for wild creatures.

These are among the benefits of this type of initiative.

- Improved urban environments attract inward investment.
- Improved environments help to encourage tourism.
- A more green urban environment can reduce journeys out of the city to experience the countryside.
- Problems of soil erosion are reduced.
- There is better support for biodiversity.
- The schemes help to recharge groundwater levels.

There is scope to increase the amount of green space in cities by, for example:

- developing 'green corridors' following transportation networks
- improving parks and gardens, playing fields and playgrounds
- planting street trees, and developing urban forestry and community woodlands
- developing community gardens and nature areas
- improving cemeteries and allotments
- 'greening' land awaiting development
- planting in public spaces
- developing roof gardens on buildings.

Although some green initiatives are located on short-term sites and necessarily have a short time-frame, in general greening initiatives should be planned on a long-term basis, and it is important to ensure that they are well integrated into a master plan. Modern landscaping opinion is generally against the use of alien species, and in favour of indigenous 'natural' landscapes, which encourage indigenous wildlife, and are usually cheaper to introduce and to maintain.

Protecting the countryside

The EC set-aside schemes have had a mixed effect on the rural environment. The current scheme, the Arable Area Payments Scheme (AAPS), introduced in 1992, requires all farmers except the smallest to compulsorily set aside a proportion of land. Unlike the earlier scheme this replaced, it will not pay for land which prior to the scheme was used as permanent grass or woodland, so it provides a disincentive for farmers to plough up permanent pasture which often has a strong environmental value. The 1991 reforms of the Common Agricultural Policy also led to the concept of long-term (20 years) set-aside land, which increases the prospect of set-aside land developing greater environmental value. The further Agenda 2000 CAP reforms in 1999 strengthened the agro-environmental aspect of the policy, introducing payment for farmers who voluntarily undertake environmental work that goes beyond normal good agricultural practice, and linking all direct payments to compliance with environmental standards. In conjunction with these, seven-year Rural Development Plans were established in all EC countries, to take effect from 1 January 2000.

Soil quality is an important issue in agricultural areas, and in 1996 the Royal Commission on Environmental Pollution published a report on *Sustainable Uses of Soil,* in response to which the government adopted a national soil protection strategy.

Land-management agreements are a tool of ensuring that rural and particularly agricultural land is managed in an environmentally sensitive way. The two major farmland conservation schemes, Environmentally Sensitive Areas and Countryside Stewardship, both work to encourage voluntary land-management agreements. In 1999 there were about 8,600 Countryside Stewardship agreements, covering around 152,800 ha of land. The aims of these agreements were to:

- sustain the beauty and diversity of existing landscapes, restore neglected land, and create new landscapes
- protect and extend wildlife habitats, and create new habitats
- conserve archaeological sites and historic features, and restore neglected ones
- improve opportunities for people to enjoy the countryside.

As well as being threatened by more intensive farming methods, some country sites suffer from their over-popularity as **tourist destinations**. There are various planning and regulatory measures that can help to protect over-used areas, including:

- demand-management policies such as 'pay and protect' access to popular open-air destinations, high admission charges to tourist attractions, reduced advertising, and the promotion of alternative destinations
- rationing policies, for example, by restricting opening hours of tourist attractions, physically closing off sites at some times of the year, or issuing visitor permits
- transport policies: restricting road capacities, limiting public transport or limiting car-parking provision.

The regulatory framework

As noted above, a very wide spread of legislation has an impact on patterns of land-use and development. Only the most immediately relevant can be mentioned here.

EC policies and regulations

EC environmental policy is, as noted before, set within the framework defined by the Fifth Community Action Plan (5th CAP) on the Environment, discussed on page 21. In part the 5th CAP has a geographical perspective, so it fits well with the general discipline of land-use planning. A major shaper of rural land use is the Community Agricultural Policy, which has led to the introduction of set-aside schemes and of Environmentally Sensitive Areas (see page 162), and which was reformed in the 1990s to move away from an emphasis on the quantity of output which tended to lead to an intensification of agricultural activity.

The EC Directive, **Environmental Impact Assessment for Certain Public and Private Projects, 1985**, has been described by the European Parliament Directorate General for Research as *'the most significant instrument in implementing the principles of Community environment policy.'* It was brought into effect in the UK in 1988, and has since been extended and amended.

Among the cornerstones of EC policy on the protection of wildlife and habitats are the **Berne Convention,** ratified by the EC in 1979, on the protection of European wildlife and natural habitats, the '**Ramsar Convention**' (The Convention on Wetlands of International Importance especially as Waterfowl Habitat), ratified in 1971 and subsequently amended, and the **Rio Convention on Biodiversity**, one of the outcomes of the 1992 Rio Conference.

There have been a number of EC regulations aimed specifically or generally at preserving habitats, most notably Directives on the **Conservation of Wild Birds 1979**, which introduced Special Protection Areas, and on the **Conservation of Natural Habitats and of Wild Flora and Fauna, 1992** (the 'Habitats Directive').

UK policies

As with the EC, environmental land issues are inextricably bound up with the entire spectrum of UK policies affecting the environment. Of particular relevance in this chapter is ***Biodiversity: The UK Action Plan***, published in 1994 in response to the Rio Convention on Biodiversity, and as one of the series of publications that have set the shape of the UK's recent sustainable development policies. It established a Biodiversity Steering Group, which has identified 38 key habitats, together covering 5% of the UK land area, that are covered by specific, costed action plans. Among the follow-up initiatives has been the Green Ministers' Action Plan, ***Making Biodiversity Happen Across Government*** (2000).

The UK Forestry Standard of 1998 sets criteria for sustainable forestry, and sets out indicators for both national development and individual forests. These cover aspects such as soil condition, water quality, net carbon sequestration, and quality of life for local people.

Planning policy guidance (PPG) publications help to set the shape of UK planning policy. Those particularly relevant to the issues discussed in this chapter include:

- *PPG6, Town Centres and Retail Developments,* issued in 1993, which signalled the end of the era of out-of-town retail developments, and set a new emphasis on considering the impact of any proposed out-of-town developments on existing town and village centres.

- *PPG9, Nature Conservation,* 1994, which considered how planning developments should take account of nature conservation and biodiversity issues.
- *PPG 13, Highways Considerations,* 1994, which introduced a new emphasis on assessing the traffic implications of new developments, encouraging development in locations well served by public transport, and on locating developments which are major traffic generators in existing centres.

Major Urban and Rural White Papers were expected in the later part of 2000. Among the forerunners of these in developing urban policy are ***Towards an Urban Renaissance*** (1999), which recommends an integrated urban planning approach including home zones with reduced speeds limits and traffic calming measures, expenditure on walking, cycling and public transport, and ***By Design: Urban Design in the Planning System*** (2000), which builds on this and dicusses design aspects in more detail.

The **UK Woodland Assurance Scheme,** launched in June 1999, is a voluntary scheme intended to support sustainable forest management.

UK legislation

Among the recent measures developing planning law are the **Town and Country Planning Act 1990** and the **Planning & Compensation Act 1991**, which among other provisions introduced the principle of planning gain, with developers either physically instigating, or paying for, the types of improvements outlined on page 168.

The **Planning (Listed Buildings and Conservation Areas) Act 1990** sets the current framework for protection of listed buildings, and buildings and trees in conservation areas.

Statutory Instruments in 1988, 1995 and 1999 (and various amendments to them) have implemented the EC **Environmental Impact Assessment** regulation outlined above. Under these regulations, major projects that can be expected to have a significant environmental impact must receive an impact assessment, and the developer must submit an Environmental Impact Statement as part of the planning and approval process. Among the types of development which require this treatment are:

- oil refineries and other fuel-processing facilities
- larger power stations
- radioactive waste handling facilities
- iron and steel works
- chemical works
- waste disposal incineration plants and landfill sites for special waste
- major developments in the transport infrastructure.

Finally, there are regulations covering developments which affect the flow of watercourses and flood plains, most notably the **Water Resources Act 1991.**

13 Environmentally friendly building

This chapter looks at ways in which new buildings can be designed, and existing buildings modified, to minimise their impact on the environment. This includes:

- consumption of resources in constructing the building
- consumption of energy by the building when in use
- the minimisation of pollution, both in construction and during use
- the general impact of the building on the health of occupants.

The emphasis is on offices and industrial buildings, but much of the material is also relevant to domestic buildings.

Environmental issues

- According to the Building Research Establishment (BRE), building construction in the UK consumes 366 million tonnes of materials per year.
- The construction industry accounts for about 7% of the UK's primary energy consumption. (About 60% of this is taken up by the production of building materials, 20% by on-site activities, and 20% by distribution of materials.)
- Buildings account for around 50% of UK's emissions of carbon dioxide.
- More than half of all offices are over 40 years old, and 35% were built before 1914. Many are buildings converted from other uses (for example, former dwellings). This factor, and the technological changes that have taken place since purpose-built buildings were first designed, mean that most are poorly suited to their current uses.
- The Association for the Conservation of Energy (ACE) estimates that the power consumption of offices increased almost two and a half times in the fifteen years to 1994. Half this consumption is of electricity, 37% of it is of gas used for heating purposes, and 11% of it is used for office appliances.
- Sick Building Syndrome has been recognised as a condition by the United Nations, the World Health Organisation, the UK Health & Safety Executive and the US National Institute for Occupational Safety & Health. It affects the health of millions of workers, leading to reduced efficiency at work and increased levels of sickness absence.

Designing buildings to be environmentally friendly

As with other manufactured items, the environmental management approach to designing buildings takes a 'cradle-to-grave' perspective, starting with the sourcing of raw materials and finishing with the ease of demolition, reuse and recycling of materials. This has obvious affinities with the integrated product policy and Design for Environment (DfE) initiatives that are discussed in Chapter15, and both these have direct applications in the design and adaption of buildings.

Building materials

An environmental cost is incurred in producing almost any building material.

- Quarrying stone consumes energy (generated at a cost to the environment), damages the physical environment, and destroys the natural environment of the quarry site. Minerals are a non-renewable (and in some cases scarce) natural resource.
- Timber is a renewable resource, but it is renewed only slowly and in many cases is being cut at more than a sustainable rate. Friends of the Earth estimate that half of the softwood used today is from non-sustainable temperate sources. Hardwood is even slower to be renewed. Some continues to derive from tropical rainforests, whose destruction has a major environmental impact (see Chapter 4), and although some derives from 'managed plantations', in many cases it is questionable whether these represent a sustainable form of activity. However, it takes less energy to turn raw timber into a usable building material than it does to produce alternative materials such as aluminium, steel and concrete, and wood is an effective insulating material with high energy efficiency, so timber is a comparatively environmentally friendly material.
- Producing metals and metal alloys is an energy-intensive and often highly polluting process, which again requires a large volume of raw material.
- Glass, plastics, concrete and other manufactured materials consume many times their manufactured weight in raw materials, consume energy in their production, and the manufacturing processes may produce dangerous pollutants.

The use of reclaimed or recycled building materials helps to save on energy usage, avoid the depletion of natural resources, and generally minimise the environmental impact. It is even more environmentally friendly to adapt existing buildings to new uses, paying due attention to energy-saving design, rather than building from scratch.

As well as using recycled materials where possible in their construction, buildings should be designed so as to encourage reuse and recycling at the end of their planned life. In terms of the waste-management hierarchy, these are among the materials that can be:

- **reused**:
  bricks
  stone
  timber
  tiles and slates.
- **recycled**:
  ferrous and non-ferrous metals
  thermoplastics
  glass.

- **rotted down or used for fuel:**
  wood (other than large pieces of timber, which should be reused)
  thatch
  paper products.

Building materials which produce particular problems in use include:

- Timber products such as plywood, chipboard and fibreboard. The glues used in their manufacture often emit formaldehyde gas, which causes problems that are discussed below and on page 210.
- Foamed polystyrene products (cavity wall foam, plastic wall and ceiling tiles) which again can emit formaldehyde.
- Products containing asbestos, no longer in general use but still found in older buildings, and a dangerous carcinogen.
- Smooth non-absorbent plastic surfacing materials, which can help to increase the number of mould spores and airborne bacteria.

Finishing materials (paints, varnishes, etc.) and timber preservatives are also frequently sources of pollution, both in their manufacture and in use.

Building design

The design process for a new building should start not with the building itself but with its site. The building should be positioned on the site not only to minimise environmental damage to the rest of the site, but also to take advantage of the natural contours of the land and vegetation, and of protection provided by other structures. The aim should be to protect the building from adverse weather conditions and to ensure that the best use is made of natural sunlight. In many cases it is desirable to improve the site, altering the natural contours, building walls or planting trees, for example.

The design of the building can do much to minimise its energy requirements. Passive solar design is the term for modifying the design of buildings so as to take the best advantage of the sun. This can have an impact on:

- heating: ensuring that the building is heated by solar radiation by orienting the building so that the areas requiring most heat are south-facing; and minimising the heat loss from shaded facades
- cooling and ventilation: ensuring that the building is designed so that no areas overheat and cause discomfort to occupants, and allowing solar heated air to assist natural convection, cutting down the need for mechanical ventilation and cooling systems
- lighting: arranging vertical and horizontal glazing so that natural light is used in preference to artificial light, while ensuring that glaring sunlight does not cause occupants discomfort.

New buildings can be designed with features such as Trombé walls or double-envelope construction, creating narrow spaces designed to trap the sun's heat by non-mechanical means.

Many old, as well as new, buildings benefit from the addition of south-facing conservatories which serve to increase insulation and to trap heat which can then be circulated around the building. Roof space solar collectors can also be retrofitted to existing buildings, and active solar energy systems can also contribute to increasing the building's energy efficiency and reducing fuel bills.

Optimising the size and position of windows does much for lighting as well as heating. New techniques such as light shelves, light pipes, mirrored louvres and holographic or prismatic glazing help to spread the impact of natural light, minimising the need for artificial lighting and avoiding excessive glare. Daylight-linked lighting controls can be used to ensure that the natural light is supplemented when necessary with artificial light.

Atria or courtyards as design features can improve both the energy efficiency of buildings and their overall attractiveness as places to work or live.

All buildings old and new should be well insulated, but the insulation should not be at the expense of adequate natural ventilation.

Buildings in areas where natural radon is prevalent should be designed to prevent radon build-up.

Building services

Recirculating air-conditioning systems can increase the amount of harmful bacteria in a building, and can cause the spread of Legionnaire's disease. Natural air circulation and ventilation is preferable, and when mechanical systems are necessary they should be designed with care and maintained properly.

Water systems should be designed to minimise the requirement for mains water and to maximise any opportunity for recycling used water. Manual-flushing lavatories are more water efficient than automatic flushing devices, and taps that operate under movement-sensor or pressure controls are more efficient than those that are capable of being left running accidentally. Water meters and regular audits of consumption should be a part of the organisation's environmental management policy.

Electrical systems too should be designed with energy saving in mind. Information on energy efficiency in general is on pages 139–42, and on energy-efficient lighting is on pages 141–2.

BREEAM

BREEAM is the Building Research Establishment Environmental Assessment Method, introduced in 1990 as a way of measuring a building's impact on the environment. The BRE will assess buildings against BREEAM criteria, and those that rate satisfactorily are awarded the BRE's Environmental Standard Award.

BREEAM standards currently exist for offices, superstores, industrial units and houses, but they can also be used for other types of building. They consider aspects such as:

- carbon dioxide emissions with quantified benchmarks
- healthy building features
- air quality and ventilation

- measures to minimise the effect on ozone depletion and acid rain
- recycling and reuse of materials
- ecology of the site
- noise
- Legionnaire's disease
- use of hazardous materials
- lighting.

Healthy and unhealthy buildings

Among the factors which can cause health problems for building occupants (apart from problems caused by industrial processes within the building) are:

- pollutants (formaldehyde, other toxic fumes, ozone, etc.) emitted by building components, hard and soft furnishings and equipment
- pollutants in the outdoor air that are carried into the building
- mould spores and bacteria
- stale air caused by lack of ventilation
- noise caused by equipment, other occupants, traffic and other sources outside the building
- poor natural or artificial lighting, causing strain or glare
- vibration of machinery
- concentrations of natural radon gas
- tobacco smoke
- dampness
- colour schemes that contribute to stress
- low-level electric fields, magnetic fields and electromagnetic radiation from electrical systems and appliances.

Some of these problems are related to building design, and although they can be avoided in well-designed new buildings, they are not easily cured in existing buildings. However, a number of relatively simple measures can be taken to improve the office environment, and most will prove cost-effective in terms of improved morale and reduced sickness absence.

Workspaces should be designed to make best use of natural light (siting computer screens to avoid glare) and with an adequate level of back-up artificial lighting.

Electronic equipment can generate ozone, a physical irritant that exacerbates common health problems, as well as dust, noise and vibration. Major pieces of equipment such as photocopiers should be sited in specific areas well removed from workstations, and all equipment should be regularly maintained, with filters being replaced at the recommended intervals. Equipment should be switched off overnight and when not in use for long periods.

Noise can be minimised by siting as much equipment as possible away from workstations (see above), by using carpets or other soft flooring materials, and by using acoustically absorbent materials on other surfaces.
Plants in the office improve the visual environment, can absorb pollutants such as formaldehyde, absorb carbon dioxide and emit pleasant odours. Among the suitable plants that fulfil some or all of these functions, while remaining relatively low-maintenance, are spider plants, ferns, parlour palms, English ivy, peace lilies, mother in law's tongue, lavender, scented geraniums, and various herbs.
Smoking should be banned entirely if possible; or at a minimum, banned in all work areas and circulation spaces, and confined to a designated smoking area.

Increasing the priority given to energy efficiency

Among the reasons suggested by ACE and others for the lack of priority given to energy efficiency in many organisations are:

- clashes of interest between leaseholders and freeholders, making both reluctant to invest in environmental improvements
- the relatively low proportion of overall costs taken up by the energy bill
- accountancy practices which, by writing off conservation investments over a time span shorter than their physical lifetime, tend to downgrade the return on investment
- lack of awareness of best practice
- lack of awareness of true energy and water costs when these are subsumed into a general charge for the building as a whole.

Among the proposals that have been made to enable organisations to improve the energy efficiency of the buildings they occupy are:

- statutory requirements for energy and water costs to be itemised
- requirements on property companies to commit to a schedule for installing individual gas and electricity meters
- statutory requirements for regular energy audits
- a possible extension of Integrated Pollution Control regulations, so that office blocks are subject to best practice requirements
- greater rights for tenants to override the landlord in undertaking energy efficiency measures.

Government regulation and guidance

The government has a number of initiatives to improve energy efficiency in households and in commercial organisations, which are outlined on pages 142–4.

Much research has been funded into the energy efficiency of buildings, and to a lesser but still significant extent into other aspects of environmentally friendly building design. The Building Research Establishment leads in this field, and the government's Energy Efficiency Office has a programme of research and guidance on energy efficiency in buildings which is operated by its sub-unit, the Building Research Energy Conservation Support Unit (BRECSU). Specific guidance has been issued on low-energy cooling technologies and on energy-efficient lighting systems, and a good practice guide, ***What Will Energy Efficiency Do for Your Business?*** is targeted specifically at the business community.

Building design is regulated through the planning system (discussed in Chapter 12) and through the **Building Regulations.** Recent and ongoing changes to the building regulations have focused on energy efficiency, and include energy labelling for new housing.

The Eco-Centre: a benchmark

Among the many environmentally friendly buildings constructed over recent years, the Eco Centre, located in Jarrow on the banks of the River Tyne, is perhaps the best example of what can be achieved. This £1.5 million office complex, opened in November 1996, was designed to be Europe's first 'self-sufficient' commercial building. It was constructed largely from recycled, second-hand and environmentally acceptable materials. Its energy sources include underground streams (a source for winter space heating), solar panels (to heat the water supply) and wind turbines (to generate electricity). With the help of these it generates almost all its own electricity. Electricity requirements are in any case low, because the building has been designed to consume only half the energy of a conventional office building.

The building is naturally ventilated; using a central wind tower in contrast to the energy-hungry air conditioning found elsewhere. It also meets most of its own water needs, using stored and recycled rainwater, and it disposes of its own waste.

The Eco-Centre, commissioned by the Groundwork organisation, is considered by them to represent a commercially viable method of building. It represents a benchmark for the environmentally friendly buildings of the next generation.

The Eco House

Leicester has been designed an Environment City for ten years, and one of its leading features is the EcoHouse, which was designed to demonstrate energy saving, recycling and other environmentally friendly building features to its more than 100,000 visitors. Among the features included in its recent refit are photovoltaic solar panels to provide most electricity needs, a rainwater storage facility which provides water for the toilets and garden, and recycled underlay for its carpets.

14 Noise

> *'In Europe overall, about 10 million people are exposed to environmental noise levels that may cause hearing loss.'*
>
> UN ENVIRONMENT PROGRAMME, *GLOBAL ECONOMIC OUTLOOK 2000*

Noise is measured in decibels (dB), a logarithmic scale, so that when the noise increases by 10 dB it sounds twice as loud. Measurements of noise are usually described in dB(A), where 'A' refers to the filter that is used in sound meters to mimic human hearing. A measurement of 0 dB reflects the threshold of human hearing, and as an indicator of practical noise measurements:

40 dB reflects the noise in the average living room.
60 dB equals the noise of a conversation heard from a metre distance.
80 dB equals the noise of heavy traffic at the roadside.
100 dB is the level of noise made by a pneumatic drill.

The World Health Organisation sets a daytime limit of 50 dB(A) (measured in a specific way) as the level above which noise levels cause annoyance. Regular exposure to noises above 90 dB can result in hearing loss, and noises above 130 dB can cause immediate and permanent hearing loss.

In practice, noise measurements attempt to capture both the level of background noise and the peaks in fluctuating noise levels.

Noise and vibration are intimately related problems, and both are considered in this chapter.

The problem of noise pollution

Low levels of noise can cause irritation, affect concentration, disturb sleep, and when prolonged, cause or exacerbate insomnia, stress and depression. Higher noise levels can cause giddiness or discomfort, and induce health problems such as tinnitus (ringing in the ears) and temporary or permanent hearing loss. Noise disrupts conversations and working ability, and outdoor noise prevents many people at home from opening windows or spending time in their gardens.

Vibration, for example of the kind experienced when operating a power tool, can damage nerves, joints, bones and muscles. Noise and vibration can also bring about machine failure and cause structural damage to buildings.

Noise is a serious and very common problem. It affects both employees working in a particularly noisy environment, and the general population who experience noise from traffic, from neighbouring buildings, and from other nearby activities. The European Environment Agency in their *Dobris Assessment* estimated that:

- 65% of the European population are exposed to noise at a level that causes annoyance and sleep disturbance.

- 17% are exposed to noise at a level that has a serious impact.
- 1.4% are exposed to noise at an unacceptable level.

An UK study in 1990 found that over half the homes in England and Wales were exposed to noise above the WHO recommended limit, and 7% of homes were above the qualifying level at which it is necessary to provide sound insulation improvements if there is to be development of a new road leading to further increases in noise levels.

Between 1983/4 and 1995/6, complaints about noise from industrial and commercial premises in the UK more than doubled. Over two-thirds of complaints to Environmental Health Officers (EHOs) were however about noise from domestic sources.

A 1995 survey found that most people considered traffic congestion and traffic noise to be much more serious issues than either the greenhouse effect or oil and gas shortages. And 32% of the respondents saw noise from traffic in towns and cities as a 'very serious' issue.

Ways to minimise the nuisance

There are both active and passive methods of reducing the problem of noise.

Changes to the source. Increasingly tight regulations (outlined below) provide a spur to the development of, for instance, quieter machinery, quieter cars, lorries and airplanes, and quieter road surfaces.

Physical controls to muffle noise and reduce vibration. This includes, for example, enclosing noisy machinery in a separate area, improving the soundproofing of its surrounding barriers, and changing the supporting structure (or building foundations) so as to reduce vibration.

Changes in structural patterns. The noise can be moved farther away, for example by introducing buffer zones along motorways or near particularly noisy factories or leisure facilities.

Personal protection. Earmuffs and earplugs can limit the noise suffered by an individual.

Limitations in hours of operation. These are used to ensure, for example, that airports do not operate at night when ambient noise levels are lower and aircraft noise is more intrusive.

General legal powers to tackle noise pollution

Producing excessive noise is an offence not only in statute law but in common law, and civil action can be taken against those who cause noise nuisance.

Many of the statutory powers to deal with noise nuisance are conferred on local authorities. Noise abatement is generally enforced by EHOs under the **Control of Pollution Act 1974** (COPA) and the **Environmental Protection Act 1990,** which defines noise coming from premises as a statutory nuisance when it is loud enough to be either a nuisance or prejudicial to health. Their powers were extended under the **Noise and Statutory Nuisance Act 1993 (NSNA).** They cover:

- noise from roadworks
- noise from construction sites (powers under the COPA)
- noise from industrial and commercial premises (powers under the Environmental Protection Act) and from audible intruder alarms (under the NSNA)
- noise from domestic premises
- noise in the street and in the environment generally.

They do *not* cover noise from traffic.

Local authorities also have the power (under the COPA) to define and implement **Noise Abatement Zones.** The purpose of these is to avoid any deterioration in noise conditions, and to secure improvements where they are practicable. However, they have proved only a limited success in practice, and the powers are not much used at present.

The **Noise Act 1996** clarified local authorities' powers to seize and confiscate noise-making equipment. Other recent legislation has introduced a specific night noise offence, and given local authorities additional powers to deal with excessive domestic noise, for example from amplified music and parties.

Noisy intruder alarms rate as a common-law nuisance, and magistrates as well as local authorities have powers to act over them.

Where noise from traffic (including roads and airports) is sufficiently bad to cause serious inconvenience and to affect property values as a result, then the affected property owners have the rights:

- to obtain noise insulation, specifically under the **1995 Noise Insulation Regulations**
- to claim compensation for the fall in value under the **Land Compensation Act 1973.**

A proposed EC **Environmental Noise Directive,** details of which were published in September 2000, outlines actions to take place over the decade to 2010 to further control environmental noise. These include:

- the harmonisation of noise indicators and assessment methods
- action plans for major transport sources of noise
- establishing an EU databank with noise maps and action plans
- the provision of information on noise exposure
- agreed medium and long-term goals for reduction in the number of people exposed to noise from transport and industrial sources
- a strategy for producing relatively quiet rural areas.

Control of specific noisy activities

Noisy activities can also be controlled through local authorities' planning powers. Planning policy guidance note 24 on *Noise* gives local authorities advice on suitable criteria for permitting noise-sensitive and noise-generating developments, and on how conditions can be attached to planning approvals that require the impact of noise generated by the development to be controlled and minimised.

Controls on noisy machinery and equipment

Both national and international regulations limit the allowable noise emissions from private cars, commercial vehicles including tractors, motorcycles and civil aircraft. New vehicles now have to meet noise regulations that limit them to about half of the noise produced by vehicles of ten years ago. Another recent European regulation has prevented the continuing operation of particularly old and noisy aircraft.

Among the other items covered by regulations or by codes of practice are:

- lawnmowers
- building site machinery
- audible intruder alarms
- ice cream van chimes
- model aircraft.

They are being developed for

- audible bird scarers
- helicopters
- rail vehicles.

The EU Energy Label which provides information about a product's energy efficiency also provides information on the amount of noise it makes in operation. It is already carried by law on new:

- fridges
- freezers
- washing machines
- tumble driers.

Other products should soon follow.

A new EC **Directive on Noise Emission by Equipment Used Outdoors** (2000) harmonises and controls noise by outdoors equipment (not including transport).

Noise at work

There are particular requirements on employers to ensure that noise at work is controlled, so as to avoid any risk to employees' hearing. The legislation that applies includes the **Health and Safety at Work Act 1974** and the **Noise at Work Regulations 1989,** which implement EC requirements.

Personal exposure noise limits are set at two levels, one to cover typical noise levels, with a limit of 90 dB(A), and one to cover the peak level, with a limit of 140 dB.

It is the responsibility of the employer to assess the risk if they have reason to believe that the specified noise limits are being exceeded. They must provide advice and information to employees, and on request must provide noise protection.

Although rules also apply to the suppliers and manufacturers of noisy equipment, it is the employer's duty to ensure that employees are protected. They may provide personal protection (earplugs or earmuffs) as a method of achieving this only if there is no reasonable alternative method of reducing the noise exposure.

Transport noise

The problem of transport noise is specifically covered under the UK government's 1998 White Paper, ***A New Deal for Transport***. As well as confirming that the government will work with the EC on expanding noise standards to cover railway equipment, it sets out policies to increase the use of quiet road surfaces, which make it sound as if the amount of traffic were halved. The policy is to use them when roads require resurfacing.

The DETR also began consultation in mid-2000 on proposals to further control the noise from civil aircraft.

15 Green consumers and green endorsements

> *'The lesson learned in practice, in some of the product areas where real progress is being made, is that a comprehensive approach towards each product market is needed, working with the market and complementing policies which promote the competitiveness of UK business.'*
>
> DETR, *CONSUMER PRODUCTS AND THE ENVIRONMENT,* 1998

This chapter looks at consumer attitudes to 'buying green' and at the various endorsement and award schemes that can help to sell a company's 'green product' credentials to its customers.

Green consumerism

If the UK is to meet its targets to cut pollution, and to pursue a sustainable development policy, then it is crucial that consumers should play their part. Many consumers are eager to do so. Research carried out for the UK Ecolabelling Board in March 1996 indicated that the following percentages of UK consumers expressed concern about green issues:

	Most concerned %	Also concerned %
Deteriorating air quality	29	37
Toxic and harmful discharges into rivers and streams	17	53
Deterioration of ozone layer	16	47
Destruction of rainforests	16	44
Global warming	10	42
Reduction in production waste	2	39
Acid rain	2	36
Use of unrenewable energy	2	29

SOURCE: *UK ECOLABELLING BOARD, ENVIRONMENTAL PURCHASING: CONSUMER MOTIVATIONS AND BELIEFS,* 1996

These percentages are tending to increase, and they are being reflected in consumer behaviour. A 1995 survey reported that 82% of German consumers, 67% of Dutch consumers and 50% of French and British consumers stated that environmental concerns helped to shape their shopping behaviour. According to another study, 67% of EC citizens had already purchased or were ready to buy green products.

Purchasing 'green' products is only one way in which consumers can help the environment. Suggestions from the environmental charity Ark for the environment-conscious consumer include, for example:

- avoiding goods with unnecessary packaging
- buying long-lived products
- buying in bulk so as to reduce the number of motorised trips for shopping purposes
- reusing plastic bags, or preferring long-life shopping bags made of natural materials
- buying in-season, organic and locally grown produce as far as possible, to reduce the impact of transporting out-of-season goods to distant markets and the harmful effects of pesticides and artificial fertilisers
- eating less meat, since the production of meat consumes a disproportionate amount of resources (compared with vegetable sources of protein).

The green product

Assessing (and improving) the 'greenness' of a product (or service) requires a change in focus. From seeing the product as an item shaped by the consumer's requirements and the dictates of the production process, it is necessary to shift to a perspective that perceives the product as just one phase in a cycle of the utilisation and wasting of raw materials. This 'integrated product' approach is broadly similar in conception to the integrated pollution control approach discussed in Chapter 5.

Design for Environment

The process of designing or redesigning products to be more environmentally friendly has become known as **Design for Environment**, or **DfE**. The process should begin by considering in depth what the customer values in the product. What needs does it fulfil, what pleasure does it give, what brand and image aspects help to sell it? It is important not to be limited in the assessment process by too much emphasis on the product as is. It may be that a quite different approach, causing far less environmental damage, would fulfil the same need. (For example, teleconferencing can replace travel to and use of conventional conference facilities, and detergent-free washing processes can replace conventional detergents.)

Once the purpose of the product has been clearly set out, a redesign process should begin with the raw material requirement, concentrating on, for example:

- the quantity of materials required
- the environmental costs of resourcing those materials
- the environmental costs of working with the materials
- the environmental costs of disposing of the materials at end of product life.

The assessment should continue to assess the production process, its energy and water requirements, its tendency to pollute and so on. It should allow for the distribution system that gets the product to the consumer. It should assess the environmental impact of the product in use, and it should end by considering the reuse or recyclability of the product and its components.

An alternative breakdown sees the process as:

- goal definition and scoping
- an inventory analysis: of inputs (materials and energy) and outputs (product, emissions and waste)
- an impact assessment: of the items in the inventory analysis
- an improvement assessment, making a similar assessment of each alternative identified.

Environmental criteria (such as the use of less hazardous materials) should be mapped against business criteria (the costs of new equipment, or of staff training) to identify areas where the two coincide and areas of conflict or risk.

Typically, an environmentally friendly product:

- will use less material than previous products fulfilling the same purpose
- will have a better performance
- will be more durable, easier to maintain, and have a longer average life
- will have a modular design to make it more easily upgradeable and repairable
- will be innovative, providing access to new markets
- will be energy efficient, making it cheaper to use
- will meet all international standards, ensuring there will be no difficulties in exporting it to any market world-wide
- will be accompanied by packaging return services and product take-back services to facilitate reuse, remanufacture and recycling
- will have all components labelled with information on their contents, to facilitate waste disposal and recycling.

Because they are efficiently designed, environmentally friendly products are also in many cases cheaper to manufacture, and any modifications needed to the manufacturing process will often pay for themselves in terms of lower material, energy or water requirements, and lower waste disposal costs. For example, Kodak succeeded in reducing the amount of material in its film canisters by 22%. Allowing for necessary equipment modifications, the modification paid for itself in four years. Electronics manufacturer Nortel invested US$1 million over three years to develop new innovative solvent-free cleaning technologies. The cheaper-to-run process paid for itself four times over a three-year period.

Other examples of the DfE process are AT&T's move away from paper labels on their equipment (which, with their adhesives and printing inks, tended to make recycling problematic) and towards moulded-in plastic labels; and Seiko and Citizen's development of a technology for battery-free quartz watches driven by the natural movement of the wearer.

Failure to reach the standard can carry heavy penalties, and not only with consumers. Failure to meet tough US car emissions standards cost European car exporters US$500 million in 1991, while the 1990 and 1992 US bans on tuna caught with nets which endangered dolphins lost an export market to Mediterranean Europe.

The DETR estimate that domestic energy consumption could be reduced by about a third if the most efficient products available were always used by manufacturers and consumers. The difference between energy-efficient products and products not designed with energy efficiency in mind can be very sizeable. For example, the most energy-efficient washing machine now on sale in the UK is rated to use 140 kWh a year, while the average machine in use consumes 270 kWh, and the least efficient new machine is rated at 510 kWh.

Integrated product policy

EC policy at the moment is based on a philosophy of 'integrated product policy', focusing on the relationship between products and their impact on the environment throughout their lifecycle. One of the triggers behind this development is a conclusion that future environmental benefits are more likely to come from focusing on consumer use of products, than on their initial production. The UK government too has signed on to this policy, but it has yet to be firmly enshrined in legislation, and their position remains that 'it is too early to judge whether [the] potential advantages will be converted into real environmental gains'.

Green endorsements

Recent research has shown that many consumers are bewildered about the 'green' claims made for products. There was considerable publicity about the misleading nature of some 'first wave' green claims (for example, that a product did not contain a harmful substance, when conventional products of the same type did not contain it either) which tended to devalue the claims and make consumers distrustful.

A convincing environmental claim can however affect customer preferences as noted above, although it tends to have a lower impact than factors such as performance and price. It can be particularly influential when it is applied to a less well established brand or to an own-brand product.

Asked by the UK Ecolabelling Board what information they needed to help them choose greener products, 58% of consumers gave a preference for specific information about the product's environmental performance. A further 31% preferred an authorised label giving a seal of approval, while most thought a 'graded label' indicating the product's performance was more useful than a simple endorsement without gradings. The preferred option was a seal of approval combined with full information about the product.

The UK government's current thinking is that efforts should be focused on providing easy-to-understand standardised information on key products, supporting this with information campaigns to improve the general level of knowledge and awareness among consumers. In the longer term, it should be possible to use information technology to help ensure that the amount of information available at the point of sale is matched to the individual consumer's requirements.

An example of early 'ecolabelling' schemes is the 'blue angel' mark, introduced in the Federal Republic of Germany in 1978. It is widely used for paper, indicating that paper with the mark consists of 100% recycled paper and at least 51% C/D low grade paper. The endorsement process also takes account of other aspects of the production process, for example whether and how the waste paper is bleached and de-inked.

A number of individual manufacturers and retailers have introduced their own ecolabelling schemes (for example, B&Q's scheme to indicate the VOC content of its paint and coating products) but the emphasis in this chapter is on schemes with institutional backing.

The EC Ecolabelling scheme

The EC's Ecolabel scheme was adopted in March 1992. It is a voluntary scheme, and was originally intended to supplement rather than replace national schemes such as the 'blue angel'. The intention was to provide assessment criteria for products (and services), enabling individual Member States to assess against the criteria products submitted to them by manufacturers (or first importers of products) for consideration. Among the aspects taken into account are:

- consumption of natural resources
- consumption of energy
- effects on ecosystems
- the noise made by the product in use
- pollution of soil, water and air
- waste handling requirements.

In addition, products are required to satisfy all EC health, safety and environmental regulations.

Ecolabelling bodies in Member States (in the UK, the UK Eco-Labelling Board) then notify the EC of products meeting the criteria, and there is an opportunity for Europe-wide objections before labelling is approved. (Goods which receive the label can display a logo.) There is also an appeal procedure.

To date, criteria have been agreed for ecolabelling:

- washing machines
- dishwashers
- soil improvers
- laundry detergents
- light bulbs
- indoor paints and varnishes
- textile products
- copier paper
- refrigerators

- bed mattresses
- footwear
- personal and portable computers.

However, the scheme is rather cumbersome and take-up has been relatively low, with the result that the EC ecolabel is still not widely recognised. It has also prompted a number of political objections, partly because there are differences of opinion between Member States (for example, on the desirability of recycled packaging) but largely because of concerns that the scheme is being used in a protectionist way to exclude or handicap non-European products.

ISO 14021

Following the criticisms of the EC scheme mentioned above, particularly by the World Trade Organisation, the International Organisation for Standardisation (ISO) developed an ISO Standard on Environmental Labels. This International Standard provides detailed guidance on the use of terms which often appear in environmental claims, such as 'biodegradable', 'recyclable', and 'reusable and refillable'. The United Nations too has been working to devise a scheme that will better balance the requirements and priorities of the developed and developing worlds.

The EC Energy Label

The EC Energy Label has become much more established, not least because it is compulsory for certain classes of equipment. 'Cold and wet' appliances such as fridges, freezers, washing machines, tumble dryers and dishwashers, must carry the label, which provides information on their energy consumption and their noise levels in operation. From January 2001 the scheme will become mandatory for light bulbs, to provide information on the energy efficiency, light output, power consumption and average life of the bulb. Other products (for example, ovens and water heaters) should soon follow.

The DETR is now issuing 'Sector Review Papers' which look at energy usage by domestic appliances, concentrating on areas covered by the EC scheme, and covering both specific product sectors and more general overviews of electricity use.

Car fuel economy labelling

EC legislation still in process of being adopted proposes to make it compulsory for purchasers of new cars to be provided with fuel economy information, including a fuel economy label that is attached to the windshield of all new cars at the point of sale.

Green Claims Code

The Green Claims Code is supported by the Confederation of British Industry, the British Retail Consortium, the Local Authorities Coordinating Body on Food and

Trading Standards and the British Standards Institution. It is designed to relate sections of the British Code of Advertising to environmental claims, with a view to eliminating spurious and misleading claims and increasing the general credibility of environmental claims. (The code applies to claims made on products, not in separate advertising material, although similar rules cover advertisements.) Published in March 1998, the code requires manufacturers to take into account the production process as well as the performance of the finished product, and discourages use of the general phrase 'environmentally friendly'. The code does not assess businesses, only their products. It requires:

- full documentary evidence to be available for all claims made, and openness about any differences of scientific opinion
- absolute claims to be avoided unless they are backed by convincing evidence that the product will have no adverse impact at all on the environment
- all claims to be explained as clearly as possible
- extravagant language to be avoided
- spurious claims (which do not indicate an advance on earlier generations of product) to be avoided
- irrelevant and insignificant (in terms of the overall impact of the product on the environment during its lifecycle) claims to be avoided
- claims to focus on the most significant of a product's impacts on the environment.

Recycled paper

There is a separate scheme for marking recycled paper, organised by the National Association of Paper Merchants. To be approved under this scheme, paper must be made from a minimum of 75% 'genuine waste fibre' of grades B, C or D. However the scheme only takes into account the recycled content of the paper, and does not consider the wider environmental impact of its production, use and disposal.

Labelling genetically modified food

Many environmentalists are concerned about the potential impact of genetically modified organisms (GMOs). The concerns are twofold: that because this is a recent innovation, food from genetically modified crops could have impacts on consumers that are not yet known, and that introduced genes may escape to have an effect on unmodified or wild crops, and in general may affect the diversity of the available gene pool. In the UK there are particular concerns about oilseed rape and sugar beet.

GMOs are regulated in the UK under an EC directive, and the government receives advice on their regulation from the Advisory Committee on Release to the Environment (ACRE). More than 300 field test sites have been approved for the trial of genetically-modified crops.

Non-product-oriented green endorsements

As well as schemes to endorse or label environmentally friendly products, there are a number of schemes which look more widely at the 'green company' or consider other aspects of its operations.

The Queen's Award for Environmental Achievement

Operated by the Queen's Awards Office (which administers the Queen's Awards for Export and for Technological Achievement) this award announced its first winners in 1993. It is awarded for significant advances *'in the application by British industry of the development of products, technology or processes which offer major benefits in environmental terms compared to existing products, technology or processes.'* There are three basic criteria for an award:

- the product or process must demonstrate technological change
- there must be demonstrable environmental benefits
- the product or process must maintain commercial competitiveness and be proven to be commercially successful.

The Award is not given to inventions or to inventors, but to companies which have demonstrated a practical application.

Unlike the other endorsements mentioned, the Queen's Award is not given to all products or processes which fulfil the criteria: it is a competitive award presented to only a few applicants each year. Among the winners in 2000 were Tesco Distribution Ltd for a reusable transport packaging system, Crosfield Ltd for systems for treating and recycling textile waste waters, and the Renewable Energy Company for 'Ecotricity'. Specific judging criteria include the difficulty of the problems that have been addressed and the potential for wider application or transfer. The awards are made by the Queen on her birthday each year (21 April) on the advice of the Prime Minister assisted by an Advisory Committee. Organisations winning an award are entitled to display the award emblem for five years.

European Awards for the Environment

These international awards, given biennially and sponsored by the European Commission and the UN Environment Programme, recognise companies which make significant contributions to economic and social development without harming the environment. Recent UK nominees have for example included BIP Ltd for developing a method of reducing emissions of VOCs, Gardner Energy Management who developed and manufacture a non-mechanical steam-trapping device, and Strattons Hotel for its environmental management practices.

Other British environmental awards include:

- The Business Commitment to the Environment (BCE) Awards
- The Engineering Council Environment Awards for Engineers

- The Civic Trust Sustainability Award.
- The Institute of Chemical Engineers Safety and Environment Awards.
- Ford Motor Company's conservation awards programme.

Government strategies

The encouragement of environmentally friendly products is a core feature of the government's sustainability strategy. Their *Sustainable Business* strategy is outlined on pages 39–41. For green products, the core elements of the strategy are:

- providing better information for consumers (using the schemes outlined above)
- working to negotiate agreements to improve industry performance
- procurement exercises to develop markets for new goods
- regulations setting minimum standards.

In general, the approach is to remove the worst-performing goods from the marketplace by raising standards so as to exclude them, while at the same time working to improve the average environmental standard of goods in use, and to encourage further improvements in standards through technological and other developments. The specific application of government policies to consumer products was discussed in a consultation paper, ***Consumer Products and the Environment***, which was published in 1998, and an Advisory Committee on Consumer Products and the Environment (ACCPE) has been set up to advise the government on sustainable consumption issues.

16 Education and training

Almost every job is in some way interfaced with the wider environment, and many jobs today are self-evidently 'in the environment field'. They vary considerably in their content and in the level of specialism required, from manual jobs requiring little training to highly professional jobs in fields such as environmental law and biotechnology.

With sustainable development a core issue today throughout industry, commerce and the public sector, there are very few working individuals who would not benefit from a degree of training in the concepts and tools of this field. In the UK, both full-time vocational training and very many specific short courses are available.

'Environmental training' currently has no specific definition in the UK, and courses which include the word 'environment' or some similar name in their title need have no specific content. Because of this limitation, and because some aspects of the field (for example, environmental building) are relatively new, there is some confusion among both employers and employees, and it is not clear whether it is always an advantage for a trainee to select a specifically environmentally-oriented course in a general professional field such as engineering or law.

There are however a growing number of bodies which accredit specifically environmental courses, such as the Institution of Environmental Sciences, and other bodies (such as the Engineering Council) are developing environmental standards and codes of practice.

The Environmental Training Organisation, started in 1996, is an industry training organisation for the environmental sector, and is co-ordinating its training, education and employment needs. It incorporates the Council for Occupational Standards and Qualifications in Environmental Conservation (COSQUEC).

It is not possible in this short chapter to outline the entire field. The focus is on providing a brief overview and pointing readers to sources of further information.

Fields of environmental employment

Jobs with a particular environmental slant include those in the following fields:

- nature conservation
- town planning
- architecture and construction
- sustainable energy
- energy efficiency
- environmental management
- water management
- pollution control
- engineering, process and product design

- environmental health (EHOs)
- organic farming
- biotechnology
- environmental law
- environmental education and training
- environmental management, auditing and accountancy.

In many of these fields there are established professional bodies that do not have a specifically environmental slant, but which nevertheless can provide much useful information. The references below are primarily to environmentally oriented groups and publications, but are not intended to exclude from consideration bodies such as the RIBA, the Construction Industry Training Board or the Chartered Institute of Transport.

Architecture and construction

Although there is as yet no specific degree in the UK in environmental architecture, most university architecture courses include a component of environmentally conscious design. MSc courses in Environmental Design are beginning to be available: for example, a course at the University of Cardiff covers passive solar design, solar geometry, thermal mass, energy-efficient air conditioning and so on. Among the specialist sources of information are the Ecological Design Association and the Association for Environment Conscious Building.

Sources particularly of environmental information in the construction field include the Construction Industry Environmental Forum, the Council for Occupational Standards and Qualifications in Environmental Conservation and the Chartered Institution of Building Service Engineers. Architecturally related conservation techniques are covered by the Association for the Conservation of Energy and the Association for Environment Conscious Building.

Energy conservation

The National Energy Foundation monitors energy standards and controls energy conservation training. They operate a course for assessors in energy conservation. The standard course is available nationwide, and needs no specific qualifications. Among the institutions offering academic qualifications in energy conservation are Cranfield Institute of Technology, De Montfort University, Middlesex University and Nene College.

Sustainable power sources

A few courses are now available at a professional level in renewable energy: for example, Reading University's MSc course in Renewable Energy for BScEng students, covering biomass, solar power, wind power, micro-hydropower, heat engines and environmental pollution. Courses in applications of solar technology are available at (inter alia) the University of Reading, the Photovoltaics Application Centre at the

University of Northumbria, the University of Southampton, which has a Solar Energy Centre, and the University College of Wales, Cardiff Solar Energy Unit.

Sources of further advice include trade organisations and other organisations (for instance, the Centre for Alternative Technology) concerned with renewable power supplies, and the professional body, the Institute of Energy.

Engineering

Environmentally conscious engineering tends at present to be a supplementary skill to the core professional skills of electronic, chemical, mechanical and civil engineering. The Environmental Council's Directory of Environmental Courses gives guidance on environmental engineering. The Engineering Training Authority, which is part of the Engineering Council, is a good source of further information.

Environmental education

A number of UK institutions specialise in training for environmental education, at all levels from the elementary to adult and further education. There is a City and Guilds Further Education Teachers Certificate Course available, and further information sources include CREATE, the National Association for Environmental Education and the Council for Environmental Education.

Law and environmental consultancy

The Foundation for International Environmental Law and Development publishes lists of courses on environmental law, and of solicitors and barristers with an interest in environmental law. Information is also available from the Environmental Law Association.

Among the sources of information on environmental consultancy is the Royal Town Planning Institute.

Environmental Health Officers

Those in the established profession of environmental health continue to play a vital role in maintaining environmental standards. The qualification for an Environmental Health Officer consists of a combination of academic study and practical training, which can be combined with work as an Environmental Health Technician.

Environmentally oriented degree courses

CRAC and other directories of degree courses can provide information on the many degree courses in the UK which now include a specific environmental element. Among the subjects on offer are:

- Agriculture and Countryside Management
- Building Environment Engineering

- Environmental Chemistry
- Coastal Management and Conservation
- Conservation Biology
- Earth Science
- Ecological Economics
- Ecological Resource Management
- Environmental Analysis
- Environmental Systems Engineering
- Environmental Technology
- Fuel and Energy Engineering
- Global Futures
- Marine Environmental Science
- Rural Environment Studies
- Wildlife Conservation.

NVQs

Modular training for NVQ qualifications is the route to vocational training for many of those below (and up to) degree standard. Although there is no specific lead body establishing NVQ syllabuses in the overall field of the environment, there are NVQ lead bodies in a wide range of environment-oriented fields, including:

- Agriculture
- Conservation
- Engineering
- Forestry
- Health and Safety
- Insulation
- Nuclear Fuels
- Waste
- Water.

Qualifications vary from Level 1 NVQs suitable for those carrying out routine tasks, to Level 5 NVQs at the equivalent of degree level. Examples of NVQ courses in the environmental field include:

- Landfill Operations
- Managing Incineration Operations
- Regulating Waste Management
- Constructing and Restoring Landscapes

- Environmental Conservation
- Managing Trees and Woodlands
- Land Administration.

Obtaining a job in the environmental field

Although there is considerable demand for many types of professional with specific environmental knowledge and qualifications, it is not easy to obtain a job in other areas, particularly in the field of nature conservation. Often, experience as a volunteer is a necessary first step.

Among the locations of job advertisements are:

- *Nature*
- *ENDS (Environmental Data Services) News*
- *New Scientist*
- National newspapers, particularly *The Guardian*
- *The Environmental Post*, an independent magazine.

Short courses

As well as courses oriented to formal qualifications, there are many short courses of vocational interest in the environmental field. The Environment Council is among the organisations offering business-oriented short courses in issues such as:

- packaging waste regulations
- working with stakeholders
- environmental management systems
- biodiversity action plans.

The Centre for Alternative Technology offers residential courses in subjects such as:

- windpower (a practical course for those wishing to install wind energy systems)
- waterpower (a practical course for those wishing to install small-scale water turbines)
- woodland management and coppice crafts
- alternative building methods
- natural sewage systems.

As well as charitable bodies, a number of commercial organisations also run training courses.

Glossary of common pollutants

acrylonitrile

A volatile, flammable liquid which is used in various industrial processes including the production of acrylic and modacrylic fibres, resins and rubbers, and as a fumigant for stored tobacco. It can also be present in cigarettes. It has been used in the production of drink and food containers (for example, margarine tubs). It is carcinogenic in animals and there is limited evidence that it is carcinogenic in humans, and it has other adverse effects on human health. The WHO considers there to be no safe limit for exposure.

alkylphenols (APs) and alkylphenol ethoxylates (APEs)

APEs degrade to their parent APs in waste water treatment processes and in the environment. The APs tend to be more toxic and can affect hormonal activity. They were used in domestic detergents and for wool-washing in the textile industry, but they are now generally being phased out.

aluminium

This metal is implicated particularly in the development of Alzheimer's disease. Human exposure comes from foodstuffs (particularly bread and tea), from aluminium cans and cooking vessels, and in a small degree from water. Aluminium sulphate is used as a coagulant during water treatment, but is normally fully removed. (Accidental discharge of it into drinking water supplies caused a poisoning incident in Camelford in 1988.)

ammonia

Ammonia is produced particularly by livestock farming. It is an ingredient of acid rain.

arsenic

A common natural element which is found in many different compound forms. It is toxic and carcinogenic. It is emitted by metal smelting processes and by fuel combustion especially of low grade brown coal, and is an ingredient of some pesticides.

asbestos

Asbestos, a fibrous mineral, occurs naturally, with asbestos minerals widely spread throughout the earth's crust. Asbestos products were used widely in buildings and elsewhere, for their strength, their resistance to heat and their inertness and relative resistance to chemical attack, before they were proven to be human carcinogens. When the fibres are inhaled (the most important exposure route for humans) they can cause asbestosis. Man-made pollution sources include:

- mining and milling activities
- the manufacture of asbestos products
- construction activities
- the transport and use of products
- product disposal.

benzene

A volatile organic compound (VOC). A colourless clear liquid, it is found in crude oil and petrol, in some plastics, inks, tobacco smoke and detergents, and is also released during the burning of wood and organic material. Environmental pollution is derived mostly from vehicle emissions, and from evaporation losses during the handling, distribution and storage of petrol. It is a known human carcinogen particularly associated with leukaemia, and the WHO sets no safe limit for exposure. Benzene was implicated in the Perrier water quality scare in 1990.

bisphenol-A
Thought to have hormonal effects, this is used in the manufacturer of polycarbonate plastics and epoxy resins, in dentistry, in water pipe linings and steel food can coatings.

black smoke
This term is given to fine suspended particles found in the air as a result of the incomplete combustion of fossil fuels., particularly coal and diesel. It includes larger particles than those defined by PM_{10} (see 'particulates' below). So named because its air concentrations are measured by determining their soiling capacity. A major source is road freight transport. Domestic emissions are also significant although they have much declined.

1,3-butadiene
A hydrocarbon used in the production of synthetic rubber for tyres, and emitted in car exhausts. A suspected human carcinogen.

cadmium
A soft silver-white metal which occurs in nature together with zinc. Cadmium compounds are used in electroplating metals, as pigments or stabilisers in plastics, in alkaline batteries and in alloy form with other metals. It enters the environment from industrial sources, waste incineration (particularly of plastic packaging), zinc production and through volcanic action. It is carcinogenic in animals and there is limited evidence that it is carcinogenic in humans, and it may cause lung and kidney disease.

carbon dioxide
A gas which occurs naturally in volume in the atmosphere, its level is increased particularly by the combustion of fossil fuels and by changes in the amount of forest cover. It is a major contributor to global warming.

carbon disulfide
An industrial chemical used in producing viscose rayon fibres and found in releases from coal gasification plants, it is toxic but not a known carcinogen.

carbon monoxide
A colourless, odourless gas produced by the incomplete combustion of carbon, and by some industrial and biological processes. Inhaling it causes hypoxia (that is, it interferes with the absorption of oxygen) which at low levels slows reflexes, impairs thinking, causes drowsiness, affects fertility and general levels of health, and at higher levels leads to death. About 100 deaths per year are caused in the UK by carbon monoxide release from faulty gas appliances. It contributes to the build-up of low-level ozone and is an ingredient of acid rain.

carbon tetrachloride
A toxic liquid which has been used as an industrial solvent and in fire extinguishers. It was used in the manufacturing process for CFCs and its presence in the atmosphere has been decreasing since their phasing-out.

cement and concrete

These corrosive alkaline substances can cause serious pollution problems in watercourses. Concrete mixing facilities should be sited to avoid the risk of pollution, and if cement or wet concrete are used in or close to any watercourse, the process must be carefully controlled to minimise the risk of any material entering the water.

CFCs – see chlorofluorocarbons

chlorine

Chlorine is widely used as a water supply disinfectant. It is effective at killing pathogens but many of the by-products it creates, chlorinated organic compounds or organochlorides (including dioxins and PCBs, and pesticides such as aldrin), have been proved to be carcinogenic in animals. Opinions vary as to whether the benefits of chlorination outweigh the risks.

chlorofluorocarbons (CFCs)

These compounds of carbon, fluorine and chlorine were widely used in aerosols and as refrigerants, solvents and cleaning fluids. Chemically inert, they have atmospheric lifetimes of over 50 years. They are significant greenhouse gases and have now largely been replaced by HFCs and HCFCs.

chromium

This grey hard metal, found widely in nature, is used in manufacturing chromic acid, in pigments, leather tanning and corrosion control (for example, as a coating for steel). It can also be found in cigarette tobacco. It enters the air through mining and production processes and by the wind erosion of shales, clay and other kinds of soil. Hexavalent chromium is carcinogenic and the WHO sets no safe level for exposure to it.

coliforms

This group of bacteria, which may be faecal or environmental in origin, are used as indicators in water of pollution especially by sewage, and thus of the possible presence of disease-causing organisms.

1,2-dichloroethane (DCE)

An artificially produced organic substance, a flammable colourless liquid used particularly in the manufacture of vinyl chloride, this becomes a pollutant through industrial use and particularly by poor disposal of 'EDC tars', vinyl chloride waste products. It is toxic at high concentrations but not thought to be a health hazard at normal exposure levels.

dichloromethane (DCM)

An organic substance, this clear non-flammable liquid is used for example as a paint remover, a polyurethane foam blowing agent, a solvent, and as a replacement for fluorocarbon propellants in aerosols. It is proven to be carcinogenic in animals, but not a fully proven human carcinogen.

dioxins

This group of 210 closely related organochlorides are highly toxic carcinogens. They also have hormonal effects, reduce immune system capacity, and can affect foetal development. Their effects are apparent at very low doses, and they are bioaccumulative: they persist in the body and in the environment. Dioxins are emitted in the production of the disinfectant hexachlorophene, and from incinerators that burn compounds containing chlorine, such as plastics and bleached paper. Research has indicated high levels in mothers' milk in the vicinity of incineration plants.

fluoride

This naturally occurring element is added to 10% of British drinking water, primarily because it is thought to reduce tooth decay in children. It is toxic when taken in quantity, and the fluoridation of water is fiercely opposed in some quarters, particularly by the National Pure Water Association.

formaldehyde

This colourless gas has a pungent odour at room temperature. It has numerous uses in household goods and building materials, including insulating materials, chipboard and plywood, fabrics and carpet backings, UF cavity wall foam, foam fillings in furniture, veneers and wood lacquers, household cleaners, synthetic fibres, adhesives, paints, PVC and other plastic floorcoverings. It is also found in cigarette smoke. Formaldehyde can be an irritant at relatively low levels of exposure, and is carcinogenic in animals, although there is no definite evidence that it is carcinogenic in humans.

halocarbons

This is the general term for chemicals containing carbon and one or more halogen (fluorine, chlorine or bromine) atoms. Some of them are ozone-depleting substances.

hydrobromofluorocarbons (HBFCs)

A general term for organic compounds of hydrogen, bromine, fluorine and carbon, ozone-depleting substances which are now being phased out of use.

hydrocarbons

A general term for organic compounds of carbon and hydrogen, the basic compounds in fossil fuels. See also VOCs, and the two specific hydrocarbons benzene and 1,3-butadiene.

hydrochlorofluorocarbons (HCFCs)

A general term for organic compounds of carbon, hydrogen, chlorine and fluorine. Although they are greenhouse and ozone-destroying gases, they have shorter lifetimes in the atmosphere than CFCs and have been used as replacements for them.

hydrofluorocarbons (HFCs)

These greenhouse gases do not deplete the ozone layer, and are used as a replacement for CFCs and HCFCs in aerosols.

hydrogen sulphide

This colourless gas, which is soluble in water, has a noxious smell. It is emitted naturally from sulphur springs and lakes and saline marshes, and from various industrial processes including coke production, viscose rayon production, some waste-water treatments, some wood pulp production processes, oil refining and tanning. An irritant at low levels, it is toxic at high levels.

iron

High levels of iron in water (from natural or man-made sources) cause staining of laundry and fitments.

lead

This naturally occurring grey-bluish soft metal enters the atmosphere mostly (an estimated 90% of total emissions) as an emission from motor vehicles using fuels with alkyl lead additives. Other significant sources of human exposure are lead water pipes (serving an estimated 8.9 million homes in England and Wales) and paints containing lead – both now not produced, but still found particularly in association with older properties – and to a lesser extent, lead manufacturing processes and the incineration of plastic packaging materials.

manganese

This abundant natural element is used in metallurgical processes, as a deoxidising and desulphurising additive and an alloying component. Much human intake is via food. It is an essential element for human health, but toxic at high concentrations. At the levels found (in water) in the UK it can stain laundry and fitments but is not normally a health hazard.

mercury

Mercury is an element produced by mining and smelting cinnabar ore. It is used in chloralkali plants, in paints, in electrical switching equipment and batteries, in measuring and control equipment, in lamps, as a fungicide and (formerly) to make tooth fillings. Atmospheric pollution is also caused by burning fossil fuels, by smelting various metals, by cement manufacture and waste disposal. Mercury is highly toxic and affects the nervous system, but it is not a known carcinogen. Methyl mercury accumulated by fish can enter the human food chain. Ingestion is dangerous, but atmospheric levels of mercury in the UK are normally not a hazard to human health.

methane

A highly potent greenhouse gas, up to 60 times more potent than carbon dioxide, and contributing approximately 16% to global warming. Major sources of emissions to the atmosphere are landfill sites, agricultural beasts and coal mining. Attempts are now being made to reduce the methane emissions from landfill by either using the gas as an energy source, or flaring, which converts it to carbon dioxide.

methyl bromide

This minor greenhouse gas is used mostly as a soil disinfectant in agriculture and as a disinfectant for agricultural products, especially strawberry and tomato crops.

methyl chloride

A significant greenhouse gas, released naturally from oceans and by human activity via the use of biomass fuels.

methyl chloroform

This was used in industry as a degreasing solvent, and acts as a major stratospheric carrier of chlorine, and thus a contributor to the destruction of the ozone layer. It has been phased out under international agreements.

nickel

This naturally occurring silvery-white hard metal is used in producing steel and other alloys, in storage batteries, electronic components, electroplating, coinage, as a catalyst, and in ceramics. Nickel emissions come mostly from burning residual and fuel oils, from mining and refining, and from municipal waste incineration. It is a known carcinogen.

nitrates

These generally long-lived compounds are widely used as agricultural fertilisers. Run-off and leaching from agricultural land leads to raised nitrate levels in fresh and marine waters. Some nitrate pollution also derives from treated sewage discharges. High levels of nitrates in marine or coastal waters can lead in some weather conditions to eutrophication, or excessive algal growth.

nitrogen dioxide and nitrogen oxide

Nitrogen oxide is oxidised in the atmosphere to the more toxic nitrogen dioxide (NO_2), which is also produced naturally by bacterial and volcanic action and by lightning. Its main man-made emission sources are power stations and road transport. There is also significant human exposure from cooking on unvented gas stoves and cigarette smoking. Nitrogen dioxide contributes to the formation of ground-level ozone, can cause respiratory illness and reduced lung function, and makes airways more sensitive to allergens such as the house dust mite, but is not regarded as a very serious health hazard. It can readily be converted to nitric acid, one of the main ingredients of acid rain.

nitrous oxide

Nitrous oxide (N_2O) is a long-lived greenhouse gas, about 270 times more powerful than carbon dioxide over a 100-year time horizon. In total it contributes about 6% to global warming. It is emitted mainly from nylon and nitric acid production plants, but also from power stations, transport and agriculture.

organochlorides

Organochloride pesticides include several that appear as List I (predominantly banned) substances, such as aldrin, lindane, dieldrin and DDT. See also under 'chlorine'.

organophosphates

Organophosphates are used in fertilisers. They are the major contributor to eutrophication, or excessive algal growth, in inland waters. See also 'phosphorus'.

ozone

A form of oxygen, occurring in the atmosphere where it is a pollutant at low levels but performs useful functions in the stratosphere. Discussed in depth in Chapters 4 and 6.

PAHs – see polynuclear aromatic hydrocarbons

particulates

A general term for small particles of matter (including dusts, acid and other materials) that are found suspended in the air. For measuring pollution the general reference is to $PM_{10,}$ that is, particles with a diameter less than 10 µm (0.01 mm). Most particulate matter is emitted by road traffic, and particularly by diesel-powered vehicles, by other combustion sources, and by industrial processes. ('Black smoke' (q.v.) is another name for this matter.) Natural sources include sea salt spray and suspended soil dust, and some particulate matter is created by chemical reactions in the air.

PCBs – see polychlorinated biphenyls

perfluorocarbons (PFCs)

A range of organic compounds containing fluorine and carbon, derived from various industrial uses, and highly potent greenhouse gases with long lifetimes.

PFCs – see perfluorocarbons

phosphorus

This element is used particularly in fertilisers, and is also found in outputs from sewage treatment works. It was used in washing powders and liquids, and the development of phosphate-free brands has helped to reduce the levels found in freshwaters in the UK. In excess, this nutrient can lead in particular weather conditions to eutrophication (excessive algal growth) in fresh waters, and to toxic algal blooms.

phthalates

These organic substances are used as plasticisers and in paints, inks and adhesives. Little is known about their environmental effects but there is some evidence that they can cause reproductive abnormalities in laboratory animals. Human exposure may be significant (although it has not been adequately measured) by leaching out from PVC items including soft toys which infants may suck.

PM_{10} – see particulates

polychlorinated biphenyls (PCBs)

These highly biologically active chemicals, which were used mostly used as plasticisers and to enhance flame retardance and insulating qualities, have not been manufactured or used in production in the UK since 1977, although some electrical equipment containing them is still being phased out of use. PCBs tend to persist in the atmosphere, and this leads to residues in the environment. They can accumulate in organisms and be passed along food chains, bringing about harmful side-effects. Contamination sources include spills as a result of improper disposal or accidents with electrical equipment, volatilisation from landfill disposal sites, incomplete incineration processes and sewage sludge.

polynuclear aromatic hydrocarbons (PAHs)

This large group of organic compounds is formed mostly by the incomplete combustion of organic materials – that is, by the use of biomass fuels, by open fires, by refuse burning, in cigarette smoke, and in car exhausts. In the past, chimney sweeps and tar workers who were heavily exposed to PAHs developed skin cancer, and they are also associated with lung cancer in coke oven workers. As some PAHs are proven human carcinogens there is no safe level for their presence in the environment.

POPs

An abbreviation for persistent organic pollutants, a term which includes substances such as DDT and PCBs.

radon

This radioactive noble gas, part of the radioactive decay chain of uranium-238, occurs naturally in parts of England (particularly in the West Country) and Wales. There is no significant man-made exposure, but the natural exposure is sufficiently high in some areas to cause a risk particularly of lung cancer, which is much higher in smokers. The fovernment issues maps showing the distribution of radon in the UK.

silt

The generic name for small particles of soil etcetera found in waters.

styrene

This man-made compound is used in the manufacture of polymers, copolymers and reinforced plastics especially polystyrene. It enters the atmosphere in emissions from the petroleum industry and from vehicles. Styrene monomer also has a tendency to migrate from polystyrene packaging to foodstuffs in contact with them, and ingestion with food probably accounts for the greatest degree of human exposure. It is thought to have adverse health effects but there is limited data available, and it is classified as Group 3 (insufficient evidence) as a possible carcinogen.

sulphur dioxide

A colourless gas with a choking smell, readily converted to sulphuric acid, this is emitted when fuels containing sulphur are burned and from natural sources such as sulphur springs. It is a major ingredient of acid rain, and can damage plants.

sulphur hexafluoride

A chemical derived from a variety of industrial uses, and a powerful greenhouse gas, present in the atmosphere in small quantities but with a long lifetime. Emissions are likely to grow in the near future, which will increase concern about its impact.

toluene

The most prevalent hydrocarbon in the troposphere, toluene is used in paints, inks, thinners, adhesives and cosmetic products, and is emitted from petroleum refining, coke-oven operation and in the production of other chemicals. At high concentrations it has irritative and health effects, but at present concentrations it is not thought to pose a major health risk.

TOMPs

Acronym for toxic organic micropollutants: applies to a range of substances including PAHs and PCBs.

tributyl tin (TBT)

Used as an antifouling agent on boats, TBT is now banned on small boats and its continued use on larger vessels is a cause of concern. It can enter the environment when ships are being cleaned and repainted, and through direct leaching from ship hulls. It is implicated in endocrine changes which damage shellfish.

trichloroethylene (TCE)

This powerful solvent is used in degreasing fabricated metal parts, in industrial dry-cleaning, printing, paint production, textile printing, household adhesives, spot removers and carpet cleaners. Evaporation in use is the main cause of emission to the environment. It is a Group 3 (impact not classifiable) carcinogen, and is not thought to have serious health effects at current environmental exposure levels.

vanadium

This metal is used mostly in alloy steel. It enters the air from natural sources, from metallurgical works, and from the burning of crude or residual oil and coal. It is an acute and chronic poison at high concentrations, but although there is a risk to workers dealing with vanadium there is no significant risk at normal environmental levels.

vinyl chloride (VC)

This gas reacts in the atmosphere to form formaldehyde, carbon monoxide, hydrochloric acid and formic acid. Its main sources are vinyl chloride production plants, PVC polymerisation facilities and product fabrication plants. It is a known human carcinogen.

volatile organic compounds (VOCs)

The generic term for a large number of compounds including hydrocarbons and oxygenated and halogenated organics. They include methane, a powerful greenhouse gas (although some definitions of VOCs for monitoring purposes treat methane separately) and other compounds which react to form tropospheric ozone. VOCs are emitted particularly by car exhausts, the evaporation of motor spirits and organic solvents used in manufacturing and applying industrial paints, and gas leakage from the natural gas distribution network. Their detailed role in atmospheric chemistry is not fully understood, but they are regarded as a pollutant.

Organisations and contact details

European Commission

200 rue de la Loi, 1049 Brussels, Belgium
for general information on EC policies:
http://europa.eu.int/

Directorate General XI (Environment, Civil Protection and Nuclear Safety)

200 rue de la Loi, 1049 Brussels, Belgium
Tel. (32) 2 299 1111
Fax (32) 2 295 0122

European Parliament Directorate General for Research

Division for Social Affairs and Employment, the Environment, Public Health and Consumer Protection
L-2929 Luxembourg
Fax (352) 4300 7720
or: 97-113 rue Belliard
B-1047 Brussels
Fax (32) 2 284 4955

European Environment Agency

Kongens Nytorv 6, DK-1050 Copenhagen K, Denmark
Tel. (45) 33 367100
Fax (45) 33 367199
http://www.eea.eu.int

Government Departments and Agencies

Ministry of Agriculture, Fisheries and Food (MAFF)

Whitehall Place, London SW1A 2HH
Tel. 020 7238 6000; Helpline 0645 335577
Fax 020 7270 8151
http://www.maff.gov.uk
Among MAFF's environmental responsibilities are:

- policies on agriculture, horticulture and fisheries in England
- protection and enhancement of the countryside and the marine environment
- flood defence and other rural issues
- registration of pesticides.
- food safety.

Executive Agencies of MAFF:

Central Science Laboratory

Sand Hutton, York YO41 1LZ
Tel. 01904 462000
Fax 01904 462111
http://www.csl.gov.uk
Technical support and policy advice on the protection and quality of the food supply and related environmental issues.

Centre for Environment, Fisheries and Aquacultural Science

Pakefield Road, Lowestoft, Suffolk NR33 0HT
Tel. 01502 562244
Fax 01502 513865
http://www.cefas.co.uk
Established April 1997, provides research and consultancy services in fisheries science and management, aquaculture, health and hygiene, environmental impact assessment and environmental quality assessment. Main laboratory in Lowestoft and three smaller specialist laboratories in Weymouth, Burnham-on-Crouch and Conwy, plus a small unit in Whitehaven.

Farming and Rural Conservation Agency

Nobel House, 17 Smith Square, London SW1P 3JR
Tel. 020 7238 5432
Fax 020 7238 5588
http://www.maff.gov.uk/aboutmaff/agency/frca
Established April 1997, and responsible jointly to MAFF and the Welsh Office. Provides professional and scientific advice on policy issues relating to agriculture and the environment, and professional services for the administration

of agri-environmental schemes. Also enforces certain aspects of the Dairy Hygiene Regulations.

Pesticides Safety Directorate

Mallard House, King's Pool,
3 Peasholme Green, York YO1 2PX
Information section: Tel. 01904 455755
Fax 01904 455711
Responsible for the evaluation and approval of pesticides and the development of policies relating to them, in order to protect consumers, users and the environment.

Department of the Environment, Transport and the Regions (DETR)

Eland House, Bressenden Place,
London SW1E 5DU
Tel. 020 7890 3000
http://www.detr.gov.uk/
http://www.open.gov.uk/detr

Environment Protection section:
Ashdown House, 123 Victoria Street,
London SW1E 6DE
Tel. 020 7890 6497
Air quality freephone: 0800 556677
website: detr/envir/aq/aqinfo.hrm

Waste Policy Division: Tel. 020 7890 6432 (Regulations administered by Institute of Environmental Awareness, Tel. 01522 540069)

Biotechnology unit: Tel. 020 7890 5275/77;
Fax 020 7944 5259
Formed in June 1997 by merging the Department of the Environment and the Department of Transport. Environmentally related responsibilities include:

- *regional development agencies and regeneration*
- *housing, construction, planning and countryside affairs*
- *environmental protection and water*
- *land, sea and air transport, including transport planning*
- *HM Coastguard and marine pollution.*

Sponsoring department for the Health & Safety Executive and the Health & Safety Commission.

Executive Agencies of the DETR:

Drinking Water Inspectorate

Floor 2/A2, Ashdown House,
123 Victoria Street, London SW1E 6DE
Tel. 020 7890 5956
Fax 020 7944 5969
http://www.dwi.detr.gov.uk
Oversees the supply of water by water companies.

Maritime and Coastguard Agency

Spring Place, 105 Commercial Road,
Southampton SO15 1EG
Tel. 01703 329100
Fax 02380 329 298
http://www.coastguard.gov.uk
Protection of life of seafarers and coastal users, and minimising marine pollution. Formed 1998 by merging the Coastguard Agency and the Marine Safety Agency.

Planning Inspectorate

Tollgate House, Houlton Street,
Bristol BS2 9DJ
Tel. 0117 987 8927
Fax 0117 987 6219
http://www.open.gov.uk/pi/pihome.htm
Joint Executive Agency of the DETR and the Welsh Office, with responsibilities including casework involving planning, housing, roads, environmental and related legislation.

Northern Ireland Assembly

Department of Agriculture for Northern Ireland

Dundonald House, Upper
Newtownards Road, Belfast BT4 3SB
Tel. 01232 520100
Fax 01232 524181
http://www.nics.gov.uk/dani

Executive Agency of the Department of Agriculture for Northern Ireland:

Rivers Agency

4 Hospital Road, Belfast BT8 8JP
Tel. 01232 253355
Fax 0289 025 3455

Department of the Environment for Northern Ireland

Clarence Court, 10-18 Adelaide Street,
Belfast BT2 8GB
Tel. 01232 540540
Fax 0289 054 0021
http://www.nics.gov.uk.doe

Executive Agency of the Department of the Environment for Northern Ireland:

Environment and Heritage Service

Commonwealth House, 35 Castle Street,
Belfast BT1 1GH
Tel. 01232 251477
Fax 02890 546660
http://www.nics.gov.uk/ehs
Concerned with the control of pollution, conservation of the natural environment and protection of the built heritage.

Scottish Executive

St Andrew's House, Regent Road,
Edinburgh EH1 3DG
Tel. 0131 556 8400

Scotland Office – London:
Dover House, Whitehall,
London SW1A 2AU
Tel. 020 7270 8754
Fax 020 7270 6812

Scotland Office – Edinburgh:
Melville Crescent, Edinburgh EH3 7HW
Tel. 0131 244 9010
Fax 0131 244 9028

Scottish Executive Rural Affairs Department

Pentland House, 47 Robb's Loan,
Edinburgh EH14 1TY
Tel. 0131 244 6022
Fax 0131 244 6116
http://www.scotland.gov.uk/who/dept_rural.asp

Scottish Agricultural Science Agency

East Craig, Edinburgh EH12 8NJ
Various functions concerned with agricultural and horticultural crops and the environment.

Scottish Fisheries Protection Agency

Pentland House, 47 Robb's Loan,
Edinburgh EH14 1TY
Tel. 0131 556 8400
Enforces fisheries law and regulations in Scottish waters and ports.

Historic Scotland

Longmore House, Salisbury Place,
Edinburgh EH9 1SH
Tel. 0131 668 8600
Fax 0131 668 8789
http://www.historic-scotland.gov.uk
Functions to protect and promote understanding and enjoyment of Scotland's historic monuments, buildings and lands.

Department of Trade and Industry

1 Victoria Street, London SW1H 0ET
Tel. 020 7215 5000
Fax 020 7222 0219
http://www.dti.gov.uk/
Environmentally-related functions include national policies in relation to energy and the development of new sources of energy.

National Assembly for Wales

Wales Office, Gwydyr House,
Whitehall, London SW1A 2ER
Tel. 020 7270 3000
http://www.ossw.wales.gov.uk/

Crown Building, Cathays Park,
Cardiff CF10 3NQ
Tel. 01222 825111
Fax 02920 825070
http://www.wales.gov.uk/

Executive Agency of the National Assembly for Wales:

CADW: Welsh Historic Monuments

Crown Building, Cathays Park, Cardiff CF10 3NQ
Tel. 02920 500200
Fax 02920 826375
Concerned with the built heritage of Wales.

Government Offices of the Regions

Established 1994, intended to promote a coherent approach to sustainable economic development and regeneration on a regional basis.

Regional Co-ordination

Eland House, Bressenden Place,
London SW1E 5DU
Tel. 020 7890 5157

Eastern

Victory House, Vision Park, Chivers Way,
Histon, Cambs CB4 9ZR
Tel. 01223 202065

East Midlands

The Belgrave Centre, Stanley Place,
Talbot Street, Nottingham NG1 5GG
Tel. 0115 971 2755

London

10th Floor, Riverwalk House,
157-161 Millbank, London SW1P 4RR
Tel. 020 7217 3456

Merseyside

Cunard Building, Pier Head,
Liverpool L3 9TN
Tel. 0151 224 6300

North-East

Room 404, Stangate House, 2 Groat Market,
Newcastle upon Tyne NE1 4TD
Tel. 0191 201 3300

North-West

Sunley Tower, Piccadilly Plaza,
Manchester M1 4BE
Tel. 0161 952 4000

South-East

2nd Floor, Bridge House,
1 Walnut Tree Close, Guildford,
Surrey GU1 4GA
Tel. 01483 882481

South-West

4th Floor, The Pithay, Bristol BS1 2PB
Tel. 0117 900 1708

West Midlands

6th Floor, 77 Paradise Circus, Queensway,
Birmingham B1 2DT
Tel. 0121 212 5000

Yorkshire and Humberside

PO Box 213, City House, New Station
Street, Leeds LS1 4US
Tel. 0113 280 0600

DTI/DETR Environmental and Energy Efficiency Technology Best Practice Programme

Helpline: 0800 585794
Fax 01235 463804
http://www.etsu.com/etbpp/
Managed by ETSU, provides free confidential advice, and free site visits for small companies.

Green Business Clubs (sponsored by the DTI/DETR)

Floor 6, Ashdown House,
123 Victoria Street, London SW1E 6DE
Tel. 020 7890 6568
Fax 020 7890 6559

Joint Environmental Markets Unit (sponsored by the DTI/ DETR)

(403 Red), 151 Buckingham Palace Road,
London SW1W 9SS
Tel. 020 7215 1055
Fax 020 7215 1089
http://www.dti.gov.uk/jemu
Encourages and supports British industries in the environment sector.

Other Public Bodies

Advisory Committee on Business and the Environment

Zone 6/E9, Ashdown House,
123 Victoria Street, London SW1E 6DE
Tel. 020 7890 6566
Fax 020 7944 6559
Committee of businessmen who make recommendations to government.

UK Atomic Energy Authority

Harwell Business Centre, Didcot,
Oxon OX11 0QJ
Tel. 01235 820220
Fax 01235 432916
http://www.ukaea.org.uk
Responsibilities include the safe management and decommissioning of nuclear plant.

British Waterways

Willow Grange, Church Road, Watford,
Herts W017 4QA
Tel. 01923 226422
Fax 01923 201400
http://www.british-waterways.org.uk
Navigation authority for over 3,000 km of canals and rivers in England, Scotland and Wales. Responsible to the Secretary of State for Environment, Transport and the Regions. Responsibilities include care of wildlife and the waterway environment.

Broads Authority

Thomas Harvey House, 18 Colegate,
Norwich NR3 1BQ
Tel. 01603 610734
Fax 01603 765710
Statutory authority set up under the Norfolk and Suffolk Broads Act 1988. Functions include conserving and enhancing the natural beauty of the Broads.

Coal Authority

200 Lichfield Lane, Mansfield,
Notts NG18 4RG
Tel. 01623 427162
Fax 01623 621955
http://www.coal.gov.uk
Manages British coal resources, including ownership of unworked coal, licensing coal mining operations and dealing with surface hazards such as abandoned mineshafts.

Countryside Agency

John Dower House, Crescent Place,
Cheltenham, Glos GL50 3RA
Tel. 01242 521381
Fax 01242 584270
http://www.countryside.gov.uk
Set up in 1968, an independent agency which promotes the conservation and enhancement of landscape beauty in England.

Countryside Council for Wales/Cyngor Cefn Gwlad Cymru

Plas Penrhon, Fford Penrhos, Bangor LL57 2LQ
Tel. 01248 385500
Fax 01248 355782
http://www.ccw.gov.uk
Statutory adviser on wildlife, countryside and maritime conservation matters in Wales, and executive authority for the conservation of habitats and wildlife.

Energy Technology Support Unit (ETSU)

159 Harwell, Didcot, Oxon OX11 0RA
Tel. 01235 433517
Fax 01235 432923
http://www.etsu.com/eebpp/home/htm
DTI-funded unit co-ordinating the development of renewable energy.

English Heritage

23 Savile Row, London W1S 2ET
Tel. 020 7973 3000
Fax 020 7973 3001
http://www.english-heritage.org.uk
Responsibilities concerning the preservation and enjoyment of ancient monuments, historic buildings and conservation areas.

English Nature

Northminster House, Northminster Road, Peterborough PE1 1UA
Tel. 01733 455000
Fax 01733 5455375
http://www.english-nature.org.uk
Established 1991 and responsible for advising the government on nature conservation in England. Promotes the conservation of England's wildlife and natural features. Selects, establishes and manages National Nature Reserves and identifies and notifies Sites of Special Scientific Interest. Provides advice and information about nature conservation, and supports and conducts research.

English Partnerships

16-18 Old Queen Street, London SW1H 9HP
Tel. 020 7976 7070
Fax 120 7976 7740
http://www.englishpartnership.co.uk
Sponsored by the DETR, and in operation since 1994, with the function of regenerating derelict, vacant and under-used land and buildings in England.

Environment Agency

Head office: Rio House, Aztec West, Almondsbury, Bristol BS32 4UD
Tel. 01454 624 400
Fax 01454 624 409
http://www.environment-agency.gov.uk
General enquiry line: 0645 333 111 (connects to nearest local office)
Emergency hotline: 0800 80 70 60
Floodline: 0845 988 1188
For information on disposal of waste oil: 0800 663366
Producer Responsibility Regulation Unit: Fifth Floor, 10 Albert Embankment, London SE1 7SP
Sponsored by the DETR, MAFF and the Welsh Office, and responsible for:

- pollution prevention and control in England and Wales
- waste regulation
- the management and use of water resources, including flood defences and fisheries.

Forestry Commission

231 Corstorphine Road, Edinburgh EH12 7AT
Tel. 0131 334 0303
Fax 0131 334 3047
http://www.forestry.gov.uk
The government department responsible for forestry policy.

Health and Safety Commission

Rose Court, 2 Southwark Bridge, London SE1 9HS
Tel. 020 7717 6000
Fax 020 7717 6717
http://www.open.gov.uk/hse/hsehome
Responsible for the reform of health and safety law, and generally the protection of people at work and the public from hazards arising from industrial and commercial activity.

Health and Safety Executive

Rose Court, 2 Southwark Bridge, London SE1 9HS
Tel. 020 7717 6000
Fax 020 7717 6717
http://www.open.gov.uk/hse/hsehome
Responsible for enforcing health and safety regulations in most industrial premises, licensing authority for nuclear installations, reporting officer on the severity of nuclear incidents.

Pesticides Registration Section: Magdalen House, Room 123, Trinity Road, Bootle L20 3QZ
Tel. 0151 951 3535
Fax 0151 951 3317

Local Agenda 21

Improvement and Development Agency, Leyden House, 76-86 Turnmill Street, London EC1M 5QU

Tel. 020 7296 6600
Fax 020 7296 6635
http://www.lgmb.gov.uk
For information on local initiatives deriving from the Rio Conference.

National Radiological Protection Board

Chilton, Didcot, Oxon OX11 ORQ
Tel. 01235 831600
Fax 01235 833891
http:www.nrpb.org.uk
Independent statutory body concerned with limiting human exposure to radiation from certain sources and electromagnetic fields, and related issues.

Joint Nature Conservation Committee

Monkstone House, City Road,
Peterborough PE1 1JY
Tel. 01733 562626
Fax 01733 555948
http://www.jncc.gov.uk
Established under the Environmental Protection Act 1990, to research and advise the government and others on UK and international nature conservation issues. Also hosts the National Biodiversity Network.

Office of Water Services (Ofwat)

Centre City Tower, 7 Hill Street,
Birmingham B5 4UA
Tel. 0121 625 1300
Fax 0121 625 1400
http://www.open.gov.uk/ofwat
Independent economic regulator of the water and sewerage companies in England and Wales, with a particular role in protecting the interests of water consumers.

Rural Development Commission

141 Castle Street, Salisbury, Wilts SP1 3TP
Tel. 01722 336255
Fax 01722 332769
http://www.argonet.co.uk/rdc
Government agency providing advice on the social and economic well-being of countryside dwellers.

Scottish Environment Protection Agency

Erskine Court, The Castle Business Park,
Stirling FK9 4TR
Tel. 01786 457700
Fax 01786 446885
http://www.sepa.org.uk
From 1996 the body responsible for various pollution and water control functions in Scotland, analogous to the powers of the Environment Agency in England and Wales.

Scottish Natural Heritage

12 Hope Terrace, Edinburgh EH9 2AS
Tel. 0131 447 4784
Fax 0131 446 2279
http://www.snh.org.uk
Concerned with nature conservation and related matters in Scotland.

Sustainable Development, British Government Panel on

5th Floor, Romney House, Turtan Street,
London SW1P 3RA
Tel. 020 7890 4962
Fax 020 7890 4959

UK Ecolabelling Board

7th Floor, Eastbury House,
30-34 Albert Embankment,
London SE1 7TL
Tel. 020 7820 1199
Fax 020 7820 1104
http://www.ecosite.co.uk/ecolabel-uk
Concerned with administration of the UK ecolabelling scheme.

Research Councils and Organisations

Atmospheric Chemistry Modelling Support Unit

University Chemical Laboratory,
University of Cambridge, Lensfield Road,
Cambridge CB2 1EP
Tel. 01223 336473

Atmospheric Research and Information Centre

Dept. of Environmental and Geographical Sciences, Manchester Metropolitan University, Chester Street, Manchester M1 5GD
Tel. 0161 247 1592/3
Fax 0161 247 6332
http://www.doc.mmu/ac/uk/aric/arichome.html
National centre for public information on air quality and acid rain.

BIBRA International

Woodmansterne Road, Carshalton, Surrey SM5 4DS
Tel. 020 8652 1000
Fax 020 8661 7029
http://www.bibra.co.uk
Involved in the assessment of toxicity of food and chemicals to humans.

Biotechnology and Biological Sciences Research Council (BBSRC)

Polaris House, North Star Avenue, Swindon SN2 1UH
Tel. 01793 413200
Fax 01793 413201
http://www.bbsrc.ac.uk
Promotes and supports research, training, knowledge and understanding in the field of biotechnology and biological sciences.

Building Research Establishment

Bucknalls Lane, Garston, Watford, Herts WD2 7JR
Tel. 01923 664206 or 01923 446767
Fax 01923 664097
http://www.bre.co.uk/

BRECSU (Building Research Energy Conservation Support Unit)

Tel. 01923 664258
Fax 01923 664787

Cleaner Electronics Research

Brunel University, Runnymede, Coopers Hill Lane, Egham, Surrey TW20 0JZ
Tel. 01784 431341
Fax 01784 472879
http://www.brunel.ac.uk
Researches ways of minimising environmental aspects of consumer electronics, such as circuit boards, including their disposal.

Climatic Research Unit

School of Environmental Sciences, University of East Anglia, Norwich NR4 TJ
Tel. 01603 592088
Fax 01603 507784
http://www.cru.uea.ac.uk

Design for the Environment Research Group

Manchester Metropolitan University, Dept of Mechanical Engineering, Design and Manufacture, John Dalton Building, Chester Street, Manchester M1 5GD
Tel. 0161 247 6248
Fax 0161 247 6326

Energy and Environment Research Unit (EERU)

Faculty of Technology, Open University, Walton Hall, Milton Keynes MK7 6AA
Tel. 01908 653335
Fax 01908 653744
Researches and encourages knowledge and education about energy use and its environmental impact.

Environmental Change Unit (ECU) Institute

5 South Parks Road, Oxford OX1 3UB
Tel. 01865 281180
Fax 01865 281202
http://www.ecu.ox.ac.uk
Research into causes of environmental damage such as domestic energy impact and land degradation and erosion.

Environmental Impact Assessment (EIA) Centre

Dept. of Planning & Landscape, University of Manchester, Oxford Road, Manchester M13 9PL
Tel. 0161 275 6873
Fax 0161 275 6893
http://www.art.man.ac.uk/eia
Also a membership association.

Environmental Strategy, Centre for

University of Surrey, Guildford GU2 7XH
Tel. 01483 259271
Fax 01483 876671
http://www.surrey.ac.uk/ces
Multidisciplinary research centre to examine environmental issues and provide education and training.

Environmental Systems Science Centre

Department of Geography, Reading University, Whiteknights, Reading RG6 2AB
Tel. 01189 318741

Institute of Food Research

Norwich Research Park, Colney, Norwich NR4 7UA
Earley Gate, Whiteknights Road, Reading RG6 6BZ
Tel. 01603 255000
Fax 01603 507723
http://www.ifrn.bbsrc.ac.uk.

Centre for Global Atmospheric Modelling

Department of Meteorology, University of Reading, PO Box 243, Earley Gate, Reading RG6 6BB
Tel. 0118 931 8315

ESRG Global Environmental Change Programme

This programme ended in June 2000, to find out any additional information go to the internet site: www.gecko.ac.uk, or alternatively telephone 01273 678935

Institute of Grassland and Environmental Research

Plas Gogerddan, Aberystwyth, Ceredigion SY23 3EB
Tel. 01970 828255
Fax 01970 828357

Hadley Centre for Climate Prediction and Research

Met Office, London Road, Bracknell, Berks RG12 2SY
Tel. 01344 856653
Fax 01344 854898
http://www.meto.gov.uk

Centre for Human Ecology

12 Roseneath Place, Edinburgh, EH9 1JB
Tel/Fax 0131 624 1972
http://www.clan.com/environment/che
Concerned with ecological ethics, environmental policy, Agenda 21 and sustainable development.

Institute of Hydrology

Maclean Building, Crowmarsh Gifford, Wallingford, Oxon OX20 8BB
Tel. 01491 838800
Fax 01491 692424

Macaulay Land Use Research Institute

Craigiebuckler, Aberdeen AB15 8QH
Tel. 01224 318611
Fax 01224 311556

Natural Environment Research Council

Polaris House, North Star Avenue, Swindon SN2 1EU
Tel. 01793 411500
Fax 01793 411501
http://www.nerc.ac.uk
Gives planning, support and encouragement to research in sciences relating to the natural environment and its resources.

Centre on Science, Technology, Energy and Environment Policy

SPRU, Mantell Building, University of Sussex, Falmer, Brighton BN1 9RF
Tel. 01273 686758
Fax 01273 685865
http://www.sussex.ac.uk/spru

Centre for Social and Economic Research on the Global Environment

School of Environmental Sciences,
University of East Anglia,
Norwich NR4 7TJ
Tel. 01603 593176
Fax 01603 250588
http://www.uea.ac.uk/env/cserge

Centre for Ecology and Hydrology

Monks Wood, Abbots Ripton,
Huntingdon PE28 2LS
Tel. 01487 773381
Fax 01487 773467
http://www.nmw.ac.uk/ite
Research institute.

Transport Research Laboratory

Old Wokingham Road, Crowthorne,
Berks RG45 6AU
Tel. 01344 773131
Fax 01344 770356
http://www.trl.co.uk

Transport Studies Unit

Centre for Transport Studies, University College London, 20 Gower Street,
London WC1E 6BT
Tel. 020 7391 1580
Fax 020 7679 1580
http://www.ucl.ac.uk/

Virology and Environmental Microbiology, Institute of

Mansfield Road, Oxford OX1 3SR
Tel. 01865 281630
Fax 01865 281696
http://www.nerc-oxford.ac.uk/

WRC Plc

Frankland Road, Blagrove,
Swindon SN5 8YF
Tel. 01491 571531
Fax 01793 865001
Research into water, waste water and environmental management.

Societies and Institutions

Aerosol Manufacture Association, British

King's Building, Smith Square,
London SW1P 3JJ
Tel. 020 7828 5111
Fax 020 7834 8436
http://www.bama.co.uk
Provides advice on the disposal of aerosol cans.

Airfields Environment Federation

Sir John Lyon House, 5 High Timber Street,
Upper Thames Street, London EC4V 3NS
Tel. 020 7329 8159
Fax 020 7329 8160
http://www.gael.net/aef
Research and campaigning on environmental issues concerning air transport.

Alarm UK: the Alliance against roadbuilding

13 Stockwell Road, London SW9 9AU
Tel/Fax 020 7737 6641

Alternative Technology, Centre for (CAT)

Llyngwern Quarry, Machynlleth,
Powys SY20 9AZ
Tel. 01654 702400
Fax 01654 702782.
http://www.foe.co.uk/CAT
Charity concerned with the search for globally sustainable, whole and ecologically sound technologies and ways of life.

Alternative Technology and Technology Assessment, Network for (NATTA)

c/o EERU, Faculty of Technology, The Open University, Walton Hall, Milton Keynes MK7 6AA
Tel. 01908 654638
Fax 01908 65858407
http://www-tec.open.ac.uk/eeru
Promotes and supports the development of renewable energies.

Aluminium Packaging Recycling Organisation

Unit 5, Gatsby Court, 176 Holliday Street, Birmingham B1 1TJ
Tel. 0121 633 4656
Fax 0121 633 4698
For details of local cash for cans recycling centres: 0845 227722
http://www.alucan.org.uk
Trade organisation aimed at increasing the recycling rate for aluminium drinks cans.

Ark Environmental Foundation

Suite 640-643 Linen Hall,
162-168 Regent Street, London W1R 5TB
Tel. 020 8444 7626
Fax 020 7734 6042
http://www.arkive.org
UK-registered charity launched 1988, to educate manufacturers and consumer about the need to innovate towards environmentally responsible products, services and industrial practices.

Battery Manufacturers Association, British

Cowly House, 9 Little College Street, London SW1P 3XS
Tel. 020 7222 0666
Fax 020 7233 0335
Provides advice on recycling portable batteries (not car batteries).

Biodiversity Network, National

c/o Joint Nature Conservation Committee, Monkstone House, City Road, Peterborough PE1 1JY
Tel. 01733 562626
Fax 01733 555948
http://www.nbn.org.uk

Bio-Dynamic Agricultural Association

Gloucester Street, Stroud, GL5 1QG
Tel./Fax 01453 759501

Biogen, British

Rear North Suite 7th Floor, 63-66 Hatton Garden, London EC1N 8LE
Tel. 020 7831 7222
Fax 020 7831 7223
http://www.britishbiogen.cok.uk/7.html
Trade association for the biomass industry.

BSI *see* Standards

BTCV *see* Conservation Volunteers

Building Service Engineers, Chartered Institution of

Delta House, 222 Balham High Road, London SW12 9BS.
Tel. 020 8675 5211
Fax 020 8675 5449
http://www.cibse.org.uk

Building Services Research and Information Association (BSRIA)

Old Bracknell Lane West, Bracknell, Berks. RG12 7AH
Tel. 01344 426511
Fax 01344 487575
http://www.bsria.co.uk
Membership organisation concerned with engineering services within buildings and to lessening the building's impact on the environment.

Business in the Environment

44 Baker Street, London W1M 1DH
Tel. 020 7268 0337
Fax 020 7486 1700
http://www.bitc.org.uk
Not-for-profit group initiated in 1989 with the aim of encouraging sustainable development through action and partnership between business and its stakeholders.

CAT *see* Alternative Technology

Chemical Emergency Centre, National (NCEC)

F6, Culham, Abingdon, Oxon OX14 3EB
Tel. 01235 463 070
http://www.neat-env.com/ncec

Chemical Industries Association (CIA)

King's Buildings, Smith Square,
London SW1P 3JJ
Tel. 020 7834 3399
Fax 020 7834 4469
Trade association.

Chemical and Oil Recycling Association

9 Parc Luned, Kinmel Bay, Rhyl,
Denbighshire LL18 5JG
Tel. 0161 439 7589
Advice on the recycling of oil, solvents and chemicals.

CHP *see* Combined Heat and Power

CIWEM *see* Water and Environmental Management

Civic Trust

17 Carlton House Terrace,
London SW1Y 5AW
Tel. 020 7930 0914
Fax 020 7321 0180
http://www.civictrust.org.uk

Clean Air & Environmental Protection, National Society for

44 Grand Parade, Brighton,
West Sussex BN2 2QA
Tel. 01273 878770
Fax 01273 606262
http://www.ww3.mistral.co.uk/cleanair

Combined Heat and Power Association

Grosvenor Gardens House,
35/37 Grosvenor Gardens,
London SW1W 0BS
Tel. 020 7828 4077
Fax 020 7828 0310
Encourages the use of district heating and CHP.

Composting Association

Avon House, Tithebarn Road,
Wellingborough NN8 1DH
Tel. 01933 227777
Fax 01933 441040

Conservation of Energy, Association for the (ACE)

Westgate House, Prebend Street,
London N1 8PT
Tel. 020 7359 8000
Fax 020 7359 0863
http://members.aol.com
Trade association formed 1981 to create an awareness of the needs for and benefits of energy conservation, help establish a national policy and programme and increase investment in energy saving measures.

Conservation Foundation

1 Kensington Gore, London SW7 2AR
Tel. 020 7591 3111
Fax 020 7591 3110
http://www.conservationfoundation.co.uk
Provides a platform for the business sector to sponsor environmental projects and awards.

Conservation Volunteers, British Trust for (BTCV)

36 St Mary's Street, Wallingford,
Oxon OX10 0EU
Tel. 01491 839766
Fax 01491 839646
http://www.btcv.org.uk
The UK's largest practical conservation charity.

Construction Industry Research and Information Association

(including the **Construction Industry Environmental Forum**)
6 Storey's Gate, London SW1P 3AU
Tel. 020 7222 8891
Fax 020 7222 1708
http://www.ciria.org.uk

CPRE *see* Preservation of Rural England

CREATE *see* Research

Council for Environmental Education

94 London Street, Reading RG1 4SJ
Tel. 0118 950 2550
Fax 9118 959 1955
http://www.cee.org.uk
Provides advice on setting up sustainable development initiatives.

Ecological Design Association

The British School, Slad Road, Stroud, Glos GL5 1QW
Tel. 01453 765575
Fax 01453 759211
http://www. salvo.co.uk/mags/ecodesign.htm
Promotes the design and use of ecologically friendly materials and products. Administers EMAS (the Eco Management and Audit Scheme).

Ecological Society, British

26 Blades Court, Deodar Road, Putney, London SW15 2NU
Tel. 020 8871 9797
Fax 020 8871 9779
http://www.demon.co.uk/bes
Promotes the science of ecology.

Effluent and Water Association, British

5 Castle Street, High Wycombe, Bucks HP13 6RZ
Tel. 01494 444544

Electric Vehicle Association

17 Westmestan Avenue, Rottingdean, East Sussex BN2 8AL
Tel: 01273 304064
Fax: 01273 390370
Trade and membership organisation.

Electronic and Electrical Equipment Recycling, Industry Council for (ICER)

6 Bath Place, Rivington Street, London EC2A 3JE
Tel. 020 7729 4766
Fax 020 7729 9121
http://www.icer.org.uk

Energy Conservation, International Institute for

21 Taven Quay Business Park, Rope Street, London SE16 7TX
Tel. 020 7237 6523
Fax 020 7257 2462
http://www.iiec.org/
Non-profit institution founded 1984, to accelerate the adoption of energy-efficient policies, technologies and practices in developing and transition countries.

Energy from Waste Association

26 Spring Street, London W2 1JA
Tel. 020 7402 7110
Fax 020 7402 7115

Energy Centre, National

Davy Avenue, Knowl Hill, Milton Keynes MK5 8NA
Tel. 01908 672787
Fax 01908 662296

Energy Information Centre

Rosemary House, Lanwades Business Park, Newmarket, Suffolk CB8 7PW
Tel. 01638 751400
Fax 01638 751801

Energy, Institute of

18 Devonshire Street, London W1G 7A0
Tel. 020 7580 7124
Fax 020 7580 4420
http://www.entech.co.uk/ioe/htm
Learned society and professional body founded 1927.

Energy Saving Trust

11-12 Buckingham Gate, London SW1E 6LB
Tel. 020 7931 8401
Fax 020 7931 8458
http://est.org.uk
Funded by the DETR and major UK energy companies, promotes energy conservation and manages energy saving schemes.

Engineering Council

10 Maltravers Street, London WC2R 3ER
Tel. 020 7240 7891
Fax 020 7240 7517

Environment and Business in Scotland, Centre for

58/59 Timber Bush, Edinburgh EH6 6QH
Tel. 0131 555 5334
Fax 0131 555 5217

Environment Conscious Building, Association for

PO Box 32, Lldysul, SA44 5ZA
Tel/Fax: 01559 370908
http://members.aol.com/buildgreen
Trade association, providing information on environmental building.

Environment Council

212 High Holborn, London WC1V 7VW
Tel. 020 7836 2626
Fax 020 7242 1180
http://www.greenchannel.com/tec/
Independent charity dedicated to enhancing and protecting Britain's environment through building awareness, dialogue and effective solutions. Includes a Business and Environment programme.

Environment and Development, International Institute for

3 Endsleigh Street, London WC1H 0DD
Tel. 020 7388 2117
Fax 020 7388 2826
http://www.iied.org.uk
Non-profit-making research organisation in sustainable development and related issues.

Environmental Management, Institute of

58/59 Timber Bush, Edinburgh EH6 6QH
Tel. 0131 555 5334
Fax 0131 555 5217

Environmental Management and Assessment, Institute of

Welton House, Limekiln Way,
Lincoln LN2 4US
Tel. 01522 540069
Fax 01522 540090
http://www.greenchannel.com/iea
Membership association.

Environmental Education, Council for (CEE)

94 London Street, Reading, Berks RG1 4SJ
Tel 01189 502550
Fax 01189 591955

Environmental Education, National Association for (NAEE)

University of Wolverhampton,
Walsall Campus, Gorway Road, Walsall,
West Midlands WS1 3BD
Tel/Fax: 01922 631200

Environmental Engineers, Society of

Owles Hall, Buntingford, Herts SG9 9PL
Tel. 01763 271209
Fax 01763 273255
http://www.environmental.org.uk

Environmental Health, Chartered Institute of

Chadwick Court, 15 Hatfields,
London SE1 8DJ
Tel. 020 7928 6006
Fax 020 7827 5865
http://www.cieh.org.uk/
Independent organisation founded 1883, representing the interests of the environmental health profession.

Environmental Industry Commission

45 Weymouth Street, London W1N 3LD
Tel. 020 7935 1675
Fax 020 7746 3455
http://www.eureco.com/eic
Incorporates the Association of Environmental Consultancies.

Environmental Information Centre (EIC)

Institute of Terrestrial Ecology,
Monks Wood, Abbots Ripton, Huntingdon,
Cambs PE28 2LS
Tel. 01487 773381
Fax 01487 773467
The NERC's data centre for terrestrial ecology and the rural environment.

Environmental Law Association, UK (UKELA)

Honeycroft House, Pangbourne Road,
Upper Basildon, Berks RG8 8LP
Tel/Fax 01491 671631
Membership association for professionals in environmental law.

Environmental Law and Development, Foundation for International (FIELD)

SOAS, University of London,
45-47 Russell Square, London WC1B 4JP
Tel. 020 7637 7950
Fax 020 7637 7951

Environmental Sciences, Institution of

PO Box 16, Bourne PE10 9FB
Tel/Fax 01778 394846
Professional body for environmental scientists.

Environmental Services Association

154 Buckingham Palace Road,
London SW1W 9TR
Tel. 020 78248 882
Fax 020 7824 8753
http://www.esauk.org

Environment Technology Centre, National (NETCEN)

F6 Culham, Abingdon, Oxon OX14 3DB

Environmental Transport Association

10 Church Street, Weybridge,
Surrey KT13 8RS
Tel. 01932 828882
Fax 01932 829015
http://www.eta.co.uk
Launched 1990, campaigns for a sound and sustainable transport system and provides breakdown and other services.

Forestry Association, Commonwealth

c/o Oxford Forestry Institute,
South Parks Road, Oxford BX1 3RB
Tel. 01865 275072
Fax 01865 275074
Membership institute promoting forestry conservation.

Forestry Society of England, Wales and Northern Ireland, Royal

102 High Street, Tring, Herts HP23 4AF
Tel. 01442 822028
Fax 01442 890395
http://www.rfs.org.uk
Educational charity.

Forestry Society, Royal Scottish

The Stables, Dalkeith Country Park,
Dalkeith, Midlothian EH22 2NA
Tel. 01387 371518
Fax 0131 660 9490
http://www.lakesnet.co.uk/forestry.html
Membership association.

Forests Forever Campaign

4th Floor Clareville House
26-27 Oxenden Street, London SW1Y 4EL
Tel. 020 7839 1891
Fax 020 7939 6594
http://www.ttf.co.uk
Campaigns for sustainable forestry on behalf of the timber and wood-using industries.

Friends of the Earth

26-28 Underwood Street, London N1 7JQ
Tel. 020 7490 1555
Fax 020 7490 0881
http://www.foe.co.uk/
Campaigning and research organisation working to change policies and practices which degrade the environment.

Friends of the Earth Scotland

Bonnington Mill, 72 Newhaven Road,
Edinburgh EH6 5QG
Tel. 0131 554 9977
Fax 0131 554 8656
http://www.foe-scotland.org.uk

Global Action Plan

8 Fulwood Place, London WC1V 6HG
Tel. 020 7405 5633
Fax. 020 7831 6244
Runs an action-at-work scheme.

Going for Green

PO Box Wigan 2100, Elizabeth House,
The Pier, Wigan WN3 4EX
Tel. 01942 621621
Fax 01942 824778
http://www.gfg.iclnet.co.uk

Green Globe

P O Box 396, Linton, Cambridge CB1 6UL
Tel. 01223 890250
Fax 01223 890258
http://www.wttc.org/
Environmental management programme for travel and tourism companies and destinations, started 1994.

Green Net

74-77 White Lion Street, Islington,
London N1 9PF
Tel. 020 7713 1941
Fax 020 7837 5551
http://www.gn.apc.org/
Non-profit organisation involved particularly with IT and its applications to environmental movements.

Greenpeace UK

Canonbury Villas, London N1 2PN
Tel. 020 7865 8100
Fax 020 7696 0012/0014
http://www.greenpeace.org.uk
International independent environmental pressure group acting against abuse to the natural world.

Groundwork UK

National Office: 85/87 Cornwall Street,
Birmingham B3 3BY
Tel. 0121 236 8565
Fax 0121 236 7356
http://www.groundwork.org.uk
UK environmental partnership organisation, active in 120 towns and cities. Charity. Devises programmes which link environmental, social and economic regeneration and contribute to sustainable development. Over 3,500 projects annually.

Henry Doubleday Research Association

Ryton-on-Dunsmore, Coventry CV8 3LG
Tel 02476 303517
Fax 02476 639229
http://www.hdra.org.uk
Organisation devoted to organic gardening.

Hydropower, British Association

Sovereign House, Bramhall Centre,
Bramhall, Stockport SK7 1AW
Tel. 0161 4409196
Fax 0161 4409273

Industrial Fuel Efficiency Service Ltd, National (NIFES)

NIFES House, Sinderland Road,
Broadheath, Altrincham,
Cheshire WA14 5HQ
Tel. 0161 928 5791
Fax 0161 926 8718
Consultants on fuel efficiency.

Intermediate Technology Development Group

Schumacher Centre for Technology and Development
Bourton Hall, Bourton-on-Dunsmore,
Rugby, Warks CV23 9QZ
Tel. 01788 661100
Fax 01788 661101
Independent charity providing information and advice on technological issues.

Landscape Institute

6-8 Barnard Mews, London SW11 1QU
Tel. 020 7738 9166
Fax 020 77350 5201
Professional body for landscape designers.

Marine Conservation Society

9 Gloucester Road, Ross-on-Wye,
Herefordshire HR9 5BU
Tel. 01989 566017
Fax 01989 567815
http://www.mcsuk.mcmail.com
Aims to increase public awareness of British marine wildlife.

National Trust, The

36 Queen Anne's Gate, London SW1H 9AS
Tel. 020 7222 9251
Fax 020 7222 5097
http://www.nationaltrust.org.uk

National Trust for Scotland

28 Charlotte Square, Edinburgh EH2 4ET
Tel. 0131 243 9300
Fax 0131 243 9301

NATTA *see* Alternative Technology

Naturalists' Association, British

1 Bracken Mews, London E4 7UT

NETCEN *see* Environment Technology Centre

NIFES *see* Industrial Fuel

Noise Consultants, Association of

6 Trap Road, Guilden Morden, Royston,
Herts SG8 0JE
Tel. 01763 852958
Fax 01763 853252
http://www.isvr.soton.ac.uk/ANC/
Trade association for consultants dealing with noise monitoring and reduction.

Nuffield Council on Bioethics

28 Bedford Square, London WC1B 3EG
Tel. 020 731 0566
Fax 020 7637 1712
Independent body researching into bioethical issues.

Oil Spill Control Association, British

4th Floor, 30 Great Guildford Street,
London SE1 0HS
Tel. 020 7928 9199
Fax 020 7928 6599
http://www.bmec.org.uk
Trade association for equipment and services to do with oil spill control.

Packaging and the Environment, Industry Council for

Tenterden House, 3 Tenterden Street,
London W1R 9AH
Tel. 020 7409 0949
Fax 020 7409 0161
http://www.incpen.org.uk
Provides information on legislation relating to the environmental effects of packaging.

Pesticides Action Network UK

Eurolink Centre, 49 Effra Road, Brixton,
London SW2 1BZ
Tel. 020 7274 8895
Fax 020 7274 9084
http://www.gn.apc.org/pesticidestrust
Charity addressing the health and environmental problems of pesticides.

Pure Water Association, National

12 Dennington Lane, Crigglestone,
Wakefield WF4 3ET
Tel. 01924 254433
Fax 01924 242380
Campaigns for safe drinking water, and especially against fluoride in water.

Quality Assurance, Institute of

12 Grosvenor Crescent, London SW1X 7EE
Tel. 02476 245 6722
Fax 02476 696 706
http://www.iqa.org.uk

Queen's Awards Office

151 Buckingham Palace Road,
London SW1 9SS
Tel. 020 7222 2277
Fax 020 7215 5770
http://www.open/gov.uk/qawards/qawardhome.htm
Administers the Queen's Award for Environmental Achievement.

Rare Breeds Survival Trust

National Agricultural Centre, Stoneleigh Park, Kenilworth, Warks CV8 2LG
Tel. 01203 696551
Fax 01203 696706
Promotes the survival of rare farm animal breeds.

Recovered Paper Association, British

Papermakers House, Rivenhall Road, Westlea, Swindon, Wilts SN5 7BD
Tel. 01793 886086
Fax 01793 886182
http://www.paper.org.uk
Trade association providing services to paper merchants.

Research Education and Training in Energy, Centre for (CREATE)

Kenley House, 25 Bridgeman Terrace, Wigan, Lancs WN1 1TD
Tel. 01942 322271
Fax 01942 322273
http://www.create.org.uk

Residual

Heath House, 133 High Street, Tonbridge, Kent TN9 1DH
Tel. 01756 709800
Fax 01756 706801
http://www.wrf.org.uk
Charity promoting energy recovery from household waste.

Preservation of Rural England, Council for the (CPRE)

Warwick House, 25 Buckingham Palace Road, London SW1W 0PP
Tel. 020 7976 6433
Fax 020 7976 6373
http://www.greenchannel.com/cpre

Rural Scotland, Association for the Protection of

3rd Floor, Gladstone's Land,
483 Lawnmarket, Edinburgh EH1 2NT
Tel. 0131 225 7012/3
Fax 0131 225 6592
http://www.aprs.org.uk

Rural Wales, Campaign for the Protection of

Ty Gwyn, 31 High Street, Welshpool, Powys SY21 7YD
Tel. 01938 552525
Fax 01938 552741

Save Britain's Heritage

70 Cowcross Street, London EC1M 6EJ
Tel. 020 7253 3500
Fax 020 7253 3400

Save-a-Cup Recycling Co Ltd

Suite 2, Bridge House, Bridge Street, High Wycombe, Bucks HP11 2EL
Tel. 01494 510167
Fax 01494 510168
www.save-a-cup.co.uk
Concerned with recycling plastic cups.

Seaside Award Office

Tidy Britain Group, 5 Chalk Hill House, 19 Rosary Road, Norwich NR1 1SZ
Tel. 01603 766076
Fax 01603 760580
Identifies well-managed beaches with good standards of cleanliness, safety and water quality.

Soil Association

Bristol House, 40-56 Victoria Street, Bristol, Avon BS1 6BY
Tel. 0117 9252504
Promotes and conducts research in organic gardening and farming

Solar Trade Association

Pengillan, Lerryan, Lostwithiel,
Cornwall PL22 0QE
Tel/Fax 01208 873518
Trade association for firms involved with solar energy.

Standards Institute, British (BSI)

Information Centre,
389 Chiswick High Road, London W4 4AL
Tel. 020 8996 7000
Customer Services: 020 8996 7111
Fax 020 8996 7960
http://www.bsi.co.uk

Steel Can Recycling Information Bureau

PO Box 18, Ebbw Vale NP23 6YL
Tel. 01495 334528
Fax 01495 350988

Survival International

11-15 Emerald Street, London WC1N 3QL
Tel. 020 7242 1441
Fax 020 7242 1771

Sustainable Energy, Centre for

CREATE Centre, B-Bond Warehouse,
Smeaton Road, Bristol BS1 6XN
Tel. 0117 929 9950
Fax 0117 929 9114
http://www.cse.org.uk
Provides insulation and energy advice.

Sustrans (Sustainable Transport)

35 King Street, Bristol BS1 4DZ
Tel. 0117 926 8893
Fax 0117 994 173
http://www.sustrans.org.uk
Civil engineering charity which designs and builds routes for cyclists, walkers and people with disabilities. Promoters of the National Cycle Network.

Tanker Owners Pollution Federation, International

Staple Hall, Stonehouse Court,
87-90 Houndsditch, London EC3A 7AX
Tel. 020 7621 1255
Fax 020 7621 1783
http://www.itopf.com
Federation founded by tanker owners to combat marine pollution.

Tidy Britain Group

Elizabeth House, The Pier,
Wigan WN3 4EX
Tel. 01942 824620
Fax 01942 824778
Independent national charity working for the improvement of local environments

Town and Country Planning Association

17 Carlton House Terrace,
London SW1Y 5AS
Tel. 020 7930 8903/4/5
Fax 020 7930 3280

Town Planning Institute, Royal

26 Portland Place, London W1N 4BE
from 1 April 2001: 41 Botolph Lane,
London EC3
Tel. 020 7636 9107
Fax 020 7323 1582
http://www.rtpi.co.uk

Transport 2000

12-18 Hoxton Street, London N1 6NG
Tel. 020 7613 0743
Fax 020 7613 5280
Federation of groups campaigning for socially and environmentally friendly transport policies.

Tree Council

51 Catherine Place, London SW1E 6DY
Tel. 020 7828 9928
Fax 020 7828 9060
Umbrella charity promoting tree warden schemes, etc.

Tree Foundation, International

Sandy Lane, Crawley Down,
West Sussex RH10 4HS
Tel. 01342 712536
Fax 01342 718282
Charity within the Tree Council (see above).

Waste Disposal Contractors, National Association of

154 Buckingham Palace Road,
London SW1W 9TR
Tel. 020 7824 8882
Fax 020 7824 8753
Trade association.

Waste Exchange Service, National

Unit 8, Douglas Close, Preston Farm
Industrial Estate, Stockton on Tees,
Cleveland TS18 3SB
Tel. 01642 606055
Fax 01642 603726
Manages a database of companies' waste streams to facilitate waste matching, chiefly of chemicals.

Waste Management Industry Training and Advisory Board (WAMITAB)

P O Box 176, Northampton NN1 1SB
Tel. 01604 231950
Fax 01604 232457
Administers certificate of technical competence scheme for the waste management industry.

Waste Management Information Bureau

AEA Technology and Environment Centre,
National Environmental Technology Centre,
F6 Culham, Abingdon, Oxon OX14 3EB
Tel. 01235 463162
Fax 01235 463004
Provides information and advice on waste management.

Waste Management, Institute of

9 Saxon Court, St Peter's Gardens,
Northampton NN1 1SX
Tel. 01604 620426
Fax 01604 621339
Charity and professional body.

Waste Watch

Europa House, Ground Floor, 13-17
Ironmonger Row, London EC1V 3QG
Tel. 020 7253 6266
Fax 020 7253 5962
http://www.wastewatch.org.uk
Charity promoting action on reducing, reusing and recycling waste.

Water, British

1 Queen Anne's Gate, London SW1H 9BT
Tel. 020 7957 4554
Fax 020 7957 4565
Trade organisation for companies in the water and waste water industry. Includes equipment suppliers and smaller specialist support firms in the water sector.

Water UK

1 Queen Anne's Gate, London SW1H 9BT
Tel. 020 7344 1844
Fax 020 7344 1850
http://www.water.org.uk
Trade association for UK water companies, formed by the merger of the Water Companies Association and the Water Services Association.

Water and Environmental Management, Chartered Institution of (CIWEM)

15 John Street, London WC1N 2EB
Tel. 020 7831 3110
Fax 020 7405 4967
http://www.ciwem.org.uk
Professional and examining body for engineers, scientists and others engaged in water and environmental management.

Water Management Society

Mill House, Tolson's Mill, Fazeley,
Tamworth B78 3QB
Tel. 01827 289558
Fax 01827 250408
Professional society to encourage sensible use and reuse of water within industry and commerce.

Water, International Association of

Alliance House, 12 Caxton Street,
London SW1H 0QS
Tel. 020 7839 8390
Fax 020 7839 8299
http://www.awq.org.uk
Membership organisation concerned with water pollution control world-wide.

WTI Training Group

Tadley Court, Tadley Common Road,
Tadley, Hants RG26 3TB
Tel. 01189 813011
Fax 01189 817000
Training in water management.

Wildfowl and Wetlands Trust

The New Grounds, Slimbridge,
Glos GL2 7BT
Tel. 01453 890333
Fax 01453 890827
http://www.wwt.org.uk

Wind Energy Association, British

26 Spring Street, London W2 1JA
Tel. 020 7402 7102
Fax 020 7402 7107
http://www.bwea.com

Wind Energy Association, European

26 Spring Street, London W2 1JA
Tel. 020 7402 7122
Fax 020 7402 7125
http://www.ewea.com

Woodland Trust

Autumn Park, Dysart Road, Grantham,
Lincs NG31 6LL
Tel. 01476 581111
Fax 01476 590808
Facilitates the conservation of native broadleaf woodland through acquisition.

World Society for the Protection of Animals

2 Langley Lane, London SW8 1TJ
Tel. 020 7793 0540
Fax 020 7793 0208
http://www.kilimanjaro.com.wspa
Organisation concerned with animal welfare issues.

World Wide Fund for Nature (WWF - UK)

Panda House, Weyside Park, Godalming,
Surrey GU7 1QR
Tel. 01483 426444
Fax 01483 426409
http://www.wwf-uk.org
Conserves species and habitat in the UK and world-wide by working to stop and reverse the degradation of the natural environment.

International Organisations

Advisory Committee on Protection of the Sea (ACOPS)

11 Dartmouth Road, London SW1H 9BN
Tel. 020 7799 3033
Fax 020 7799 2933
http://www.acops.org
Forum for the study of marine pollution, with representatives from government and non-government organisations in 18 countries.

Atomic Energy Agency, International (IAEA)

Vienna International Centre,
Wagramerstrasse 5, P O Box 100,
A-1400 Vienna, Austria
Tel. (43) 1 20600
Fax (43) 1 20607
http://www.iaea.or.at/worldatom

Energy Agency, International

9 rue de la Fédération,
75739 Paris Cédex 15, France
Tel. (33) 18 4057 6554
Fax (33) 18 4057 6559

European Environmental Bureau (EEB)

26 rue de la Victoire, 1060 Brussels, Belgium
Tel. (32) 2 539 00 37
Fax (32) 2 539 0921
Federation of approximately 130 major non-government organisations from 24 countries.

European Organisation for Testing and Certification

rue d'Egmontstraat 15, 1000 Brussels, Belgium
Tel. (32) 2 511 2589
Fax (32) 2 511 5666
http://www.emas.lu

Maritime Organisation, International

4 Albert Embankment, London SE1 7SR
Tel. 020 7735 7611
Fax 020 7587 3210
http://www.imo.org

Meteorological Organisation, World

41 Avenue Giuseppe Motta, P O Box 2300, 1211 Geneva 20, Switzerland
Tel. (41) 22 730 8284
Fax (41) 22 733 1270
Also hosts the Intergovernmental Panel on Climate Change (IPCC) established jointly by the WMO and UNEP.

Standardisation, International Organisation for (ISO)

1 rue de Varembé, Case postale 56, CH-1211 Geneva 209, Switzerland
Tel. (41) 22 749 01 11
Fax (41) 22 733 34 30
http://www.iso.ch/

United Nations Convention on Biological Diversity (CBD)

Secretariat: World Trade Centre, 413 Rue St Jacques, Bureau 630, Quebec H2Y 1N9, Canada
Tel. (1) 514 288 2220
Fax (1) 514 288 6588

United Nations Convention on International Trade in Endangered Species (CITES)

Secretariat: 13 Chemin des Anemones, CH-1219 Chatelaine-Geneva, Switzerland
Tel. (41) 22 979 9139
Fax (41) 22 797 3417

United Nations Economic Commission for Europe (UNECE)

Palais des Nations, 8-14 avenue de la Paix, 1211 Geneva 10, Switzerland
Tel. (41) 22 9172893
Fax (41) 22 9170036
Responsibilities include development of regional environmental policies, promotion of international environmental legislation, promotion of environmentally sound products and technology, management of hazardous chemicals, energy efficiency, sustainable development.

Convention on Long-Range Transboundary Air Pollution (LRTAP)

Environmental and Human Settlements Division, Palais des Nations, 1211 Geneva 10, Switzerland
Tel. (41) 22 917 2354
Fax (41) 22 907 0107
http://www.unece.org.env/

United Nations Environment Programme

P O Box 30552, United Nations Avenue, Gigiri, Nairobi, Kenya
Tel. (254) 2 621234
Fax (254) 2 226890
Established 1972, encourages international co-operation on environmental matters, analyses trends, etc. Conducts the Earthwatch environmental assessment programme and the Global Environmental Monitoring System. Also the address for the Ozone Secretariat which services the Vienna Convention for the Protection of the Ozone Layer and the Montreal Protocol.

Europe office:
Geneva Executive Center 5, Chemin des Anemones, CH1219 Chatelaine-Geneva, Switzerland.
Tel. (41) 22 979 9302
Fax (41) 22 797 3420
http://www.unchs.unon.org.unep/conv.htm

UNEP Working Group on Sustainable Product Development (UNEP-WG-SPD)

3rd Floor, J. H. van't Hoff Institute, Building B, Nieuwe Achtergracht 166, 1018 WV Amsterdam, Netherlands
Tel. (31) 20 525 6268
Fax (31) 20 625 8843
http://www.unep.frw.uva.nl/

United Nations Framework Convention on Climate Change (UNFCCC)

Secretariat: Haus Carstaien, Martin Luther King Strasses 8, D-53175 Bonn, Germany

United Nations Food and Agriculture Organisation (FAO)

Via delle Terme di Caracalla, 00100 Rome, Italy
Tel. (39) 6 52251
Fax (39) 6 5225-3152
Responsible for the chapters of Agenda 21 relating to water resources, forests, sustainable agriculture, etc.

United Nations Scientific Committee on the Effects of Atomic Radiation (UNSCEAR)

Vienna International Centre, Wagramerstrasse 5, P O Box 500, A-1400 Vienna, Austria
Tel. (43) 1 21345 4330
Fax (43) 1 21345 5902

World Conservation Monitoring Centre

219 Huntingdon Road, Cambridge CB3 0DL
Tel. 01223 277314
Fax 01223 277136
http://www.wcmc.org.uk/
Joint venture between the International Union for the Conservation of Nature and Natural Resources (IUCN), the United Nations Environment Programme (UNEP) and World Wide Fund for Nature (WWF). Supports conservation and sustainable development through providing information on the world's biological diversity.

World Conservation Union (IUCN)

rue Mauverney 28, CH-1196 Gland, Switzerland.
Tel. (41) 22 999 0001
Fax (41) 22 999 0002
Membership association to assist conservation societies.

World Health Organisation

Division of Environmental Health:
20 avenue Appia, 1211 Geneva 27, Switzerland.
Tel. (41) 22 7912111
Fax (41) 22 7910746
Provides global co-ordination of environmental health matters.

Regional Office for Europe:
Scherfigsvej 8, DK-2100 Copenhagen 0, Denmark.

WWF International

avenue de Mont Blanc, 1196 Gland, Switzerland
Tel. (41) 22 364 9111
Fax (41) 22 364 3239
Concerned with conservation of nature and ecological processes, biodiversity, sustainable development, etc.

Hotlines

Aluminium can recycling centres
0345 227722

BIO-Wise
0800 432100

BSI Environmental Help Desk
020 8996 7111

BRECSU Enquiry Bureau
01923 664258

Business Link
0345 567765

DETR Environment and Energy helpline
0800 585794

Energy efficiency hotline
0345 277 200

Energy helpline for small businesses
0541 542 541

Energy Technology Support Unit (ETSU)
Enquiry Bureau
01235 436 747

Environment Agency General Enquiry Line
0645 333 111

Environment Agency emergency hotline
0800 807060

Floodline
0845 988 1888

MAFF helpline
0645 335577

Disposal of waste oil
0800 663366

Bibliography

EC legislation

Regulations:

(note: this is an indicative sample only)

1734/88/EC, Export and import of certain dangerous chemicals.

1210/90/EC, Establishment of a European Environment Agency and European Environment Information and Observation Network.

594/91/EC, Substances that deplete the ozone layer.

1973/92/EC, Setting up an environmental fund (LIFE).

880/92/EC, Community Eco-Label Award Scheme.

793/93/EC, Evaluation and control of the risks of existing substances.

1836/93/EC, Allowing voluntary participation by companies in the industrial sector in a Community Eco-Management and Audit Scheme.

3093/94/EC, Substances that deplete the ozone layer.

716/96/EC, Over Thirty Months Scheme for cattle.

925/99/EC, Noise from subsonic civil jet aircraft

1257/99/EC, Rural development.

2278/99/EC, Protection of forests against atmospheric pollution

Directives:

(note: this is a selection only of relevant directives, and in particular most amending directives are not listed.)

70/157/EC, Permissible sound level and the exhaust system of motor vehicles.

75/440/EC, Quality of surface waters intended for the abstraction of drinking water.

75/442/EC, Waste (framework directive).

76/160/EC, Quality of bathing waters.

76/464/EC, Pollution caused by dangerous substances discharged into the aquatic environment.

78/319/EC, Toxic and dangerous waste.

78/659/EC, Freshwater fish.

79/113/EC, Determination of the noise emission of construction plant and equipment.

79/409/EC, Conservation of wild birds.

79/923/EC, Quality of shellfish waters.

80/51/EC, Noise emissions from subsonic aircraft.

80/68/EC, Protection of groundwater against pollution caused by certain dangerous substances.

80/778/EC, Quality of water for human consumption.

80/779/EC, Air quality limit values and guide values for sulphur dioxide and suspended particulates.

82/884/EC, Limit values for lead in the air.

83/189/EC, Standstill directive.

84/360/EC, Combating air pollution from industrial plants (framework directive).

84/631/EC, Supervision and control within the Community of the transfrontier shipment of hazardous waste.

85/203/EC, Air quality standards for nitrogen dioxide.

85/337/EC, Assessment of the effects of certain public and private projects on the environment.

86/118/EC, Protection of workers from risks related to exposure to noise at work.

86/278/EC, Sewage sludge used in agriculture.

87/217/EC, Prevention and reduction of environmental pollution by asbestos.

88/609/EC, Limitation of emissions of certain pollutants into the air from large combustion plants.

89/369/EC, Prevention of air pollution from new municipal waste incineration plants.

89/429/EC, Prevention of air pollution from existing municipal waste incineration plants.

90/219/EC, Contained use of genetically modified organisms.

90/220/EC, Deliberate release into the environment of genetically modified organisms.

90/1210/EC, Establishment of an European Environment Agency.

91/156/EC, Waste (framework directive).

91/157/EC, Batteries and accumulators containing certain dangerous substances.

91/271/EC, Urban waste water treatment.

91/414/EC Marketing of plant protection products.

91/676/EC Water pollution by nitrates.

91/689/EC, Hazardous waste.

92/43/EC, Conservation of natural habitats and of wild flora and fauna.

92/72/EC, Air pollution by ozone.

92/880/EC, Community Eco-label Award Scheme.

93/1836/EC, Voluntary participation by companies in the industrial sector in a Community Eco-Management and Audit Scheme.

94/2/EC, Labelling of refrigerators and freezers.

94/62/EC, Packaging and packaging waste.

95/12/EC, Labelling of washing machines.

96/57/EC, Minimum efficiency standards for refrigerators and freezers.

96/61/EC, Integrated pollution prevention and control.

96/62/EC, Ambient air quality assessment and management (air quality framework directive).

96/737/EC SAVE II scheme.

97/35/EC, Release into the environment of genetically modified organisms.

98/69/EC, Emissions from petrol-engined and diesel-engined passenger cars and light commercial vehicles.

98/70/EC, Quality of petrol and diesel fuels.

98/83/EC, Quality of water intended for human consumption.

98/101/EC, Batteries and accumulators containing certain dangerous substances.

99/13/EC, Limitation of omissions of volatile organic compounds due to the use of organic solvents.

99/31/EC, Landfill of waste.

99/32/EC, Sulphur content of certain liquid fuels.

99/96/EC, Emission of gaseous pollutants from diesel engines.

99/125/EC, Reduction of carbon dioxide emissions from passenger cars.

200/140/EC, Noise emission in the environment by equipment for use outdoors.

UK legislation

Acts (and bills in progress):

(note: this is a selection only and excludes specific Scotland and Northern Ireland legislation)

Town and Country Planning Act 1947.

National Parks and Access to the Countryside Act 1949.

Countryside Act 1968.

Land Compensation Act 1973.

Control of Pollution Act 1974.

Health and Safety at Work Act 1974.

Energy Act 1976.

Transport Act 1980.

Wildlife and Countryside Act 1981.

Food and Environmental Protection Act 1985.

Control of Pollution (Amendment) Act 1989.

Electricity Act 1989.

Environmental Protection Act 1990.

Planning (Hazardous Substances) Act 1990.

Planning (Listed Buildings and Conservation Areas) Act 1990.

Town and Country Planning Act 1990.

Land Drainage Act 1991.

Planning & Compensation Act 1991.

Radioactive Material (Road Transport) Act 1991.

Water Industry Act 1991.

Water Resources Act 1991.

Traffic Calming Act 1992.

Noise and Statutory Nuisance Act 1993.

Clean Air Act 1993.

Radioactive Substances Act 1993.

Home Energy Conservation Act 1995.

Environment Act 1995.

Noise Act 1996.

Road Traffic Reduction Act 1997.

Pesticides Act 1998.

Waste Minimisation Act 1998.

Road Traffic Reduction (National Targets) Act 1998.

Food Standards Act 1999.

Pollution Prevention and Control Act 1999.

Water Industry Act 1999.

Utilities Act 2000.

Energy Efficiency Bill 2000.

Marine Wildlife Protection Bill 2000.

Recycled Content of Newsprint Bill 2000.

Renewable Energy Bill 2000.

Urban Regeneration and Countryside Protection Bill 1999.

Statutory Instruments:

(note: this is an indicative selection only)

SI 80/1709, Control of pollution (special waste) regulations.

SI 86/1510, Control of pesticides regulations.

SI 87/2115, Control of asbestos at work.

SI 88/1241, Highways (assessment of environmental effects) regulations.

SI 88/1657, Control of substances hazardous to health (COSHH) regulations.

SI 88/1199, Town and country planning (assessment of environmental effects) regulations.

SI 89/1790, Noise at work regulations.

SI 89/1148, Surface water (classification) regulations.

SI 91/324, Control of pollution (silage, slurry and agricultural fuel oil) regulations.

SI 91/472, Environmental protection (prescribed processes and substances) regulations.

SI 91/1597, Bathing waters (classification) regulations.

SI 92/2383, UK Eco-Labelling Board regulations.

SI 92/588, Controlled of wastes regulations.

SI 92/337, Surface waters (dangerous substances) (classification) regulations.

SI 94/440, Ozone monitoring and information regulations.

SI 94/1057, Surface water (river ecosystem) (classification) regulations.

SI 94/2841, Urban waste water treatment (England and Wales) regulations.

SI 94/3246, Control of substances hazardous to health (COSHH) regulations.

SI 95/417, Town and country planning (environmental assessment and permitted development) regulations.

SI 95/418, Town and country planning (general permitted development) order.

SI 96/972, Special waste regulations.

SI 97/189, Plant protection products (basic conditions) regulations.

SI 97/648, Producer responsibility obligations (packaging waste) regulations.

SI 97/2560, Surface water (dangerous substances) (classification) regulations.

SI 97/3043, Air quality regulations.

SI 98/389, Surface water (dangerous substances) (classification) regulations.

SI 99/ 743, Control of major accident hazards (COMAH) regulations.

SI 99/293, Town and country planning (environmental impact assessment) (England and Wales) regulations.

SI 99/1361, Producer responsibility obligations (packaging waste) (amendment) regulations.

SI 99/1676, Energy information (dishwashers) regulations.

SI 2000/97, Air quality (Scotland) regulations.

SI 2000/227, Contaminated land (England) regulations.

SI 2000/928, Air quality (England) regulations.

SI 2000/1280, Home energy efficiency scheme (England) regulations.

SI 2000/1973, Pollution prevention and control (England and Wales) regulations.

Draft SI, Air quality (England) regulations 2000

Official publications

Green and White Papers:

The Air Quality Strategy for England, Scotland, Wales and Northern Ireland – Working Together for Clean Air, 2000.

A Better Quality of Life: A Strategy for Sustainable Development for the United Kingdom, 1999.

Biodiversity: The UK Action Plan, 1994.

Climate Change: Draft UK Programme, 2000.

Conclusions of the Review of Energy Sources for Power Generation and Government Response to Fourth and Fifth Reports of Trade and Industry Committee, 1998.

Down to Earth, A Scottish Perspective on Sustainable Development, 1999.

A Fair Deal for Consumers: Modernising the Framework for Utility Regulation, 1998.

A Framework for Contaminated Land, 1994.

A New Deal for Transport: Better for Everyone, 1998.

Safer Ships, Cleaner Seas: Report of Lord Donaldson's Enquiry into the Prevention of Pollution from Merchant Shipping, 1994.

Sustainable Forestry: The UK Programme, 1994.

The UK Draft Programme on Climate Change, 2000.

Waste Strategy 2000 for England and Wales, 2000.

EC publications:

European Commission, *Action against Noise: Green Paper*, online summary, 1998.

European Commission, *Agenda 21: The First Five Years. EC Progress on the Implementation of Agenda 21, 1992–97*, 1997.

European Commission, *Agriculture and the Environment*, 1990.

European Commission, *Energy for the Future: Renewable Sources of Energy*, 1996.

European Commission, *Environmental Liability*, 2000.

European Commission, *Inclusive Cities: Building Local Capacity for Development*, EC Regional Policy document, 2000.

European Commission, *The SAVE II Programme*, online document, 1997/8.

European Commission, *A Strategy for Revitalising the Community's Railways*, White Paper, 1996.

European Commission, *Towards Sustainability: The EC's Fifth Programme of Policy and Action in Relation to the Environment and Sustainable Development*, 1992.

European Commission, *Towards Sustainability: The EC's Progress Report and Action Plan on the Fifth Programme of Policy and Action in Relation to the Environment and Sustainable Development*, 1997.

European Commission, *Transport Services: Current Position and Outlook*, online document, undated.

European Commission, *The Union's Policies – Energy Policy*, online document.

European Commission, *The Union's Policies – Environment Policy*, online document.

European Commission, *The Union's Policies – Trans-European Networks*, online document.

European Commission, *The Union's Policies – Transport*, online document.

European Consultative Forum on the Environment and Sustainable Development, *Employment and Environment*, online document, November 1998.

European Environment Agency, *Europe's Environment: The Dobříš Assessment*, Copenhagen 1995.

European Environment Agency, *Air Pollution in Europe 1997*, Copenhagen 1997.

European Parliament Directorate General for Research, *Working Document W14: The European Parliament and the Environment Policy of the European Union*, 1995.

European Community, *Progress Towards Fair and Efficient Pricing for Transport*, 1997.

European Community, *The 'Citizen's Network' – Fulfilling the Potential for Public Passenger Transport in Europe*, 1997.

Other official publications

BRECSU (Building Research Energy Conservation Support Unit), *Energy-Efficient Lighting*, DETR, 1998.

BRECSU, *What will Energy Efficiency do for Your Business? Good Practice Guide* 285, 2000.

Centre for Environment and Business in Scotland/Institute of Environmental Management, *Developing Successful Business with the Environment in Mind: Theory and Practice*, CEBS/IEM, 1996.

Department of the Environment, Transport and the Regions (DETR), *Acid Rain: Acidification in the UK*, online document, DETR, 2000.

DETR, *The Air Quality Strategy for England, Scotland, Wales and Northern Ireland: A Consultation Document*, DETR, 1999.

DETR, *Breaking The Logjam*, DETR, 1998.

DETR, *British Shipping: Charting a New Course*, DETR, 1998.

DETR, *Chemical in the Environment: The Chemicals Strategy*, DETR, 1999.

DETR, *Code of Practice on Conservation, Access and Recreation: Consultation Draft*, DETR, 1999.

DETR, *Consumer Products and the Environment*, DETR, 1998.

DETR, *Control of Noise from Civil Aircraft*, consultation paper, 2000.

DETR, *Control and Remediation of Radioactively Contaminated Land*, DETR, 1998.

DETR *Consultation Draft, Environmental Reporting Guidelines for Company Reporting on Water,* online document, 2000.

DETR, *Consultation Paper on Recovery and Recycling Targets for Packaging Waste in 2001*, online document, 2000.

DETR, *Design of a Tax or Charge Scheme for Pesticides*, DETR, 1999.

DETR, *Digest of Environmental Statistics no. 20, 1998,* The Stationery Office, 1998.

DETR, *Energy Efficient Consumer Products, A 'Market Transformation' Strategy for More Sustainable Consumption,* DETR, 1998.

DETR, *Energy Saving Guide for Small Businesses,* DETR, 2000.

DETR, *Environmental Assessment,* online document, 1998.

DETR, *Environmental Reporting: Guidelines for Company Reporting on Waste,* online document, 2000.

DETR, *From Workhorse to Thoroughbred: A Better Role for Bus Travel,* DETR, 1999.

DETR, *The Government's Sustainable Development Strategy: What Does it Mean for Business?,* DETR, 1999.

DETR, *Green Claims Code,* DETR, 1998.

DETR, *Increasing Sustainable Developing Awareness Across Government,* online document, 2000.

DETR, *Land Use Change in England,* online document, 2000.

DETR, *Less Waste, More Value: Consultation Paper on the Waste Strategy for England and Wales,* DETR, 1998.

DETR, *Making Biodiversity Happen Across Government: Green Ministers Biodiversity Checklist,* online document, DETR, 2000.

DETR, *Opportunities for Change: Consultation Paper on a Revised UK Strategy for Sustainable Development,* DETR, 1998.

DETR, *Proposed Groundwater Regulations: Consultation Paper and Compliance Cost Assessment,* DETR, 1998.

DETR, *Quality of Life Counts, Indicators of Sustainable Development for the United Kingdom,* DETR, 2000.

DETR, *Recent Statistics* (Quarterly - various dates), online documents.

DETR, *Reducing Catering Costs through Energy Efficiency, Good Practice Guide 222,* DETR/BRECSU, 1998.

DETR, *Regeneration Programmes – The Way Forward, Discussion Paper,* DETR, 1997.

DETR, *Report by the United Kingdom on Intentions for Action at the National Level to Implement to OSPAR Strategy with Regard to Radioactive Substances*, DETR, 1999.

DETR, *The Road Traffic Reduction Act 1997: Draft Guidance to Local Traffic Authorities, Public Consultation Exercise,* DETR, 1998.

DETR, *Rural England: A Discussion Document,* DETR, 1999.

DETR, *Sites of Special Scientific Interest: Encouraging Positive Partnerships,* consultation paper, 2000.

DETR, *Tackling Climate Change in the UK,* online document, 1999.

DETR, *Tomorrow's Roads: Safer For Everyone*, DETR, 2000.

DETR, *Towards an Urban Renaissance,* online document, 1999.

DETR, *Transport 2010: The 10 Year Plan,* The Stationery Office, 2000.

DETR, *Transport Statistics Great Britain 1999*, The Stationery Office, 1999.

DETR, *Transport Trends,* The Stationery Office, 2000.

DETR, *UK Strategy for Radioactive Discharges 2001-2020, Consultation Document*, DETR, 2000.

DETR, *Vehicle Speeds in Great Britain 1998*, Statistics Bulletin (99)17, DETR, 1999.

DETR, *Water Quality: A Guide to Water Protection in England and Wales,* online document, DETR, 1998.

DETR, *Water Related Energy Savings, Good Practice Guide 228*, DETR/BRECSU, 1998.

DETR, *Water Charging in England and Wales – A New Approach: Response to Consultation*, DETR, 1998.

DETR, *Water Industry Act 1999: Delivering the Government's Objectives,* DETR, 1999.

DETR Advisory Committee on Releases to the Environment, *The Commercial Use of Genetically Modified Crops in the United Kingdom: The Potential Wider Impact on Farmland Wildlife,* online document, DETR, 1999.

DETR Urban Task Force, *Towards an Urban Renaissance,* DETR, 1999.

DETR/Welsh Office/Scottish Office, *Control and Remediation of Radioactively Contaminated Land: A Consultation Paper,* DETR, 1998.

DETR/Welsh Office/Scottish Office/Dept. of the Environment N. Ireland, *Economic Instruments for Water Pollution: A Consultation Paper,* DETR, 1997.

DETR/ Dept. of the Environment N. Ireland/National Assembly for Wales/ Scottish Executive, *UK Strategy for Radioactive Discharges 2001–2020, Consultation Document*, DETR, 2000.

Department of the Environment (DoE), *Climate Change and the Demand for Water,* HMSO, 1996.

DoE, *EC Eco-Management and Audit Scheme: A Participant's Guide,* DoE, 1997.

DoE, *Energy from Waste: Getting More Value from Municipal Waste*, DoE, 1996.

DoE, *Greening the City: A Guide to Good Practice,* HMSO, 1996.

DoE, *Indicators of Sustainable Development for the UK,* HMSO, 1996.

DoE, *Pesticides in Water*, DoE, 1996.

DoE, *Planning Policy Guidance note (PPG) 6: Town Centres and Retail Developments,* HMSO, 1993.

DoE, *PPG 9: Nature Conservation,* HMSO, 1994.

DoE, *PPG 13:Highways Considerations,* HMSO, 1994.

DoE, *PPG 23: Planning and Pollution Control,* HMSO, 1994.

DoE, *PPG 24: Planning and Noise,* HMSO, 1994.

DoE, *The Producer Responsibility Obligations (Packaging Waste) Regulations 1997: How do They Affect You? Summary,* DETR, 1997.

DoE, *A Review of UK Environmental Expenditure*, DoE, 1993.

DoE, *Sewage Collection, Treatment and Disposal in the UK, One World Information Sheet,* DoE, 1996.

DoE, *Water Resources and Supply: Agenda for Action*, DoE, 1996.

Department of Health, *Quantification of the Effects of Air Pollution on Health in the UK*, The Stationery Office, 1998.

Department of Trade and Industry (DTI), *Bioguide*, online document, 1998.

DTI, *Consultation on an EC Directive on End-of-Life Vehicles*, DTI, 1998.

DTI, *Digest of UK Energy Statistics 1999,* The Stationery Office, 1999.

DTI, *The Energy Report: Shaping Change, Vol. 1,* DTI, 1997.

DTI, *Environmental Technology Best Practice Programme: A Guide for Potential Host Companies and Researchers,* DTI, 1994/7.

DTI, *New and Renewable Energy: Prospects for the 21st Century*, DTI, 1999.

DTI, *The Queen's Awards for Export, Technological and Environmental Achievement: General Background Note,* DTI, 1997.

DTI, *Unwanted Computer Equipment: A Guide to Reuse*, online document, DTI, 1999.

DTI, *Unwanted White Goods: A Guide to Reuse*, online document, DTI, 1999.

Drinking Water Inspectorate, *Nitrate, Pesticides and Lead 1995 and 1996*, DETR/Welsh Office, 1997.

Drinking Water Inspectorate, *Drinking Water 1999: A Report by the Chief Inspector*, Drinking Water Inspectorate, 2000.

EcoTec et al. for DoE/DoT, *Reducing Transport Emissions Through Planning*, HMSO, 1993.

Energy Technology Support Unit (ETSU), *An Assessment of Renewable Energy for the UK*, HMSO, 1994.

Environment Agency (EA), *The Agency's Contribution to Sustainable Development: Case Studies*, EA, 1997.

EA, *The Agency's Contribution to Sustainable Development: Waste Minimisation*, EA, 1997.

EA, *Derelict and Contaminated Land*, online document , 1998.

EA, *Endocrine-Disrupting Substances in the Environment: What Should Be Done?*, EA, 1998.

EA, *An Environmental Strategy for the Millennium and Beyond*, EA, 1997.

EA, *Groundwater Pollution: Evaluation of the Extent and Character of Groundwater Pollution from Point Sources in England and Wales*, EA, 1996.

EA, *Heavy Industrial Processes*, online document, 1998.

EA, *Prevention of Pollution Guidelines (PPG) 1: Prevention of Pollution of Controlled Waters: Sites*, EA, 1997.

EA, *Radiation Dose to the Public*, online document, 1998.

EA, *Riverside Owners' Guide: A Guide to Planning and Regulations Requirements and Legal Responsibilities for People Living near Rivers and Streams*, EA, 1996.

EA/Scottish Environment Protection Agency (SEPA), *PPG5: Works In, Near or Liable to Affect Watercourses*, EA, 1998.

EA/National Water Demand Management Centre, *Saving Water: On the Right Track 2: A Summary of Current Water Conservation Initiatives in the UK*, EA, 1999.

EA/SEPA, *PPG6: Working at Construction and Demolition Sites*, EA, 1997.

EA/SEPA, *PPG9: Prevention of Pollution of Controlled Waters by Pesticides*, EA, 1997.

EA, *PPG11: Preventing Pollution on Industrial Sites*, EA, 1997.

EA, *Producer Responsibility Obligations (Packaging Waste) Regulations 1997: Explanatory Notes (draft)*, EA, 1997.

EA, *Protected Areas*, online document, 1998.

EA, *The State of the Environment of England and Wales: Land*, The Stationery Office, 1999.

EA, *The State of the Environment of England and Wales: Coasts*, The Stationery Office, 1999.

EA, *The State of the Environment of England and Wales: Fresh Waters*, The Stationery Office, 1998.

EA, *The State of the Environment of England and Wales: Atmosphere*, The Stationery Office, 2000.

EA, *Urban Air Quality*, online document, 1998.

EA, *Water Abstraction*, online document, 1998.

EA, *Wildlife, Biodiversity and Conservation*, online document, 1998.

Environmental Technology Best Practice Programme (DTI/DETR), *Summary, 1997.*

European Environment Agency (EEA), *Europe's Environment: The Second Assessment*, EEA, 1998.

EEA, *Environmental Management Tools for SMEs: A Handbook*, EEA, 1998.

Forestry Commission (Redfern, D. B. et al.) *Forest Condition 1998, Forestry Commission Information Note 19,* Forestry Commission, Edinburgh, 1999.

Intergovernmental Panel on Climate Change (IPCC), *Climate Change: The IPCC Scientific Assessment,* Cambridge, Cambridge University Press, 1990.

IPCC, *Second Assessment Synthesis Report and three Summaries for Policymakers,* IPCC, 1995.

Joint Environmental Markets Unit (JEMU) (DTI/DETR), *Business Plan: 1998–2001,* JEMU, 1998.

Ministry of Agriculture, Fisheries and Food, Scottish Executive Rural Affairs Department, Department of Agriculture and Rural Development (Northern Ireland) and National Assembly for Wales Agriculture Department, *Agriculture in the UK 1999,* The Stationery Office, 2000.

National Rivers Authority, *Water: Nature's Precious Resource, an Environmentally Sustainable Water Resources Development Strategy for England and Wales,* 1994.

Royal Commission on Environmental Pollution (RCEP), *Sustainable Uses of Soil,* RCEP, 1996.

RCEP, *Energy – The Changing Climate,* RCEP, 2000.

UK Climate Change Impact Programme, *Climate Change: Assessing the Impacts – Identifying Responses,* UK Climate Change Impact Programme, 2000.

UK Ecolabelling Board (UKEB), *Environmental Purchasing: Consumer Motivations and Beliefs,* UKEB, 1996.

UK Round Table on Sustainable Development, *Fifth Annual Report,* DETR, 2000.

UN General Assembly, *Resolution S-19/2, Programme for the Further Implementation of Agenda 21,* 1998.

United Nations Environment Programme (UNEP) *Global Environment Outlook 2000*, Earthscan, 1999.

United Nations Environment Programme, *Earthwatch Strategic Framework for Environmental Observing, Assessment and Reporting,* UNEP, 2000.

World Commission on Environment and Development, *Our Common Future,* Oxford University Press, 1987.

World Health Organisation (WHO), *Air Quality Guidelines for Europe*, Copenhagen, WHO, 1987.

World Resources Institute, United Nations Environment Progeramme, United Nations Development Programme and World Bank, *World Resources 1998–1999: Environmental Change and Human Health*, Oxford University Press, 1998.

Other publications

Association for the Conservation of Energy (ACE), *Briefing Note 98/4: A Strategy for Making Offices More Energy Efficient in the UK*, online document, 1998.

Banister D. (ed.), *Transport Policy and the Environment*, London, E. & F. N. Spon, 1998.

Berry, C., *Marine Health Check: A Report to Gauge the Health of the UK's Sea Life,*. WWF, 2000.

Borer P., *Environmental Building Factsheet,* Powys, Centre for Alternative Technology (CAT), 1998.

Bradnam L., *Solar Energy Factsheet,* Powys, CAT, 1998.

British Social Attitudes 16th Report, Aldershot, Ashgate, 1999.

Brown, L. R., Flavin, C., French, H. et al., *State of the World 2000,* Earthscan, 2000.

Brown, L. R., Renner, M. and Halweil, B. (ed. L. Starke), *Vital Signs 1999-2000,* Earthscan, 1999.

Buchdahl, J., *Glossary of Global Climate Change,* Atmospheric Research & Information Centre (ARIC), online document, 1997.

Buchdahl, J., *Potential Effects of the Climate Change in the UK,* ARIC, online document, 1997.

Business in the Environment, *The Index of Corporate Environmental Engagement*, BiE, 1998.

Centre for Alternative Technology (CAT), *Bright Ideas: A Guide to Energy Efficient Lighting: Tipsheet,* Powys, CAT, undated.

CAT, *Where the Wind Blows An Introduction to Wind Power,* Powys, CAT, 1997.

Chartered Institute of Environmental Health (CIEH), *How to become an Environmental Health Officer (EHO),* CIEH online document, updated 2000.

Collier, U., *The UK's Climate Change Programme – FoE briefing,* FoE online document, undated.

Countryside Commission/Blunden, J., Curry, N. et al., *A People's Charter: Forty Years of the National Parks and Access to the Countryside Act 1949,* London, HMSO, 1990.

Croner's Environmental Management, Croners (1991 and updates)

Dalton, R. J., *The Green Rainbow: Environmental Groups in Western Europe,* New Haven, Yale University Press, 1994.

Davies, H. W. E., Gosling, J. A. and Hsia, M. T., *The Impact of the European Community on Land Use Planning in the UK,* London, Royal Town Planning Institute, 1994.

Davison, G. and Hewitt, C. N., *Air Pollution in the UK*, Cambridge, Royal Society of Chemistry, 1997.

Earth Summit 1992: The UN Conference on Environment and Development (includes a shortened version of Agenda 21), London, Regency Press, 1992.

Energy from Waste Foundation (EfW), *Energy, Waste and the Environment,* EfW, 1998.

Environment Council, *A Manager's Introduction to Product Design and the Environment,* online document, 1998.

Environment Encyclopaedia and Directory 1998, London, Europa Publications, 1997.

Environmental Transport Association (ETA), *Cycling Factsheet,* online document, 1998.

ETA, *Motorcycling Factsheet,* online document ,1998.

European Wind Energy Association, *European Best Practice Guidelines for Wind Energy Development,* EWEA, undated.

Friends of the Earth (FoE), *The Acid Test: The UK Government's Policy on Acid Rain,* FoE. 1991.

FoE, *Air Quality Briefing,* FoE, 1990.

FoE, *Cars Cost the Earth*, FoE, 1996.

FoE, *Forests and Climate Change: FoE Briefing,* online document, undated.

FoE, *Paper, Wood and the World's Forests,* FoE, 1997.

FoE, *Reaping the Double Dividend – Climate Change and Jobs, FoE Briefing,* online document, undated.

FoE, *Road Transport, Air Pollution and Health: Briefing Sheet*, FoE, 1997.

FoE, *Summertime Smog: Briefing Sheet,* FoE, undated.

FoE, *Up in Smoke: Why FoE Opposes Incineration: Briefing Sheet,* FoE, 1997/8.

FoE, *Water Quality: the Role of European Community laws,* FoE, 1991.

FoE, *What is Earth Summit II? – FoE Briefing,* online document, 1997.

FoE, *Your Drinking Water is Being Polluted,* FoE, 1993.

Gandy, M., *Recycling and the Politics of Urban Waste,* London, Earthscan, 1994.

Golub, J. (ed.), *Global Competition and EU Environmental Poliy,* London, Routledge, 1998.

Glazier, K., *SGS New Environmental Index*, SGS online document, 1998.

Grayson, L., *Environmental Auditing: A Guide to Best Practice in the UK and Europe,* Cheltenham, Thornes, 1994.

Hardstaff, P., *Forests and Climate Change: Briefing Sheet,* FoE, 1997.

Hester, R. and Harrison, R. M. (eds), *Waste Treatment and Disposal,* Letchworth, Royal Society of Chemistry, 1995.

Horne, B, *Power Plants: Biofuels Made Simple,* Powys, CAT, 1996.

Howes, C, *The Spice of Life: Biodiversity and the Extinction Crisis,* London, Blandford, 1997.

Institute for Environmental Assessment and Landscape, *Guidelines for Landscape and Visual Impact Assessment,* London, E. and F. N. Spon, 1995.

Jones, B. (ed.), *Tolley's Environmental Handbook: A Management Guide,* Tolley, 1994.

Kronsell, A., *Greening the EU: Power Practices, Resistances and Agenda Setting,* Sweden, Lund University Press, 1997.

Lawton Smith, H. and Woodward, N. (eds), *Energy and Environment Regulation,* London, Macmillan, 1996.

Lees, N. and Woolston, H., *Environmental Information: A Guide to Sources,* (2nd edn), British Library, 1997.

McCormick, J., *The Global Environmental Movement* (2nd edn), Chichester, Wiley, 1995.

Nicholson, M., *The New Environmental Age*, Cambridge, Cambridge University Press, 1987.

Nuffield Council on Bioethics, *Genetically Modified Crops: The Social and Ethical Issues, Invitation to Comment,* Nuffield Council, 1998.

Our Common Future: A Reader's Guide, the Brundtland Report Explained, IIED/ Earthscan, 1989.

Royal Town Planning Institute (RTPI), *Energy Planning: a Guide for Practitioners,* RTPI, 1996.

RTPI, *Planning for Biodiversity,* RTPI, 1998.

Selman P, *Environmental Planning: The Conservation and Development of Biophysical Resources,* London, Paul Chapman, 1992.

Seymour, J. and Girardet, H., *Green Planet: How You Can Take Practical Action Today to Fight Pollution,* London, Dorling Kindersley, 1987.

Shepherd, A., *Careers and Courses in Sustainable Technologies: How to Get a Job that Doesn't Harm the Planet,* Powys, CAT, 1995.

Starke, L. (ed.), *Vital Signs 1997/98,* London, Earthscan, 1997.

Stauffer, J., *Safe to Drink? The Quality of Your Water,* Powys, CAT, 1996.

Sydenham, M., *The Green Office Action Plan*, Edinburgh, FoE Scotland, 1996.

Warhurst, A. M., *An Environmental Assessment of Alkylphenol Ethoxylates and Alkylphenols*, FoE, 1994.

Index